THE

# BIG PICTURE

# The Big Picture

The authority and integrity
of the authentic
Word of God

## David W. Norris

*Authentic Word*

First Edition 2004

ISBN 0-9548425-0-2

Printed and published in the UK by

*Authentic Word*

99 Mount Street, Hednesford, Cannock, Staffordshire,
WS12 4DB, England

# Contents

# Preface

*"The fear of the Lord is the beginning of knowledge: but fools despise
wisdom and instruction."*
(Proverbs 1:7)

What is to be known of the faith we share with all genuine
believers down through time. Certainly, this book does not
pretend to be original in the sense of being novel. Indeed, this
would be a negative signal to the reader. Whilst I have tried to
ensure that my arguments are academically sound, ultimately
the conviction that when we take up the 1611 *Authorised
Version* of the Bible we are reading the authentic Word of God
depends on the testimony of the Holy Spirit to our hearts. The
purpose of this book is less to answer critics of the *Authorised
Version* than to strengthen the faith of God's people in the
inspired Word given to them. Despite this, we can but pray
that some doubters, some who have previously given these
matters but scant attention, and some opponents, may
perhaps be persuaded.

I have many books in my library, some good, some bad, some
indifferent, some I have read, some not, and a few I ought to
have thrown away many years ago. What constitutes the best
of books is fairly easy to define, it will be one that drives us to
that one book by which all others are to be measured, the
sacred Scriptures. We ought not, as C. H. Spurgeon wittily
remarked, to confine ourselves to that light which falls on
Scripture because of a crack in our own roof! For more than

forty years, I have drunk deeply at wells I have not digged and thank God continually for the insight on His Word that He gives His saints. We must remember that we are not the only ones to whom our gracious Saviour has revealed Himself through His Word. In writing this book, I owe a debt to others that I am happy to acknowledge. The work of others has been used by God to strengthen my own faith in Christ and in the Bible, particularly in times when my own faith was under severe attack, as for example during the time spent at various universities.

It may appear unusual to the reader to find few quotations from other authors. This has been quite deliberate. I do not want to convey the impression I am constructing an apologetic for any one theological direction, nor do I wish to suggest that my views are those of authors consulted, which would be patently inaccurate. Also my intention has been to avoid raising unnecessary prejudices in some readers that would obscure the light of the truth. Rather, I would that the reader do what I have done, test all things directly by Scripture.

It is difficult to underestimate the help of friends whose words have encouraged me to continue at moments of doubt. I cannot mention all, but my special thanks must go to my good friend Wes Trotman of Toronto, who, despite a busy life as pastor, took the time to read the long manuscript of the first draft of the book. His comments have proved most helpful. My thanks go too to my wife, Valerie, who is able to make comments no one else would dare to express and whose patience enabled me to be at work in my study when I ought to have been doing other things.

*David W. Norris*

# Introduction

*"I have not shunned to declare unto you all the counsel of God."*
(Acts 20:27)

Two people encounter a wristwatch for the very first time in their lives. Perhaps it could happen, even today, in remoter parts of the world. The first man finds a complete watch. He is fascinated by the second hand moving around the face of the watch, he does not see that the minute and the hour hands are also moving around the face in the same direction. This being his first encounter with a timepiece of any kind, he does not have a clue as to the purpose behind this delicate mechanism. If he would make use of the watch, it must be explained to him why the watchmaker constructed it, its relationship to day and night, that there are twenty-four hours in each day, and that the fingers move around the face twice each day. He needs to know that hours are divided into minutes, and minutes into seconds, but he does not really need to know very much about how a watch is put together in order to read the time from it.

The second man encounters his first wristwatch in quite different circumstances. The watch he sees has been completely taken apart and lies in pieces on the watchmaker's bench. At first he does not see that any of these curious little pieces of metal spread out in front of him bear any relationship one to the other. There is a little wheel with spikes all around the edge and a strange small disc with unusual markings on its face. Indeed, on their own, separated from each other, they serve no useful purpose. It does not matter how long this man ponders over each separate item, looking at each piece singly will not yield up to him any meaning for its existence. The watchmaker now takes down a complete watch and opens up the back; gears are meshed one with the other to turn the fingers on the face. Each small item is essential to the proper working of the watch; nothing can be left out. The meaning of the greatest as of the smallest component is inter-linked to serve the one purpose: that the owner of the watch may know what time of day it is.

If we consider the world God has made as a whole (which, incidentally, He does not wind up and leave to run on its own like a watch), then clearly, as with the man who found the complete watch, we stand in need of some explanation. We need to know what we are to make of creation, what of ourselves, of the One who made it all and sustains it, and of the nature of our relationship to Him. We too do not need to know or understand everything. As the second man, who encountered his first wristwatch laid out in pieces, we will see that our universe is made up of countless different parts. We also observe different events happening to different people at different times. The meaning of the particular component is derived from its place in the universal whole. To understand the individual components of the watch, this man needs the 'big picture'. Meaning and purpose of a particular thing or event cannot be culled from it by considering it in isolation.

No single truth, no isolated historical event, can be seen for what it really is outside the 'big picture' given us in God's Word. The individual details of creation are what they are by virtue of the 'whole' of God's eternal purpose. Each and everything is connected one thing with another in, and all things and events derive meaning from, this one eternal purpose. Ultimately, the purpose of everything happening and existing is to bring praise and glory to God. Without the whole, the individual facts and truths are indistinguishable one from the other and bear no relation to one another. The Christian faith stands or falls *as a whole*.

> *Either all things are as the Scriptures say they are, or we are left with a series of unrelated meaningless truths and historical facts with nothing to link one to the other.*

Any debate about an individual teaching, such as the resurrection of Christ, will inevitably involve a debate about the truth of *the whole of Scripture*. The Bible as the revelation of God constitutes for believers the final authority for every fact and detail of our existence. Facts are what they are only by virtue of what God makes them to be. All facts testify to the truth of the Scriptures.

The human personality has been created by God to receive His revelation of truth. This means that even the Christless mind calls for a unified knowledge of the created world. Yet, because he lives in total rebellion against God, the godless man directs all his efforts to rejecting the Word of God. Having rejected God, he has no alternative but to look for meaning within the world He created. Therefore, an unbeliever will take one aspect of reality and seek to make it the explanation of everything else. It is rather like taking a single item of our watch, the face, the spring, or a gear wheel perhaps, and making it the explanation of the whole. This will, of course, lead nowhere. On its own, each item eludes the search for meaning and cannot even be described properly. To explain all creation from one single aspect deifies it. It is to put it in the place of God as the source of all meaning. Everyone who does not worship the true God worships the creature and creation. The created universe on its own, which includes man and all his faculties, cannot be the source of its own meaning. This is because all things were created *by* God and *for* God and they continue to exist only by His will. The meaning of all things existing and every event of history has been predetermined by the place it has in the eternal purpose of God. If we would have understanding, we must seek to discover what God has revealed of this purpose in the Bible.

The question, *'What is it?'* can only be answered if we already have some previous understanding of its use or begin with some previous hypothesis of our own, otherwise we can say nothing about what the purpose of any particular thing may be. The unbeliever, unwilling to accept the truth, has to construct his own alternative interpretation *before* he can say anything about anything. To begin this process, he will generally assume that only that which he can perceive with his physical senses is real and he will build his explanations on this. He has no grounds other than pure conjecture for beginning in this way. He has no proof, nothing gives him reason to make the assumption that nothing exists beyond the reach of his physical senses. He chooses this route because of his rebellious and sinful predisposition. The important point for the unregenerate man is that the self-sustaining, self-existent God of Scripture is *excluded* at the beginning of any interpretation of reality. God, should He exist, will be subject to the same observation and testing by the physical senses as everything else. The God of the Bible is ruled out by the unbeliever before he begins thinking about anything. *What* replaces God is initially less relevant. What the unbeliever considers 'evidence' is all that is left after that which he has previously arbitrarily decided cannot exist has been ruled out. He has removed in advance all evidence to miracle, the resurrection, and all else in the Bible. His 'evidence' is in fact based on prejudice against, and a deep hatred of the truth of God. There is no way in which the unbeliever is going to permit his sinful state and continued wilful rebellion to be exposed for what it is.

Further, every unbeliever assumes that there is nothing problematic about what his senses and his reason tell him. In reality, both his senses and his reasoning powers have been considerably weakened and distorted by the fall. The believer is regarded by the unbeliever as stupid and ignorant because the believer builds his understanding on a self-contained, self-revealing God, the authority of whose Word he does not question. Yet, everything the unbeliever looks at is perceived in a distorted way and his conclusions are unreliable because of the effects of sin on all that he is.

What the unbeliever seeks to do is to remove the eternal plan of God and replace it as a whole with an alternative interpretation produced by his own fallen and weakened intellect in order to bring the unity and meaning he needs to the diversity of the universe. This process will enable him to avoid the authority of God and replace it with his own. It is impossible to argue the *individual aspects* of what we believe, such as creation, miracles, the resurrection, with unbelievers. Each side will try to show the 'errors' of the other system, by testing it according their own presuppositions. The unbeliever measures by what he assumes his senses and reason tell him, the believer measures all things by God's revealed Word. Each will begin, therefore, from a starting point irreconcilable with that of the other, making agreement on details impossible. We must begin by questioning the assumptions of the unbeliever, and show the absurdity into which his thinking leads him. We must present the truth of Scripture.

The counsel of God is a whole, is one, and is already established from eternity to eternity. It is all-inclusive. Nothing in the universe is self-creating or self-explanatory, nothing happens by chance, unexpectedly, or as an afterthought. God has the 'big picture'. The real authority, the real infallibility of Scripture is rooted in the fact that it is a revelation to us of what God wants us to know of His one eternal infallible purpose. The meaning of everything is derived from its place in this plan. A cohesive view of God's universe, unity in diversity, the unity of all particular things is found here. Dispense with God's plan and we are left with no more than a series of unrelated particulars, none of which has any meaning in itself. If we believe all these many things came into being by chance, and that the occurrence of all historical events is purely random, we face a similar problem to that of the man looking at the watch lying in pieces on the watchmaker's bench. If these single bits and bobs have just popped up any old how, they each can bear no relationship one to another and consequently will yield to us no meaning. The unbeliever cannot find meaning in the detail except by giving away the whole to an endless series of particulars or by losing the particulars in the whole. There can be no unified understanding of the universe apart from that of the One who created it. All godless systems of thought *must* therefore end in irrationality and madness.

It is from the heart of the God of the Bible that His eternal thoughts are revealed to our finite human hearts through the medium of Scripture. There is no other such book and we ought to take it in our hands with great reverence and take its teaching into our souls with great care. It impossible for any fact in the universe to be out of line with what God has revealed in Scripture. Its veracity is secure; its authority is final. One can only assume that those who treat this book lightly, adding to it, changing it, forever translating it until it says something that pleases them better, do not appreciate what they hold in their hands.

# CHAPTER 1

# Two Foundations

*"Therefore whosoever heareth these sayings of mine, and doeth them, I will liken him unto a wise man, which built his house upon a rock: And the rain descended, and the floods came, and the winds blew, and beat upon that house; and it fell not: for it was founded upon a rock. And every one that heareth these sayings of mine, and doeth them not, shall be likened unto a foolish man, which built his house upon the sand: And the rain descended, and the floods came, and the winds blew, and beat upon that house; and it fell: and great was the fall of it"* (Matthew 7:24-27)

Sometimes when buildings outlive their usefulness or fall into a state beyond repair, it becomes necessary to demolish them. If the building is relatively small, such as a house, it can perhaps be flattened with a crane and a bulldozer. In the event of the building being somewhat larger, it may be necessary to use explosive charges. This latter course of action demands skill and a good knowledge of building construction. Simply to place explosives in inappropriate positions would be dangerous and irresponsible. Charges need to be placed at those strategic points upon which the whole building rests. Detonating the charges then brings the whole edifice crumbling down in a cloud of dust. Some structures are more difficult to demolish than others. Many buildings will collapse with just a little physical encouragement. This will almost certainly depend not just on the structure but also on the foundation. Too much of the wrong kind of sand, too little cement, and the structure raised stands on shaky ground indeed. An unstable foundation will secure rapid demolition.

To build our faith upon anything other than the solid rock of God's Word is to set out the footings for predictable and irretrievable disaster. We build on God's Word *or* we build on the sands of the pretended autonomy of human reason. There can be no mixture of these two. It is easy to deceive ourselves, thinking we build on the Scriptures whilst we are at the same time filtering everything we read through a fine mesh of personal opinions and prejudiced assumptions. We cannot build a structure of faith upon a foundation of reasoning from a position outside Scripture. All too often, this is exactly what we do in seeking to answer arguments handed to us by the demands of our opponents. We face a twofold task: not only must we establish our own foundation from Scripture, but we must also set explosive charges at those points of the enemy's foundation where his structured system of belief is most vulnerable. There is very little point to chipping away at massive reinforced concrete walls with a hammer and chisel however hard we may wallop the hammer.

## *Two ways of thinking, two kinds of people*

Although there are many different belief systems in the world, many different philosophies, there are actually just two ways of thinking: one way is according to the truth, the other according to falsehood. The first way of thinking reflects the truth of God that rules in the light of His kingdom; the second reflects the lie with which Satan has seduced the hearts of men and that rules in the darkness that is his kingdom. We begin with the revealed thoughts of God recorded in Scripture or we begin with thoughts and judgements arising in our own hearts apart from God. We can build upon only one of these two foundations.

As there are two kingdoms, two ways of thinking, so there are two kinds of people. There are those who are part of the kingdom of God and there are those who are outside it. There are those who have been regenerated, born anew, who have been enlightened so that their inward being has been transformed. Those outside the kingdom of God, whose minds remain in the darkness of their natural state, deny this and will not accept that it is possible for anyone to have insights they do not also possess or to have an ability to understand things they cannot also grasp. The Scriptures are clear: *"But the natural man receiveth not the things of the Spirit of God: for they are foolishness unto him: neither can he know them, because they are spiritually discerned"* (1 Corinthians 2:14). The 'natural' and the 'spiritual' are states of human consciousness, each inwardly different from the other. A different content arises in the consciousness of the regenerate than in that of the unregenerate so that he who is born of God's Spirit will look at everything around him in a very different way and be moved by different impulses. There are two kinds of human life, two kinds of consciousness, and two kinds of knowledge. A denial of the fall of man and of regeneration and the consequential effects of both must lead to a rejection of the Christian faith as a whole. Those within the kingdom of God, because of what they have now become, think in a completely different way than those outside it.

If we are to arrive at conclusions that are according to the truth, we must begin with the fact that what God has revealed in His Word is the truth. We must take seriously the words, *"thy word is truth"* (John 17:17). We must build on the bald statements of Scripture. As an example, the Bible says incontrovertibly that God created the world in six days and rested on the seventh; we know therefore evolution in all its forms cannot possibly be true. Having consulted Scripture, we then look at the world in which we live and interpret it bearing in mind what we have already read in the Bible.

The unbeliever builds on another foundation. As Satan before him, he says to himself, I can decide on my own what is true and not true, *I am as God*. This is an implicit denial that he is but a finite creature. Not only does the unbeliever make no distinction *between men*, regenerate and unregenerate, he will also insist that no essential distinction can be made *between the being of God and that of men*. Whether God in some way created him, or whether man is the product of an accidental process of evolution, in both cases the unbeliever will say that there is no distinction to be made between him and God, or between him and all other men. All being is the same. There can be no attributes of essential being possessed by deity that he as a man does not also possess in some measure. This is to appropriate to himself those divine attributes which make God distinct from all that which He has created. At the same time, it is to deny that any such distinguishing attributes can exist. This immediately raises man to the level of God and brings God down to the level of man. If I am made in God's image, so the unregenerate mind reasons, then it must equally be true that God is made in my image. God cannot be anything other than I am, except perhaps in measure. This means that the unbeliever assumes that as a human being he can know and reason according to the truth independently, autonomously, in and of himself, and without reference to God. Truth is neutral and 'out there', accessible to God and to man in the same way. This is at the heart of Satan's lie to our first parents in Eden that they could be as 'gods'. It is then not surprising to find men saying, I can decide all on my own whether the Bible is what it claims to be. I do not need to refer to God or to the Bible first in any matter in order to arrive at the truth. If I can make mistakes, then so can God.

The unbeliever thus implicitly denies his finitude, but he also *denies that he is a sinner by nature.* He may admit to having sinned, but he will find an alternative explanation for the fall of man, or he will deny it altogether. Whether he is a modern Roman Catholic humanist follower of the teachings of Aquinas, or whether an Enlightenment rationalist, what he will most certainly deny is that such a fall can have in any way *inherently impaired* his ability to know and to reason. If he cannot think as he ought then it will be for some reason *external* to himself and not something that is part of his human nature as a direct result of sin. He denies emphatically any effect of the fall on his mind.

If unregenerate men think in a different way than regenerate, then it is because they are different. All spiritual matters are foolishness to anyone still in his natural state; the Gospel is hidden from him because Satan, the god of this world, has blinded his mind.

> "But if our gospel be hid, it is hid to them that are lost: In whom the god of this world hath blinded the minds of them which believe not, lest the light of the glorious gospel of Christ, who is the image of God, should shine unto them."
> (2 Corinthians 4:3-4)

Such blindness inflicted by the power of Satan can be removed only by the power of God. Only then can anyone respond to the Gospel. Until this point, they walk in the vanity of an unregenerate mind. Living within Satan's kingdom, they imagine there is nothing closed to them; there is no area of knowledge they cannot explore; and very little they cannot eventually achieve. What can there be that a Christian believer knows that they cannot know? They are indignant at the very idea! If the unregenerate heart recognises no essential difference between itself and God, so too will it deny any difference the Bible makes between believers and unbelievers. The rejection of Christ by unbelievers is evidence enough of their inability to comprehend spiritual matters and until the Holy Spirit lifts the veil, the truth of the Gospel is closed to them. *"Having the understanding darkened, being alienated from the life of God through the ignorance that is in them, because of the blindness of their heart"* (Ephesians 4:18). We must not expect those outside Christ to see things the way we do or to understand what we are saying as long a there is a veil over their hearts. We may bring convincing and careful arguments, but they will not be persuaded. The reason for this is that the way in which they look at everything prevents them from accepting what we say. Not only does Satan blind their minds to the Gospel, but also, as a direct result of the fall, their hearts are naturally predisposed to reject the truth and to interpret all things in a way that is in harmony with the sinful state they regard as 'normal'. Can they have a more pressing reason to deny their descent from Adam?

Until they are born of God, unbelievers will reject all our arguments outright, regarding them as foolish. They need the Word of God, the incorruptible seed through which men are born again. Until there is a change within, a move into the kingdom of God, they will remain blind and antagonistic to the truth. The unbeliever rejects any need to be 'born again' in order to apprehend things that are presently beyond him. He sees nothing amiss within himself. Unbelievers assume all things are now as they always were, *"all things continue as they were from the beginning of the creation"* (2 Peter 3:4). Only before the fall of man in Eden was everything 'normal'. Adam lived in submission to the revealed Word of God, exercising his mind, his reason, in harmony with it. If he accepts the fall at all, the unregenerate man will reject any suggestion that it brought about any disturbance in his ability to think and reason. To him the present state is 'normal' and his mind unimpaired.

Because the unregenerate are so blinded, how then are they to be reached with the Gospel? Separation from God is never total, for without the grace of God no one could continue to live; He *"maketh his sun to rise on the evil and on the good, and sendeth rain on the just and on the unjust"* (Matthew 5:45) to the end that His goodness should lead to repentance (Romans 2:4). There is, however something more: within the human consciousness of everyone, there remains ineradicable knowledge of God.

> *No one fights against a God in whom they do not believe.*

All are thus without excuse *"Because that, when they knew God, they glorified him not as God, neither were thankful; but became vain in their imaginations, and their foolish heart was darkened"* (Romans 1:21). Even as Satan has a toehold in the human heart because of its fallen bent towards sin, so too has God. All men possess an inborn knowledge of God and of the law of God as part of their human constitution; they are not human without it! They *"... shew the work of the law written in their hearts, their conscience also bearing witness, and their thoughts the mean while accusing or else excusing one another"* (Romans 2:15). The preaching of the Word of God is to be set in this direction, to stir the *conscience* rather than convince a *darkened mind* that is generally occupied accusing others and excusing itself! God's Word is certainly received through the mind, but the conscience will respond first. Every time the Bible is read, every time the Gospel is preached, the heart will be reminded to its own discomfort of that which it already knows about God, but desperately works at suppressing every moment of the day. Every son, every daughter of Adam is inherently 'theophobic'. What men do *not* know is the way to God through faith in Christ, for this they need the Scriptures. Without them, they will not come to know the truth nor exercise faith in Christ, "...*faith cometh by hearing, and hearing by the word of God*" (Romans 10:17). There can be no way around this. Those who refuse the testimony of the Scriptures, those who cannot and will not see the truth, are demonstrating one thing, that they are sinners in need of God's salvation. With regeneration a man will recognise himself at once to be God's creature, he will also acknowledge that he is a sinner. Turning from sin to Christ, he recognises that all that he is by nature is finite and sinful. His desire then becomes to live to God's glory and to interpret all things according to the Word of God. Despite the fact that in this he may not be altogether successful due to the remnants of sin still within him.

When we preach the Gospel, we speak to the dead, the deaf, and to the spiritually blind. There is no life, no hearing, no sight of the Gospel. The heavens may rejoice as the Word of salvation in Christ is preached, but the dead around us do not hear it, nor can they. The world lies in wickedness, our hearers are as the valley of dry bones, *very dry* bones (Ezekiel 37). Yet even as we cry, "*O ye dry bones, hear the word of the Lord*", God Himself causes breath to enter them and live. Without this work of God, no one will respond in faith. "*The just shall live by faith*" (Romans 1:17). The Word is preached and the bones live. At the influx of spiritual life, Christ Jesus "*of God is made unto us wisdom, and righteousness, and sanctification, and redemption*" (1 Corinthians 1:30).

We believe the truth or we believe a lie. Many mistakenly believe that dividing these two irreconcilable kingdoms is an expanse of no-man's land. Here it is thought to be possible for each side to meet and somehow work out any differences, everyone on the same level. Knowledge is neutral and all that is required is to present the facts of the Gospel, the evidences for God, for creation, for the Bible, and unbelievers can be convinced, can decide for themselves. What is overlooked is that when the human mind is presented with such 'facts' it will unfailingly interpret them according to the pre-programmed perspective from which it sees them. A sinner, as long as he is still in rebellion and constantly given over to finding excuses for his sin, must and will interpret all that he comes across in a manner that supports his sinful status. The alternative is to capitulate, to admit his need of Christ, and this he will not do. He is 'Christophobic'. Because of the inherent tendency to misinterpret everything coming its way, unregenerate judgement is unstable and unreliable and is certainly no judge of the contents of God's Word.

Were we by skilful argument to persuade a sinner of the truth of God's Word, even this would not of itself constitute evidence of a change of heart. The sinner already knows something of the truth and rejects it! The human mind must *submit to the authority* of God and *all* He has revealed, accept that it is true because of who has revealed it, and then live by it. To be persuaded that God exists is good, but *"the devils also believe, and tremble"* (James 2:19). The great danger is that the sinner may be persuaded to accept the truth based on his own unregenerate reasoning, but this still leaves his own mind as the ultimate authority, rather than being submitted to the authority of God's Word. Such will continue to subject the Scriptures to his or her own judgement, instead beginning with God's Word. Paul's preaching, *"...was not with enticing words of man's wisdom, but in demonstration of the Spirit and of power: That your faith should not stand in the wisdom of men, but in the power of God"* (1 Corinthians 2:4-5).

Only when born again by the Spirit of God, hearing and believing the Word of God, will anyone lay down his arms and begin to think according to the truth, no longer reserving the final word for himself.

## Mounting the heavenly throne

The early chapters of Genesis show us how our first parents in Eden were led a step at a time from complete trust and confidence in the revealed Word of God to mistrust, denial, and *reliance upon their own powers of judgement as decisive*. The original Word had been given to *"the man"* (1:16), to Adam, she had not been present. This is underlined by the use of the second person singular, *"thou"* — used only when addressing just one person. Adam would have repeated to Eve what God had said. The Word of God came to Eve first through her husband, reminding us of Adam's unique role within the original created universe. In his fall, Adam sinned against God and against his calling. Satan was the first to whisper the lie, inferring to Eve that what God said was not the truth, and so this conflict began. God was made out to be the liar and deceiver and Satan presented himself as the representative of the truth, itself a lie. God had said that to eat of the tree of the knowledge of good and evil meant certain death, *"thou shalt surely die"* (Genesis 2:17) — there could be no doubt about it.

First, Satan plants **doubt** in the mind of Eve as to exactly what God had said. He suggests to Eve, *"Yea, hath God said?"* (3:1). Is this really what God meant to say? Doubt leads to **denial** as surely as defiance of God leads to death. This is where Satan took Eve, *"Ye shall not surely die"* (3:4), which was precisely the opposite of what God had originally said. This was not before Eve had added her bit of embroidery, *"neither shall ye touch it, lest ye die"* (3:3). This was the first 'revised version' of the

Word of God! There is no record of God having said any such thing to Adam. Is there not a hint here that Eve thinks that God is being somewhat unreasonable in not even letting them touch the fruit of this tree? We should note: Adam and his wife lived in a perfect environment. They could not blame their environment or their parentage for their fall into sin. They had only themselves to blame. Everything they could have possibly wanted was theirs and they still fell into sin.

The one thing that God forbade was what they wanted - simply because God had forbidden it, and this is at the heart of all sin and rebellion. Paul makes this point in Romans 7. *"But sin, taking occasion by the commandment, wrought in me all manner of concupiscence. For without the law sin was dead"* (Romans 7:8). Prohibition provokes the rebel heart to sin. Eve's new slant on the Word of God has the effect of undermining rather than underlining the certainty of what God had said. It dilutes it, the words God spoke *"thou shalt surely die"* are far stronger than *"lest ye die"*.

Satan now moves from denial to the **defamation** of God, suggesting God was deliberately keeping something good from them. God, who had given them all things, was to be blamed; He had ulterior motives. *"For God doth know that in the day ye eat thereof, then your eyes shall be opened, and ye shall be as gods, knowing good and evil"* (Genesis 3:5). The suggestion was that God was keeping from them something they had a right to know, something that would make them as gods. Knowing good and evil would put them in a position to decide matters for themselves, to judge for themselves with no reference to God Himself and still come to an knowledge of the truth — a wicked and quite impossible lie. Note that Satan uses the nominative plural 'ye', applying his remarks to both Eve and to her husband.

This leads us now to the crux of the whole encounter with Satan. Eve faced a dilemma. She could accept without question what God had said because of *who* was saying it, confessing that God alone knows all things as they truly are. On the other hand, she could accept the word of Satan, not because it was Satan who was speaking, but simply by examining *what* he was saying. Eve and her husband could then decide for themselves whether what was said was true or false. The focus of the unbeliever will inevitably be upon *what* is said rather than *who* is speaking and upon whether that person – in the case of Scripture, God – speaks with authority. Is God in a position to know what He is talking about and therefore to be trusted and believed? In doubting someone's word, we are suggesting that there is a possibility they could be wrong. Those who barter with evidence claiming to show that the Bible is true have already moved onto the ground of doubt and denial because evidence is only required in a situation where the claims made are being questioned, could be false, and need to be tested. The ground of faith says there is no possibility of God's Word being anything other than true, for the simple reason that God cannot lie or be deceived and His knowledge as Creator is both infinite and comprehensive. To doubt the Word of God, or even to feel the need to test it, is to say that God could have made a mistake. Something we know to be true does not require proving to us. We have faith in God and His Word, or we have faith in the powers of fallen human judgement to ultimately determine what can be true or false.

We cannot doubt someone's word without at the same time saying something about the *person speaking*. At very least, we will be suggesting our source is not wholly reliable. Putting God's Word to the test is the same as saying that we do not trust Him to tell us the truth! To focus attention on *what* is said rather than *who* is saying it places the recipient of those words in a position to judge for himself whether what is before him is true or false. It rules out any consideration that the words must be true purely from the fact of who is speaking. Eve was at the point where she would say that what is said is true because *she* judged it so. She now became determinative of what could be true and what false in the place of God. Now she and her husband would be the authority as to what could be accepted as true or false. They would now imagine themselves to be sitting indeed in God's seat, they would see themselves as being *as gods!* Without first passing through the screen of human reason, nothing could be said to be true.

We accept what God says based on His own authority or we replace His authority with our own. There is no third way. The fact that Eve had already placed herself in a position where there was even thought to be a choice to make demonstrates to us that she had already set aside the absolute authority of God. She had already believed the LIE. She had made herself in her own mind to be the source of wisdom and authority in God's place! She was to test the veracity of what God had said against her own powers of judgement. She would put God on trial to see whether He was telling the truth. It is, of course a lie, a satanic lie, she was in no position to do no such thing – but since that day, this is how men have imagined themselves to be, *as gods!*

> *Unregenerate men will not accept God's authority purely on the basis that He is God, despite the fact that the God of whom we read in the Bible can only speak with absolute authority.*

Unbelievers will always subject what God says to their own judgement. Because they measure God's Word based on assumptions that cannot possibly leave room for its truth, they will unfailingly reject it. To profess faith in God and at the same time to subject the authority of given Scripture to tests of our own contrivance is a contradiction in terms. To question Scripture is to reject its absolute authority. Rejection of the authority of Scripture as the only authoritative Word is at the same time a rejection of Him who gave it. Those who truly know God will live after the pattern of our Saviour, who said, *"If any man will do his will, he shall know of the doctrine, whether it be of God, or whether I speak of myself"* (John 7:17). Men speak from God, or they speak of themselves, they cannot do both. They believe God and trust His Word, or they have believed the lie of Satan with respect to themselves. From that sad moment in Eden to this present time men have made themselves instead of God the measure of all things. They have followed hard on the heels of their diabolic master and persuaded themselves: *"I am a God, I sit in the seat of God"* (Ezekiel 28:2).

## A foundation of sand or solid rock?

The understanding of unregenerate men *is built upon heavily biased assumptions* about reality that exclude God as ultimate *without reason or evidence.* This amounts to disallowing all evidence except that which appears to support their own case. It takes for granted the existence of a pattern in all things that can be uncovered by an application of the human mind to the processes of nature. The ground of their position is a rebellious desire to be rid of God. By contrast, the believer sees God as being the source of all things and of all events, and accepts His infallible revelation to us in Scripture of Himself and His eternal counsel as the only basis for a cohesive understanding of the created world.

Ironically, even the most logical godless scientist inconsistently relies in his work upon the truth of that which he denies. He could not even carry on his God-denying work had not *God* created the world and were *God* not still actively sustaining it. He could formulate no 'natural laws' were it not for the faithfulness of God in maintaining the natural world. What we mean by 'laws' in nature are in fact the usual ways in which we observe God working in creation. *"And he is before all things, and by him all things consist"* (Colossians 1:17). *"Who being the brightness of his glory, and the express image of his person, and upholding all things by the word of his power..."* (Hebrews 1:3). That we can rely on these 'laws' in nature to operate in the same way each time is due to God's faithfulness. There are *no fixed laws* for God to obey. God is at liberty to work in a different way at any time He may choose and when He does so, this we call miracle. Therefore, our Lord along with Peter could walk on water when usually human bodies sink. Creation bears constant testimony of God's glory to the scientist. The fact that God is inescapable everywhere he looks stings the unregenerate conscience. Such a man *faces God every day* in His world and is thereby provoked thereby into God-denying explanations. Men can admit to the truth only when God by His Holy Spirit removes the blindness of mind obscuring his vision.

Until someone has been regenerated and reconciled to God, he or she will persist in offering 'scientific' objections to the Bible. In seeking to reply to these objections with yet more 'science', we only lend support to the objector by meeting him on his terms. We thus validate his false presuppositions by using them ourselves. At the same time, we are overlooking the real problem – just what he wants! A God who has created all things and calls all men to account is the last person the unbeliever wants to come across in his investigations. After beginning by eliminating God without any grounds for doing so and when the whole of creation points in the opposite direction, unregenerate minds continue to build up an explanation of all things without Him, falsely calling it 'science'. They then claim to have a 'proven' case! The boffin or bishop who turns to scoffing and irrational invective against 'creationism' is telling us no more than which side he is on in this battle to the death. Following the ancient credo of Pharaoh, – *"Who is the Lord, that I should obey his voice?"* (Exodus 5:2) – the unbeliever moves forward hoping he will be unchallenged by God's absolute authority. The basic belief of the regenerate man is that we move about in a world where God is inescapable, where every fact testifies of God, where the Word of God provides a foundation for our understanding of those things God wants us to know.

As the unregenerate mind has already concluded that the structure of the physical world is ultimate, that nothing exists outside it, he has thereby made it impossible to give account of anything that actually does exist outside it. All his ideas, including any about God, must be interpreted within his own 'big picture' of the physical universe, one that he has constructed himself. Anything that does not fit within it does not exist. It now becomes almost impossible to explain any idea of purpose or personality in such a context. Having rejected the possibility of an uncreated, self-contained God, the unbeliever must transfer those same attributes to creation. Having rejected the Creator, it is 'nature' that must provide from within itself its own answers. Every fact, every possibility, can only be understood in natural terms. Everyone and everything is equally ultimate and God is just part of the universe like everyone and everything else. If He exists, He may be a little wiser or a little more knowledgeable than man, but that is all. He too must learn about the universe of which He is a part. Everything, including God, is swallowed up in a common self-sustaining world.

Furthermore, this purely natural physical world is also said to be constantly in flux, changing continually, every second is unique. This will, of course, also be true of God as part of this one world. Heraclitus of Ephesus (c. 500 BC) put it like this, *"You cannot step twice into the same river"*. Accordingly, Jesus Christ cannot be *"the same yesterday, and today, and for ever"* (Hebrews 13:8). There can be no once-for-all creation. Things that are entirely new, that have not existed previously, are said to appear constantly. Of course, such a world could not exist by eternal decree and so any notion of a comprehensive divine plan is denied. Instead, the universe is thought to be entirely unpredictable and uncontrollable, ruled largely by *chance occurrences*. Our senses tell us everything is in constant change, but only reason, it is said, can discover permanent and stable truths. Only reason can bring order into this slippery chaos. Nothing is fixed, not even God Himself. All being is said then to be both natural and in continual change, nothing is ever the same except change! There can be no fixed, final, absolute truth. Nothing is today as it was yesterday, or will be tomorrow as it is today – we are always 'moving on'. Man's own experience of this change is the only real authority. We must 'modernise' to keep up, new doctrine, new bibles.

The believer takes the statements of the Bible seriously and here we learn that God exists and the world He has made. There is nothing else outside this. The Bible opens with the most profound statement, *"In the beginning God created the heaven and the earth"* (Genesis 1:1). We must always maintain a clear distinction between God and the 'natural' created world. Unlike all creation, God is sufficient in and of Himself, dependent on no one and nothing that is outside Himself. Rather, God sustains all things. God exists and acts in the way He does because, as God, He can be and do nothing else. Man is what he is and does what he does by virtue of being a creature *dependent* upon God. That men are able to deceive themselves sufficiently to believe that this is not so, changes nothing. The world God brought into being at creation out of nothing continues as it does only by His providence and fulfils His purposes in every detail, even down to the falling of a sparrow from the sky. This provides for the Christian a unified outlook on the whole of human life the unbeliever does not have.

The unbeliever has no such comprehensive view, but *vacillates between pure chance, and rigid determinism.* The only thing of which many unbelievers appear to be certain is that a unified view of the universe is not possible and can have no meaning. The Bible teaches that the whole of creation is unified by the one purpose and plan of God and everything without exception is kept by Him. This is the only order in the universe and from this all things derive their meaning. Remove God, remove His plan, and the world sinks into an abyss of contingent meaninglessness.

Having begun with two very different foundations, there will always be an unavoidable clash at every point rather than a meeting of minds between subjects of the kingdom of light and those of the kingdom of darkness. There is no common ground upon which believers and unbelievers may stand together to begin discussions; this is because both starting points cancel each other out at the start. For there to be any discussion one or other of the sides must abandon his starting point: the believer his trust in the authority of God's Word, or the unbeliever his trust in the authority of his pretended autonomous reason. This is something neither side can afford to do. We are facing two opposing 'faiths'. The humanistic materialism of the average unbeliever must be seen as a pagan 'faith'. What unbelievers try to do is to replace the sovereign purposes of God with a scheme of their own. All things are *already* part of a rational system by virtue of God's plan and have no need of being organised into such a system by a human mind that is at enmity with God. As believers, we argue and reason beginning with the truth given us in Scripture. All things are to be explained from statements we find there and nowhere else. We do not seek to prove or disprove a hypothesis we have thought up for ourselves. We begin, therefore, with the God of Scripture and His eternal counsel and what has been revealed to us of it in Scripture. To begin elsewhere would be to begin with something other than the truth.

If men do not recognise what God has put straight under their noses for what it is, it is due to a difficulty within them. They ought to see it, the Bible says so, and by right they ought, not simply to be aware of some supernatural being, but of the God of Scripture. Whether unbelievers like it or not, whether they receive it or not, the Bible comes to *all* men as: *"Thus saith God the Lord, he that created the heavens, and stretched them out; he that spread forth the earth, and that which cometh out of it; he that giveth breath unto the people upon it, and spirit to them that walk therein"* (Isaiah 42:5).

CHAPTER **2**

# Man the Measure of his World

*"And the people gave a shout, saying, It is the voice of a god, and not of a man. And immediately the angel of the Lord smote him, because he gave not God the glory: and he was eaten of worms, and gave up the ghost."* (Acts 12:22-23)

Those who have striven to seat themselves upon the throne of God do not see His glory in all created things. The glory that is God's, they call by another name. They have also closed their eyes to the ineradicable image in which they are made; they decline His crown of honour and glory. Speaking of man the Psalmist says, *"For thou hast made him a little lower than the angels, and hast crowned him with glory and honour"* (Psalm 8:5). In setting God aside, godless men downgrade themselves. Those who refuse the rule of Christ at the same time condemn themselves to be ruled by their own blind passions and prejudices; the sinful aspirations of their own hearts replace God's purpose.

Within his soul, the man without God seeks endless freedom – for his mind, for his passions, for his will. Yet, he will die in chains, although freedom is upon his lips. In setting free unbridled passion, all embracing reason, and an irresistible will, men destroy themselves. The man at war with God is at war with himself. They are not gods, as their physical limitations constantly remind them. They see the body as the prison of the soul. To try to free his soul a man will destroy himself, but he drops in truth into the eternal fires of hell.

Rejecting Him, the man without God must now set to and draw up a picture of the world after another blueprint, one lifted from the world created by the One whom he is so swift to deny.

> *In the place of the being of God, men make their own souls the measure of their own world.*

There can be few better examples of this than the teachings of Plato (427-347 BC). In a very literal sense the soul of man is replicated in a world that becomes one created in man's own image. In *The Republic* the perennial scourge of human conflict is overcome by the rule of an aristocracy of intellectuals, whom Plato judged to be the most suited to rule others (Gk. *ariston* + *kratos* = rule by the best). His system begins with an analogy drawn between the human soul (*psyche*) and the city (*polis*). What he understands to be the form of the human soul is replicated in the order of the wider community of men and their dealings with each other. The community of men was to exemplify the human heart; it could therefore only glorify man and not God.

According to the psychology of the day, the soul consisted of three parts. The rational element of the *mind* we use to reason, to argue and deliberate. Next, there was the spirited element making one courageous or cowardly, and giving strength of *will*. Finally, there remains *emotion*, the appetitive element of desires and passions. Accordingly, the three classes of men within human society were made to correspond with these three perceived elements of the soul. The class to which any individual member of society belonged was determined by which of the three characteristics of the soul was dominant in them. If all three parts of the soul functioned harmoniously *with reason in overall command* then that person was judged 'sound in mind'. Few men were thought able to achieve this balance perfectly. These were deemed philosopher-rulers or *guardians* of society, fitted to rule wisely and according to reason. Then there were those in whom the spirited element of the soul was dominant rather than reason; these were the wilful spirited class of soldiers called *auxiliaries*. They needed the reason of the ruling class to guide them and keep them in check. Finally, at the bottom of the pile there was the third and largest group, the *economic class*. As these people were ruled by the desires and passions of the soul, they needed both the wisdom of the rulers and the force of the auxiliaries to make them submit to reason; left to themselves they would not do this. Such a city, according to Plato, would be a just or righteous one. Evil is not defined as an offence against the holy character of any God. It is more psychological than moral in any generally accepted sense. Evil is thought of as an exaggeration of one of the elements of the soul, particularly that of the appetitive or lower part. It is a personality imbalance requiring remedy, a psychological defect.

This view of the individual, evil, and human society has persisted and is alive and kicking today. *The Republic* remains a standard text in our universities. It is found in Mozart's *Magic Flute* and Freemasonry in general. It is inherent in the political philosophy of 'globalism' and 'the new world order'. It has guided the development of the European Union and long before this found its way into the Arab world. Those individuals and nations should rule, it is said, who are most fitted to do so. There is an establishment trained and fitted to rule; there are those who execute and enforce the will of that rule, soldiers, police, university professors, teachers training our children to become 'good citizens', Then there are all the others, the mass economic class, there to fulfil an economic function in the great machine. It is a substitute kingdom of God, a kingdom of darkness that parades as a kingdom of enlightenment. It is a kingdom that condemns itself because the fallen soul of man is its measure.

## Man the measure of his fate

Before the Reformation got underway, a movement began in Italy around 1350, spreading later to northern Europe. We know it as the *Renaissance*. Medieval thinking up to this point had been dominated by the writings of Augustine of Hippo (345-430). Now the Renaissance began to change the way in which men had previously viewed themselves and the world in which they lived. Literally, the word 'renaissance' means 'new birth'. The classical word 'renovatio' or 'renewal' was used to describe something contemporary that resembled something ancient. Although the term is sometimes restricted to the world of painting, sculpture, and literature, the scope of the Renaissance was actually much wider. There was no area of life left untouched by its influence: philosophy, politics, theology, science, jurisprudence, and education. The motto of the Renaissance, 'man the measure of all things', was derived from the famous dictum of Protagoras of Abdera (b. 481 B.C.) and it pervaded all the very practical areas of life such as architecture and rudimentary science.

A central figure in the early days of the Renaissance movement was Franciscus Petrarch (1307-74), a wanderer, collector of manuscripts, and writer. Petrarch is thought to have originated the term 'dark ages', intended as a description of the times between classical antiquity and his own day. They were 'dark', not because they lacked Christianity as is often said, but because they lacked pre-Christian classical Roman values and virtues. Petrarch rediscovered Latin texts by Cicero whilst rummaging through monastic libraries. Cicero had said that the word for man *(vir)* is that from which the word virtue is derived *(virtus)*. It is this special quality of human 'virtue' that is to be developed through education, thus to become the *vir virtutis*, the truly manly man. This perspective, called 'humanism', stressed the creature power of man. Its goals were to be achieved through the development of a new educational programme centred in a classical revival of the study of the 'humanities' — grammar, rhetoric, history, poetry, and moral philosophy. The new humanist ideal dispensed with the specialist, the ideal had become to imitate 'Renaissance man', one who aims to excel in all things. This explains the interest of Leonardo da Vinci in everything from painting and drawing, sculpture, to literature and science. For man to exercise his own noblest characteristics was to possess god-like qualities. This unsurpassable excellence was worthy of honour, glory, and praise. Despite a thin cloak of Christian belief, the Renaissance developed an utterly man-centred goal that gave to man honour and glory belonging rightly only to God. *Glory to man in the highest!* The greatest aspiration for a man of letters was to become worthy of glory and gain immortality for his name. To this day, following the Renaissance precedent, university students pursue 'honours' degrees. Whilst they *may* have some value elsewhere, remembering their origin, we ought in all seriousness to question the growing place such man-glorifying accreditations are given today in the church of Christ.

A further development was taking place, not only was everything around man to be cast in his own mould, but now *even the unfolding of time was understood in terms of the measure of the human will rather than being attributed to divine providence as previously.* Following Augustine, the dominant thinking up to that time had been that God raised and disposed of earthly kingdoms, that he intervened in the affairs of men with earthquake, wind, and fire. Pre-Christian classical belief had seen life as a struggle between man's will and the wilfulness of fortune. The Romans had worshipped Fortuna, the daughter of Jupiter. She had been portrayed as turning a wheel, the wheel of fortune. The turning of this wheel determined the fate of men. Being a woman guided by feminine caprice, men of true *virtus* could woo and even subdue her. In this way, their 'fate' could be influenced and changed. Augustine vehemently attacked this heathen teaching in *Civitas Dei*. He insisted upon the all-pervading providence of God and denied that events on earth happen 'rashly or at random'. What virtue men may acquire, said Augustine, would be solely a gift of God's grace. The superstition is still with us that the controlling factor of human events is the unpredictable power of fortune rather than divine providence. Augustine viewed history as being a linear unfolding of the purposes of God for the world he created. Aristotle and the humanists of the Renaissance, totally in tune with the idea of Fortuna, viewed history as a series of recurring cycles — from where we obtain the idea of history repeating itself. Even although no longer embodied in the figurehead of a goddess, many still believe the 'wheel of fortune' turns for them.

It seemed that man had now found the route whereby he could be the master of his fate, could command the outcome of history. There was much written and spoken at this time about the 'freedom of the will', by which was actually understood the *autonomy* of the human will. Man alone within creation could mould his own character; he alone had the power of choice whereby he could determine his own destiny. It was not long before the figure of Fortuna herself disappeared, to be replaced by impersonal chance. The teaching grew that man on his own could mould the flux of events in a manner not previously envisaged. This meant that the causes of men's sorrows were within themselves, rather than simply being the outcome of fickle fortune.

> *Such is his arrogance that, in his own eyes at least, man now sits upon the throne of God governing the affairs of a kingdom built after the measure of his own soul. He rules the universe by his own reason; even the unfolding of events must bend to his will.*

## The light that was darkness

Few in 17th century Europe would have denied that Scripture spoke of real things. Nevertheless, already in the 13th century scholastic theology had divided human life into two spheres, that of faith and that of nature. The same idea is found in this extract from the writings of the Englishman, Francis Bacon (1561-1626),

> "Man by the Fall fell at the same time from his state of innocence and from his dominion over nature. Both of these losses, however, can even in this life be in some part repaired; the former by religion and faith, the latter by the arts and sciences." *(Novum Organum)*

Bacon understood the fall of man to have had a double aspect. There was spiritual separation between man and his Maker, but there was also a separation — and he likened it to a divorce — between the natural world and the human mind; more precisely, between the impressions gained by the senses, and reason. There being two spheres, the spiritual and the natural, there were for Bacon also two kingdoms, the kingdom of God and the kingdom of man. Entrance into the kingdom of man he maintained *"is not much other than the entrance into the kingdom of heaven, whereinto none may enter except as a little child."* A precursor of later romanticism, Bacon claimed we need the 'purity and integrity' of a child's mind, with *"the understanding thoroughly freed and cleansed, the entrance into the kingdom of man, founded on the sciences."* The mind must be cleansed of anything that would distort or obscure the *"commerce between the mind of man and the nature of things"*. There must be a fully open channel between nature and reason; this is the 'redeemed mind'. All blockages, preconceived 'idols or phantoms', must be eliminated.

> "And all depends on keeping the eye steadily fixed upon the facts of nature and so receiving their images simply as they are. For God forbid that we should give out a dream of our own imagination for a pattern of the world; rather may he graciously grant to us to write an apocalypse or true vision of the footsteps of the Creator imprinted on his creatures..."
>
> *(The Great Instauration)*

Any idea of the observed facts of the natural world coming to us as pre-interpreted by the eternal purposes of God and revealed in Scripture is thereby ruled out. This pattern of the world would reveal itself to impartial, unfettered, uncluttered, and unaided human reason. The one is made to fit the other. In *The Great Instauration* Bacon celebrates the approaching marriage of the 'redeemed' mind to the external world of nature. This 'bridal song' is pre-emptive of the 'spousal verse' in the *Prospectus* of the English romantic poet, Wordsworth, celebrating the wedding of man's mind *"to this goodly universe"*.

> My voice proclaims
> How exquisitely the individual Mind
> (And the progressive powers perhaps no less
> Of the whole species) to the external World
> Is fitted ...

However, Bacon drew his line of distinction in the wrong place. Reality is one; both the spiritual and the natural make up *one* world created by God. The real distinction to be made is between the kingdom of darkness and the kingdom of light.

> "The light of the body is the eye: if therefore thine eye be single, thy whole body shall be full of light. But if thine eye be evil, thy whole body shall be full of darkness. If therefore the light that is in thee be darkness, how great is that darkness!" (Matthew 6:22-23)

All our physical senses, our mind, all our thoughts are affected by and biased by inherent sinfulness and *so cannot even see natural things aright!*

It is still often suggested that when we need to know about God, we read the Bible, but when we need to know about all other things we only need to use our five senses. Once more, an excursion is made into the mythical no-man's land between faith and unbelief. The truth is that all that can be known is as the Bible portrays it, we can no more do without God in the realm of science or psychology, or anything else, than we can when we are seeking our soul's salvation. There is nothing in the universe that God has not made; and therefore to know anything truly we need to know it as God does. What the Bible has to say affects all of life, again, *because God made all things.* "*For of him, and through him, and to him, are all things: to whom be glory for ever. Amen*" (Romans 11:36). All things were created to the everlasting glory of God. To know anything truly we must begin by acknowledging: "*Thou art worthy, O Lord, to receive glory and honour and power: for thou hast created all things, and for thy pleasure they are and were created*" (Revelation 4:11).

To assume that what we know may be drawn from both revelation *and* reason independently of each other is a serious mistake. First, because human knowledge is derivative and must replicate God's knowledge; but second, as a fallen and rebellious creature the sinner has every reason to deny and suppress any revelation of the God who calls him to account. The human mind cannot operate autonomously and be right, and furthermore in its fallen state it will inevitably pervert and misinterpret all that which enters its consciousness. Unregenerate men only know anything of the truth because they are inconsistent and are not completely successful in suppressing the truth. Every historical fact, every scientific fact, *every fact of the universe belongs to God*. No judgements made in independence of God can be true judgements. Every fact, every unfolding event in the universe is testimony to the truth of Scripture, it testifies to the reality of the existence of the God of Scripture. Every fact presupposes the eternal counsel of the omnipotent, omniscient, eternal God. Nothing could otherwise exist.

The Reformers did much to combat Renaissance humanism. However, by the 18th century, the Reformation had lost the momentum it once had and there was a resurgence of humanism in *'the Enlightenment'*. Few did more to propagate the lie of Enlightenment thinking than Immanuel Kant (1724-1804). This is the well-known opening to his essay *What is Enlightenment?*

> "Enlightenment is the withdrawal of man from his self-inflicted intellectual immaturity. This immaturity is the inability the use his own reason without being guided by someone else. It is self-inflicted immaturity whenever its cause does not lie in a lack of reason, but in the resolve and courage required to use it without the guidance of another. sapere aude! Have the courage to make use of your own reason! is then the watchword of the Enlightenment."
> (Kant's *Gesammelte Schriften*, Band VIII, our translation)

Lest anyone be inclined to doubt that what we are facing in Kant is anything other than a deliberate and conscious refusal of Christ and an acceptance of the original Satanic lie in Eden of the presumed ultimate authority of the human heart and mind, let them read the following comments on Kant by the modern writer, Iris Murdoch.

"How recognisable, how familiar to us, is the man so beautifully portrayed in the *Grundlegung* (ed. *Grundlegung zur Metaphysik der Sitten*, Kant,) who confronted even with Christ turns away to consider the judgement of his own conscience and to hear the voice of his own reason. Stripped of the exiguous metaphysical background which Kant was prepared to allow him, this man is with us still, free, independent, lonely, powerful, rational, responsible, brave, the hero of so many novels and books of moral philosophy...
In fact, Kant's man had already received glorious incarnation nearly a century earlier in the work of Milton: his proper name is Lucifer." (from *The Sovereignty of Good over other Concepts*)

The authority of Christ is ultimately replaced by that of Satan. The claim is that if man is to be capable of pure thought, he must be freed from the outside influence of others, even including the voice of God in Christ Jesus! Reason alone rules, all else must be stripped away. This was the original promise of the Serpent: think for yourself; choose for yourself — apart from God!

*Let those who would reject the easy yoke of Christ to 'be as gods' and rule a world of their own creation remember that in so doing they will be all their lifetime subject to the bondage of Satan and share his end.*

Other names associated with the Enlightenment are Descartes, Hobbes, Hume, and Diderot. Prominent at this time in England was John Locke (1632-1704). He went up to the University at Oxford when Puritanism was at its height and the godly John Owen was vice-chancellor. According to Locke the mind can only work with what is perceived through the senses, yet like many in the movement, he was reluctant to relinquish all Christian beliefs. His book on Christianity, *The Reasonableness of Christianity* (1695), was widely read, but in attempting to defend Christianity against the sceptics he only succeeded in undermining it yet further because he would accept revelation only if he could sift it first through the mesh of human reason. As in Eden, everything must be brought before the bar of human judgement, to which end Locke devised a number of categories of reason. The existence of one God he deemed *reasonable*, the existence of more than one God *contrary to reason*, but the resurrection of the dead was *above reason*. Up until the Enlightenment, as we observed in Francis Bacon, reason had been confined to nature, the part of the universe that could be looked at like a machine subject to laws of cause and effect. With Locke and the Enlightenment, reason began to nibble away at things spiritual. Once reason was let loose in this way it soon encompassed everything, there was nothing left lying outside it.

Descartes (1596-1650) began not with the self-contained God of the Bible, but with ultimate, self-contained man. He began with himself, *'cogito ergo sum'* — I think, therefore I am. Nature and God were to be examined and proved from this starting point. The only certain knowledge which man can possess is to be found within his own mind. Beyond that, nothing could be proved objectively. God, the universe, and all that is in it, all that is to be known, actually or potentially, *have become reduced to the measures of the human mind*. In the end, God too becomes a part of the universe existing within the mind of man. Descartes then attempted to recreate the world after the image of a mathematical pattern.

True knowledge could thus originate only within the human consciousness. The world begins and exists first, not in the consciousness of God, but within human consciousness. God and all things are contained within the consciousness of man, not God. This is a complete reversal of the truth and is at the heart of Satan's lie and we must be very clear about where this thinking leads. By contrast, the Bible tells us that it is *within the heart and consciousness of GOD* that all things have their origin and by which they continue to exist. Only as the eternal purposes of God unfold in the human consciousness through the enlightening work of the Holy Spirit can that which is the truth be known and understood. It is within this process that the Scriptures have their place. They form a necessary link between that which is in God's heart and which He wills to reveal to our hearts.

The English philosopher, Thomas Hobbes (1588-1679), shared Descartes mathematical view of the world, but left no room for an autonomous will in practical human activities, leaving man subject to the same mechanical causality ruling nature as a whole. In seeking an illegitimate route to freedom, man was now completely caught up in 'the machine'. With the differential and integral calculus of Leibnitz (1646-1716), nothing was beyond the reach of the human mind, not even chance. Physics saw the world as a huge machine that in time would succumb to total explanation and with it would come complete intellectual and practical mastery of man's environment. The work of evolutionary biologists like Darwin, Huxley, and Spencer drew the activities of living organisms into the same framework. At this same time the experimental psychology of Wilhelm Wundt reduced thought itself to a physical base, explaining it in terms of organic stimulation and nervous impulse. The mind as such is now dead and gone, everything is physical, or it is nothing. Wundt's work remains to this day at the heart of the modern pedagogical methodology, of learning as stimulation and response rather than the acquisition of knowledge. Children respond to stimuli provided by the teacher like a dog to Pavlov's little bell. Teaching has degenerated into being little different than training a troop of circus monkeys. The mind is indeed now effectively dead, reduced to a cocktail of chemicals and electrical impulses. Is the God of the Bible dead? Then it will not be long before man too is carried out on a bier!

At the turn of the 19th to the 20th century, the pendulum began to swing in the other direction and the previous optimism faced insurmountable challenges. The strongly held assumptions about the nature of the physical world were being seriously undermined. In 1900 Max Planck put forward the radical new hypothesis that the emission of light might not be a continuous process, but that light was emitted and absorbed in packets or quanta, thus challenging the assumption of classical physics that continuity rules. The discovery of X-rays by Röntgen, developments in atomic and nuclear physics, all made mechanistic determinism look increasingly improbable. Early studies of the structure of the atom were carried out by Ernest Rutherford at Manchester University in England. He likened electrons orbiting a nucleus to planets going around a sun. His Danish associate Niels Bohr demolished this analogy by suggesting that the movement of electrons within atoms was not predictable but infinitely random. There was an irreducible uncertainty in the behaviour of atomic particles rendering the universe indeterministic and completely unpredictable. These movements could not be explained by the laws of mechanics and the old 'common-sense' picture of cause and effect.

The crumbling of positivistic optimism was being felt in spheres other than science. There was a growing cult of the irrational that subordinated conscious reasoning to unconscious instinct and vitalistic intuition. Central to this movement was Friedrich Nietzsche (1844- 1900). Reason was not unassailable and self-sufficient as had been previously taught; science was not sovereign. Unbridled reason had killed man off. He preached in place of reason the sovereignty of the *living* man, self-sufficient, a law unto himself, a man of action, where *will* prevailed over reason. Objectivity, unbiased knowledge, scholarship, all elements of modern civilisation, paralyse the human will; they beset it about with self-doubt and restlessness. The stripping away previously inflicted upon the mind was now enacted upon the will. Man must know the complete independence of decision, choice, the brave joy of willing. Nothing must obstruct it. Yet another element of the human soul is thereby deified. *The human will is now god in the place of reason.*

To set out along this new road all remnants of romanticism and sentimentality must go, only the real, the facts, the here and now, have any value. There must be, in Nietzsche's view, an *Umwertung aller Werte*, a transvaluation of all values. So, God is dead, Christ is the enemy of life, morality is a lie, truth is a fiction. What is left is the untrammelled Dionysius life, life without illusions and sham, a destiny men must accept with joy. Yet, what we have before us is a nihilistic lack of values and an affirmation of the meaningless of all existence. We see again, in Nietzsche, a conscious fist held in the face of God, a changing of the truth into a lie. So the scene was set in the 19th century for the progressive unravelling tragedy that was the 20th century, precursor of the disintegration, disaster, and judgement that must yet inevitably await us.


## *The dead-end dilemma*

Thankfully by the grace and mercy of God, men are never able to follow their presuppositions to any real conclusion. The consequences of the extremes of a completely deterministic or a completely random universe are unacceptable to a man still bearing about him even a marred image of God. Therefore, what all godless systems of thought, all vain 'imaginings', attempt to do is to reconcile these two contradictory directions in some way, interpreting one by the other, or by holding both apart as Kant tried to do. This thinking has spawned an evil culture, corrupt 'values', all of which will be judged and swept away by God.

The fact that man is made in the image of God and has an inherent, if partial, knowledge of the truth, means that he revolts against the result of his own reasoning. The sinner is inconsistent in the way he reasons, he swings to and fro between a world that is ruled by utter chance happenings and a world that is bound by inescapable natural law, between the chaos of total irrationality and the frigid logic of icy reason. His belief in the randomness of all existence ties him to a view of the world that is entirely irrational. At the same time, he seeks to subdue the chaos by describing all things in terms of the rule of natural law. Attempting to enclose all things within mathematics produces a world bound by logic. It is a rational yet irrational world at the same time. The irresistible determinism of both worlds deprives man of his much-cherished freedom. Man is slave to physical natural law; he is to be explained entirely in terms of chemical reactions, DNA, inherited genes. He has no non-physical aspect, no mind, and no immortal soul. On the other hand, he is said to be wholly free to move and decide as he will, but even here, he is captive to chaos.

Neither world appeals to the sinner on its own and so his efforts are directed at striking a balance at some point between them, somewhere between the meaningless of absolute diversity, where everything is free and one thing unrelated to another, and the rigidity of absolute unity. All godless views of the world, where man is placed at its heart, are caught in this dilemma. The consequence is that every worldly philosophy thought out by sinners is arbitrary and unstable because of the necessity of continually swinging about somewhere in the middle between these two extremes. The final arbiter as to the point of balance is the assumed autonomy of the human mind. The data is finite, assumed absolutes are arbitrary, the judgements tenuous and difficult, and are at rock bottom utterly subjective.

Whether we take the side of chaos and irrationality, or whether we swing the other way towards determinism and the finality of natural law, man disappears; he simply loses his humanity. God is dead, and man is dead too. Everything becomes devoid of meaning and life is absurd. In seeking to place himself at the centre of all things, man now finds his world disintegrating around him. Despite this, because he is made in the image of God, because he knows he is more than a mathematical and chemical formula, he revolts. His own conclusions are abhorrent to him. Man has begun by now, not simply to deny the existence of God, but finds it necessary to try to prove his own. Still refusing to submit to the Gospel, many seek to find something beyond the material in mysticism, in 'new age' Gnosticism, in the occult pseudo-spirituality of the Pentecostal charismatic movement. The 20th century existentialist philosophers Heidegger, Jaspers, Sartre, Camus recognised the absurdity of life, its meaninglessness. They spoke of nausea, *Angst*, fear, agony, boredom, becoming. Some sought an 'ultimate experience', one that would finally demonstrate to them the reality of their own being. This was sought in the psychedelic drugs of the sixties and even in suicide. What else is there to do otherwise? We can just sit in our dustbins and watch the world go by, like Samuel Beckett's two characters waiting for Godot, who never turns up.

## *A finite copy of the thinking of God*

We see then that the unbeliever imagines he can understand and interpret all things by his own fallen, unaided human reason, now perverted and misdirected by sin. The sinner sees himself as surrounded by an irrational world that came into being on its own, simply by chance, without any underlying purpose and into which he must bring some order by use of his reason. The believer, by contrast, sees the universe as created, as sustained by God and fulfilling His eternal purpose. Every fact comes to us pre-interpreted by its place in God's plan. So the believer calls for reason, fallen or regenerate, to submit itself unreservedly to the Word of God.

The work of God's self-revelation originates in His own heart and consciousness, what He reveals is first found there. Through the inspired writers it passes onto a written page, we read it from the page, and as it is illuminated to our mind, so it unfolds within *our* consciousness. This work, carried through from start to finish by God's Spirit, is *one* work. No one aspect of this work constitutes the whole, and yet without each of the separate parts the work cannot take place. This self-revelation of God is only completed when that which has its origin in the consciousness of God is identically reproduced in our human consciousness. God still speaks to men today, and He does so in the marvellous way we have just described, yet only *through Scripture!* In Scripture He has said all He has to say. It is here that we begin; it is to Scripture we submit. Apart from this, what is in the heart and mind of God cannot be known. There is that which God wants us to know, but also that which has come forth because of God's action of revealing it.

> *The content of that which God reveals AND the manner in which He brings it to us, namely in the written book we now hold in our hands, both are a revelation of God.*

We are conscious of ourselves and of everything around us only because first God is a self-conscious being and we are made in his image. To deny God is to deny ourselves, for if God does not exist neither can that which is made in His image. It is also to deny the possibility of knowing anything. Only because we are made in God's image can we receive that which God reveals to us; only because *our mind is a finite copy of God's mind* can we think as He does and so know the truth.

> *Only in a world where every detail of our life and existence is ruled by the all-encompassing plan of a sovereign God can we enjoy any kind of real freedom and be rescued from the only other possibility, that of being thrown about by the vagaries of a purposeless and chance existence or imprisoned by the cold determinism of fate.*

Only in a world unified by the plan and purpose of God can there be a once-for-all certain and finished act of redemption with consequences for the whole race of men. Unregenerate men will not tolerate under any circumstances a God who has ordained all things by eternal decree and spoken authoritatively concerning them and whose authority they cannot countermand or even question. They will spend their life's energy denying this truth.

The only alternative to the eternal plan of God is that of a meaningless world coming into existence by pure chance from materials that always existed. This is a universe of a seemingly endless variety of disconnected facts. How can one chance 'fact', one disconnected occurrence, bear any relation to another? It cannot. The universe is reduced to some gigantic lottery to be explained by trying to enclose it all in an immeasurable mathematical calculation. Remove the Genesis account of creation and we are left with an irrational, meaningless, contingent universe with no order and *no real connections between any facts in it.* On the one hand, pure reason, logic, is said to exist as an eternal principle which even God, should He exist, must observe. On the other hand, everything is governed by chance. What the godless thinker must try to do is make rational statements about that which appears to be intrinsically irrational. It cannot be done. *He claims at the same time to believe in a structured and an unstructured universe.* The 'post-modern' route out of this dilemma is to assert that any system of interpretation is equally valid and none is ultimately authoritative. Our own view of reality can be true only for us. All forms of authority thus disappear. Applied to the world of moral behaviour this relativism has wrought untold havoc in the western world. Applied to Christian belief from any rank liberal to the fervent evangelical who says 'this is God's Word *to me*', objective authority has gone and spiritual anarchy has replaced the Gospel of Christ. Whilst hanging on for dear life to the fraying threads of a belief that all things are accessible to the human mind, there is at the same time an admission that things as they truly are can never be known to the human mind. God is dead, man is dead, knowledge is dead.

In seeking to shake off the authority of a sovereign God, in seeking to escape what God has beforehand decreed, in the mistaken belief it deprives him of his ability to decide and act freely, the sinner refuses the providence of a loving heavenly Father. He exchanges this for the impersonal total captivity of a deterministic world ruled by chance and simultaneously bound by the cruel logic of inescapable natural law. Instead of seeing himself as *"the offspring of God,* lovingly fashioned in God's image, he permits himself to be explained away entirely in the cold impersonal terms of chemical reactions, DNA, and inherited genes. If he follows the dictates of his own fallen mind, he must always end up a captive.

The believer is committed to the doctrine of Scripture, infallibly and verbally inspired, to its final authority for *all* men in *all* matters. The believer does not accept that there is *any sphere* of life where Scripture does not bring its authority to bear and where reason is sufficient without it. There is no place for reason to operate apart from under the authority of Scripture. He is so committed because to doubt God's Word is also to doubt in the Person whose Word it is. We have regard for our Saviour only as we have regard for His Word. If we believe *Him* to be reliable, able to save to the uttermost, we shall believe that what He tells us in His Word is equally reliable.

## *If the Son therefore shall make you free...*

The eighteenth century French libertarian and libertine, Jean-Jaques Rousseau, wrote, *"Man is born free; and everywhere he is in chains"*. This perfectly describes the persistent dilemma for godless men, although not in the sense intended by Rousseau. What Rousseau did not see is that man is born fettered in sin and can be freed only by Him *"who bled for Adam's helpless race"*. Whilst revolution raged throughout infidel France, in godless England, Charles Wesley wrote the following words of testimony.

> Long my imprisoned spirit lay
> > Fast bound in sin and nature's night;
> Thine eye diffused a quickening ray,
> > I woke the dungeon flamed with light;
> My chains fell off my heart was free;
> I rose, went forth, and followed Thee

In seeking to be free of God, man has lost what freedom he thought he had, becoming now being the plaything of chance, or the object of soulless determinism. Of course, in truth he is neither, his view of the world is a complete myth. He is born free only to sin. With no sovereign God, with no sovereign plan, there can be no certain salvation *and no freedom of any kind for men at all!* Only a *sovereign* God, One who can ensure all that He wills and all that He promises will surely come to pass, only the God of the Bible, can make it possible for us to exercise our wills in a way that has meaning, can enable us *freely* to love and serve Him. He has determined that this should be so; nothing is left to 'chance'. Without the sovereign God of Scripture, heaven would forever remain empty.

When thinking of God, we are faced with choosing one of two possibilities. First, either God is fully conscious of all things and sovereign, and nothing exists or happens of itself; or second, God Himself is dependent upon other things around Him that exist or take place apart from Him and totally unpredictably. He then needs to wait and see what will occur, or wait upon what man will decide before taking action. This second option is not the God of Scripture. All this has very serious implications for the reliability of Scripture. Should we choose the second option, because God Himself can never be quite sure how things will turn out, His Word can hardly be relied upon with respect to events now or in the future. This has particular relevance for the certainty of our salvation and the ultimate triumph of our Saviour. If we take the first option, then we must conclude that, being made in the image of God, when our minds are enlightened by God's self-revelation, the nature of our knowledge will be a finite replica of God's own knowledge and so we can know with a certainty that escapes the godless. We can express the same idea by saying that what is in the consciousness of God replicates itself in our finite consciousness within the limited parameters of our finitude and that which He has willed to reveal to us. If we are to know anything for sure, we need the Bible.

> *We cannot function without the Word of God – because it is the sole physical instrument, which by His Spirit, links our finite hearts and minds to the eternal heart and mind of God.*

It is the way, according to God's will and purpose, that which is in His heart to tell us is made clear to us. Without God's Word, we can be sure of nothing.

At first glance, what we have been saying appears to be leading us towards the same dilemma as that faced by human philosophy, of swinging between a completely deterministic universe and a completely contingent one. We appear at first, on the one hand, to face God's complete control over all things in a way that removes any meaning from the free actions and thoughts of men; yet on the other, to face unpredictable, contingent human actions, which God may foresee but can do nothing to prevent. Were these assertions truly the teaching of the Bible, there is little doubt but that we are no better off than were we to adopt some human philosophical system in the place of Scripture, but this is not what the Bible says at all.

It is true that there are those who describe the sovereignty of God in such terms so that it is effectively reduced to little more than a form of fatalism. It is not surprising to find a practical antinomianism among these people. They cannot help being sinners and they continually bewail their sinful lot before God, whilst at the same time they use the cover of a fallen nature as an excuse for all kinds of unloving and ungodly behaviour. Andrew Fuller, friend of the missionary pioneer William Carey, faced such a distressing situation in his first pastorate at Soham, near Cambridge. A member of his Church repeatedly excused his drunkenness by protesting he had a sinful nature and so could not help himself. The teaching of Scripture is that He who demands, *"Be ye holy; for I am holy"* has also made provision that even now we may *"be holy in all manner of conversation"* (1 Peter 1:15-16). If we are unable to take full responsibility for our own sin, then we must put the blame at God's door for making us sinners in the first place! Perish the thought! Gospel preaching is *far more* than calling in the 'dead elect'. This is hardly a biblical expression. All sinners are under the same condemnation until snatched as brands from the burning, hopelessly lost and facing the judgement of God. *"Among whom also we all had our conversation in times past in the lusts of our flesh, fulfilling the desires of the flesh and of the mind; and were by nature the children of wrath, even as others."* (Ephesians 2:3) The offer of salvation to *all* men lost in sin is a perfectly genuine one.

On the other side, there are those who, thinking to spare God the blame for all the evils in the world, have put Him at the mercy of events it is said He cannot control. They have made Him a dependent God, helpless before the 'sovereign will' of man. This is clearly in conflict with all that the Bible teaches about God. If by 'freewill' we mean thoughts and deeds that are beyond the sovereign plan of God, then we have already gone beyond Scripture. There can be nothing floating about somewhere in time and space all on its own. Whilst such sentiments may be well intentioned, they are unnecessary and unbiblical, and implicitly amount to a denial that *"all things were made by him"*. Against this view, the Scriptures teach, *"There are many devices in a man's heart; nevertheless the counsel of the Lord, that shall stand"* (Proverbs 19:2 1).

It is only by the will of God that the will of man stands, so that it makes no sense to set the one against the other. Even as the mind of man is a finite mirror image of the mind of God, the same is true of the will. There are, however, some essential differences. First, the will of man does not operate outside the will of God, indeed the freedom that it does have is possible *only because* of the will of God. Second, since the fall, the will of man has a perverted bias because of sin. To be in full accord with the teaching of Scripture, and at the same time to avoid the dilemma within human philosophy, we must maintain that all things are determined by the counsel and will of God. At the same time, we must *insist strongly upon the meaningful and free actions and thoughts of men as being made possible only because God is sovereign.* Only a personal and truly sovereign God can rescue us from the impersonal determinism of fate and the uncertainty and meaninglessness of pure chance that dominates modern godless thinking by creating us free agents, the guarantee of that freedom being His own sovereignty. There can be no meaningful human freedom outside the sovereign will of God; elsewhere we remain imprisoned. Anything originating on its own outside God's purposes can have no possible meaning, no possible freedom.

The extent of human freedom is finite and determined by the man's nature. The will of God is infinite, but is equally determined by all attributes of His nature. God, being good, cannot create that which is evil; fallen man, being sinful, cannot please God, *"...they that are in the flesh cannot please God"* (Romans 8:8). Sinful man is naturally inclined neither to choose God nor to want to live for Him. Faith in Christ on the part of a lost sinner presumes a work of God's Spirit having already begun in the heart drawing him to Christ. Whilst it is true that *"no man can come unto me, except the Father which hath sent me draw him"* (John 6:44), equally we read, *"whosoever shall call upon the name of the Lord shall be saved"* (Romans 10:13). The one truth does *not contradict but enables* the other.

Those who press God's sovereignty or man's freedom beyond the bounds of Scripture do not have different but *identical misconceptions* about both of these doctrines. This is because they all believe that one cannot exist where the other is present. They feel that where God is sovereign, man can have no say, or where man is free God's will does not prevail. The problem is that *both* these extremes tend to think of God's sovereignty in quasi-fatalistic terms and the operations of the human will as unbridled contingency. Thinking in this way means that where God is sovereign man cannot act freely out of his own will and where man makes a free choice of will God's sovereignty is implicitly denied. Certainly, if set out in this way they cannot co-exist but this is not what is taught in Scripture. Men do not naturally exercise faith in Christ, not because they are not free agents, but because they are sinners and not inclined to do so.

Men exercise their wills freely and take responsibility for their thoughts and actions, despite the fact that they cannot do so beyond the boundaries of their own fallen and finite personalities. Limitations are no denial of responsibility and free agency. God's sovereignty *guarantees* the free agency of the human psyche. God has decreed it shall be so. Were God not comprehensively sovereign man could have no freedom of any kind, but would be reduced to being a limp puppet on a string. Such freedom as man enjoys is God's gift and part of being made in the image of God. Indeed, only in this way can man be saved from the deterministic tyranny of the humanist world always swinging between a cold calculated logic and the chaotic irrationality of a universe ruled by chance occurrences. That men choose to abuse this freedom cannot be blamed on God. If men sin, it is because they want to, and so they are held responsible for their sin. *No one ever sinned who did not want to,* so if we claim our freedom let us not try to place the blame for sin elsewhere. To blame what we do on anyone or anything other than ourselves is to *deny* our freedom and to return to the humanist world of determinism. It is ultimately to blame God, saying to our Maker, *"Why hast thou made me thus?"* (Romans 9:20) If the actions of men are always shot-through with sin, then it can only be because they are sinners. When they freely think and act, they do so in accordance with a fatal flaw in their nature, there because of the fall, there because of a deliberate sin, something that can now only be changed by the redemption that is in Christ Jesus. Equally, we must also say that no one ever came to Christ who at some point did not become willing.

It is important that we perceive the sovereignty of God and the free agency of man not as ruling each other out, but as the latter being possible only because of the former. This affects the way we understand the unfolding of God's purposes in human history, including the inspiration of the Bible. Unless we see the human will as operating freely within the compass of God's sovereign will, when considering verbal inspiration we shall be left with the unsatisfactory alternatives of a theory of mechanical dictation in which man is a passive instrument, or of a thoroughly human Bible.

We must remember, *God does not reveal to us all He has in mind* and we ought not to expect Him to do so. God gives to us all that we need to know whilst withholding many things. *"The secret things belong unto the Lord our God: but those things which are revealed belong unto us and to our children for ever, that we may do all the words of this law"* (Deuteronomy 29:29). Only in God is comprehensive knowledge possible. Such an aspiration on the part of man is ungodly and impossible. By His self-revelation, He entrusts man with a systematic knowledge of Himself and the universe He has made, that is, to the extent that He wills us to know it. Whilst such a systematic knowledge is a replica of God's own knowledge, it is not comprehensive, nor will it ever be. Against this, unbelievers assume that what is knowable to God is knowable to them. We do not have the complete picture so that from time to time we shall meet *apparent* contradictions. As there can be no internal contradictions within God's being God, so there can be no external contradictions with respect to His actions. All things being subject to Him, there can be no real contradictions only apparent ones.

> **We are in no position as God's creatures to demand of Him an answer to every stupid question that occurs to us.**

If there is no answer in Scripture, we do not need to know it! The Bible gives us all that God wants us to know; it does not reveal all that is to be known.

If God's eternal plan is immutable, why then should we pray, still less say that prayer changes things? It is true that the events and occurrences on earth cannot be regarded as being something new in and of themselves. This would be to attribute to 'history' the ability to produce something out of nothing. This would be to deny what the Bible teaches about creation and the idea of God controlling world events in His providence. Such occurrences, were they possible, being unrelated to God's eternal purpose could consequently have no meaning. God sanctifies and ordains the means to His end as well as the end itself and prayer must be seen in this light — a means to God's ends in which we are privileged to have real participation, and involving *our* wills and *our* genuine desires. We do not deny the unchangeable purpose of God by insisting that prayer changes things, nor do we deny the free agency of men by insisting that God's will is unchangeable. This does not deprive us of the privilege of prayer and persuasion with God. Any contradiction can only be an apparent one, often because we are not in possession of all the facts. We cannot judge the works of God using our own incomplete knowledge and limited understanding of the situation. God must be God for prayer to be answered. Again,

God's sovereign will *enables* prayer rather than contradicts it. God cannot answer prayer if it is always possible for His will to be countermanded. We do not establish the free agency of man by denying the sovereignty of God, but we *do* thereby deprive all such actions of any real meaning and make it impossible to be certain that God is ever able to answer our prayers!

There is another common misunderstanding: *we must not think that when sin entered the world, something occurred which God did not foresee.* How could it? We must not think that here was an event He could not possibly have anticipated and after which He was forced to look about for some means of recovering His losses. Nothing could be further from reality. First, this simply does not coincide with the picture of God given in Scripture, whose knowledge extends to every detail as it is, was, or ever will be, but also ever *could be.* Second, it does not account for the fact that the remedy was prepared before the calamity. The Lord Jesus is *"the Lamb slain from the foundation of the world"* (Revelation 13:8) and those who believe are chosen *"in him before the foundation of the world"* (Ephesians 1:4). This is the only certainty we can have that we shall of our own volition believe in the Lord Jesus and cast our all upon Him. It is the only certainty we can have that having believed we shall be saved. The certainty of our faith even as the certainty of our hope lies with God.

The question now arises, if God not only saw evil coming, but also included it in His plan, then surely He must be to blame for it? No, not at all. God and God alone is good, so that evil cannot originate with Him. This would introduce a contradiction within the being of God; it would require that God do something of which He is not capable. It would make Him both good and evil at the same time. God being man's Creator, it is impossible that there could be any evil present at the time of creation. Therefore, sin and death are not normal attributes of this world, but are unnatural and the results of the wilful transgression of man at the instigation of Satan. To assume that the current state of affairs in the world is normal is to deny that man is responsible for bringing this calamity upon himself and instead places the blame squarely with God. This would mean that man's present moral consciousness is also normal and reliable; it would also preclude the possibility of salvation. We would then need no revelation, no Bible, no Saviour from sin. It is quite impossible that God should even think to do evil let alone originate it. This is not the same as saying that, for reasons He has chosen not to reveal to us, evil is not, despite this, an integral part of His eternal purpose and that it is made to fulfil His ends to the letter.

Whilst we cannot say, that evil necessarily appears so that good may be identified as such, there are things we can learn from the appearance of evil in the world, and perhaps in this we can begin to have some faint understanding as to why evil was permitted by God. We have a practical demonstration before us that however evil may prosper, even the worst evil imaginable cannot prevail. It cannot thwart or overcome God's purpose, it cannot overcome our conquering Saviour, and it is not greater than His sacrifice for sin. Evil is made to serve God and in conquering it, glory is brought to our Saviour's Name.

We live in a personal universe in the sense that God is personally involved with all that goes on. He has not given His creation over to impersonal natural laws. God, Paul tells the Athenians, is *"...not far from every one of us: for in him we live, and move, and have our being; as certain also of your own poets have said, For we are also his offspring. Forasmuch then as we are the offspring of God..."* (Acts 17:27-29). As we have seen, this is in contrast to heathen, impersonal, godless fatalism. Let us now summarise some of the points we have been considering. First, the free-agency of man is established by the fact that we are finite replicas of God Himself – *in Him we have our being, we are His offspring* – and therefore will have a will that is a finite version of His will. Second, it is the sovereign will of an omnipotent Father that is the guarantee of our own ability to make free decisions and undertake actions under the constraint only of our nature, be it a fallen one to sin, or regenerate to serve God. It is God's perfect plan and purpose that frees us from the grip of heathen determinism, that rescues us from being thrown hither and thither by fickle fortune. We move by the regenerative work of God's Spirit from a state of constant rebellion, in which we *willingly* sin, to one of life in Christ where we begin *willingly* to serve Him. We then love God because it is our own fervent desire to do so. *"We love him, because he first loved us"* (1 John 4:19). Our love to God is a finite copy of that love with which He first loved us; it is free. We love Him simply because we want to love Him.

When speaking of the will of man and human responsibility, its true freedom does not lie in being able to function autonomously outside the sovereign will of God, but in the ability, when regenerate, to act positively in response to the revealed will of God rather than being obliged by an unregenerate and fallen nature continually to sin. The sinner is free only from righteousness, being the servant of sin; the believer is free from the dominion of sin and is a servant of righteousness. Herein lies the freedom of the human will. It is not an ability to make autonomous choices. True freedom *exists only for the believer* in that he is now freed from sin to serve the living and true God in righteousness. *"And ye shall know the truth, and the truth shall make you free. ...If the Son therefore shall make you free, ye shall be free indeed"* (John 8:32, 36). *"Being then made free from sin, ye became the servants of righteousness. ...For when ye were the servants of sin, ye were free from righteousness"* (Romans 6:18, 20).

Our belief in a reliable and authoritative Word is grounded in the belief in a God who is sovereign. Were our God not sovereign, we would be left with an unreliable Bible. Those who suggest we have an imperfect and unreliable Bible are saying that our God is not sovereign; that His purposes can fail and His knowledge is lacking. They suggest that He also does not possess the power to give and preserve for us a reliable Word in a language we can understand, despite being the Creator of every language ever spoken! Indeed, such a God would care little for us since He is quite willing to let us be misled by a book containing errors, large or small, something He could do little to prevent. Our belief in a reliable and authoritative Word is grounded in the belief in a sovereign God.

> *When we read in Scripture of God's love, because we read it there, He must therefore have always loved us. Never ever was there an instant in God's eternal existence when this could not have been so.*

Scripture is the means to an opening up in human hearts what has eternally existed in the heart of God.

CHAPTER 3

# Only One God, Only One Plan

*"I, even I, am the Lord; and beside me there is no Saviour."*
     (Isaiah 43:11)

A t the fall, man placed himself in his own mind at the centre of his own world. This delusion now became the mainspring of his living. In seeking to reserve to himself the final judgement in all things, man says, as did Satan before him, *"I am a God, I sit in the seat of God"*. God reminds everyman, even before the day of final reckoning *"yet thou art a man, and not God, though thou set thine heart as the heart of God"* (Ezekiel 28:2). Today, men still place themselves where God alone belongs; they *"worship and serve the creature more than the Creator"* (Romans 1:25). Those who by God's infinite grace have been born from above by His Spirit, who have thus moved from rebellion to being ruled by Christ Jesus, now truly worship and serve their Creator. They live with a true picture of the way things are because they now interpret all things with the Word of God in their hands. We do not add the Bible to what we can discover for ourselves using our physical senses, but instead we *measure all things we encounter by the Bible*. God has nothing more to say to us than is found within its pages.

At the heart of a truly biblical faith is the belief in one eternal, self-sustaining God, antecedent to all other beings and things, all of which, without exception, were made by Him. *"All things were made by him; and without him was not any thing made that was made"* (John 1:3). This is the sum total of reality, that God exists and all the things He has made. There is nothing else. Nothing exists outside God that He has not made. God exists in and of Himself and is distinct from all the things He has made. All things owe their present existence to His continued active presence in the world and without Him, they could not continue to exist for a second longer. He upholds *"all things by the word of his power"* (Hebrews 1:3). God Himself, however, exists necessarily and is as He is for reasons that lie entirely within Himself.

Clearly, a God who exists in and of Himself can in no way be dependent upon anything outside His own being, anything that He has Himself created. In addition, there can be nothing beside Him with which He can be compared that can tell us what He is like. There is nothing and no one the same as He is, as there is nothing precisely the opposite from which we can deduce who He is by comparison. We cannot look at anything around us and say, "God is the same as, or the opposite of, this or that". Isaiah asks,

> "To whom then will ye liken God? or what likeness will ye compare unto him?
> … It is he that sitteth upon the circle of the earth, and the inhabitants of the earth are as grasshoppers."
> (Isaiah 40:18, 22)

God cannot be explained by referring to anyone or anything other than to Himself. It is thus quite impossible for us, from within ourselves, to create within our minds, let alone with our hands, anything even approaching a true image of God. It is not possible for anything real or imagined outside God Himself to be used as a representation that will provide for us a definition of God. To attempt to construe God by projecting heavenwards what we know about ourselves leaves us with a human mythological god and not the God of Scripture. God is not the reality behind the highest notion we can have of God.

It follows from this that it is only possible to know anything of God when He chooses to reveal Himself to us. He reveals Himself in us, around us in creation, and to understand this revelation and all else He wants us to know, He has revealed Himself verbally in Scripture. We can say that what understanding of God we have as a direct result of His self-revelation in the Bible and the enlightenment of the Holy Spirit upon it will be a finite copy of God's own understanding and therefore true. *We need the infallible revelation of Scripture to know God.* It is here *and only here* that we possess an objective and verbal revelation of God; there is no other route. Furthermore, everything God has made, everything that occurs within His created universe, is as it is by virtue of the one eternal plan forever present within His being. *We need, the infallible revelation of Scripture to know the purposes of God.* Nothing can occur, nothing can exist, outside the purposes of God; they encompass all things and all events. God *"worketh all things after the counsel of his own will"* (Ephesians 1:11). The God of the Bible is the necessary presupposition of all things existing and occurring on earth, including all human activity. Our knowledge of God is by faith in Him, we trust implicitly what He says in Scripture about Himself and everything else, and we think and act according to what we find there.

Only the God of the Bible is God; there is and can be no other. It is this uncompromising insistence that so infuriates multicultural humanists and the adherents of heathen religions. The 'gods' of other religions, even seemingly 'monotheistic' ones such as Islam, are emphatically not the God of the Bible. They can, therefore, only be myths, the products of human imagination or the evil projections of demons upon the mind. The God we find in Scripture is alone God and no other. Scripture is uncompromising.

> "The Lord he is God; there is none else beside him. . . the Lord he is God in heaven above, and upon the earth beneath: there is none else." (Deuteronomy 4:35 & 39)
>
> "Look unto me, and be ye saved, all the ends of the earth: for I am God, and there is none else." (Isaiah 45:22)
>
> "I am God and there is none else; I am God, and there is none like me." (Isaiah 46:9)

There is and can be none like He. Such statements abound in the Old Testament, where God demonstrated this truth in His dealings with Israel and the Gentile nations. This truth is, however, reiterated in the New Testament in many places.

> "But to us there is but one God, the Father, of whom are all things, and we in him; and one Lord Jesus Christ, by whom are all things, and we by him." (1 Corinthians 8:6)
>
> "For there is one God, and one mediator between God and men, the man Christ Jesus." (1 Timothy 2:5)

Only as we consider who God is, *who it is who speaks*, only then can we begin to appreciate the true authority in Scripture. As this one God has revealed to us His thoughts in this book, the Bible as *His* Word must therefore likewise be unique. As there is only one God and there is nothing created with which to compare Him, as He can be known only as He reveals Himself, and because He has revealed Himself in this one book, today, it alone can be the source of our knowledge of Him. Without the Bible, we must remain ignorant of God and the way of salvation in His Son.

God is infinite. He exists in a boundless fullness of being. His existence is limitless in all aspects. With respect to God's infinity in relation to time, He is eternal. In relation to space, He is omnipresent. Both time and space are part of creation. Being uncreated, God can know nothing of the limitations imposed by space and time upon the created world. We cannot really speak of God as living in an eternal 'present' for this too is a time-bound expression. With God, the beginning is as the end and the end as the beginning.

> "I am the Alpha and Omega, the beginning and the ending, saith the Lord, which is, and which was, and which is to come, the Almighty." (Revelation 1:8)

> "Before the mountains were brought forth, or ever thou hadst formed the earth and the world, even from everlasting to everlasting, thou art God." (Psalm 90:2)

> "But, beloved, be not ignorant of this one thing, that one day is with the Lord as a thousand years, and a thousand years as one day." (2 Peter 3:8)

God is eternal. God is omnipresent and at the same time transcendent, not part of space yet present everywhere in it in all His fullness — and it cannot be sufficiently emphasised — *at the same time remaining distinct from all He has made.*

> "Whither shall I go from thy spirit? Or whither shall I flee from thy presence? If I ascend up into heaven, thou art there: if I make my bed in hell, behold, thou art there."
> (Psalm 139:7-8)

Before the world existed God was already there, Father, Son, and Holy Spirit. Being alone God, He was and is dependent upon no one and nothing. He finds all that He needs within Himself. He had no inherent *need* to create the world; this would make Him less than *perfect*. All God needs to be God is found within Himself and nothing can be added. Such a God as is found in Scripture cannot be thought of as at any time never having ever existed. This cannot be said of the world He has made, for it was once created by God out of nothing and into nothing.

> "Through faith we understand that the worlds were framed by the word of God, so that things which are seen were not made of things which do appear." (Hebrews 11:3)

As God only is God and alone exists in eternity, that which He created must of necessity have at some point not existed or else it would be part of God Himself. In other words, to claim the eternity of matter, of created things, is to raise them to the level of God Himself, whether they be the lower things of the creation, the earth the sun, the moon, the stars, or the higher things, man himself. This is unashamed pantheism. It is to worship and serve the creation not the Creator and is the worst kind of error and idolatry. We note too, that the worlds were *"framed by the word of God"* (Hebrews 11:3). The Word of God gives first expression of that which is in His heart to do.

Eternity does not exist as some place where God lives over against time and space where we live. Eternity exists only in the being of God, for He alone is eternal. This means that when creating the world, God could not have used pre-existent materials for in eternity only God is there. He must have created all things into and out of nothing to have created at all. There is no other way in which God could create. Matter had a beginning and is not indestructible, the God who brought it into being out of nothing can also reduce it once more to nothing should He so wish, a statement of monumental scientific significance. On this count alone, modern evolutionary theory cannot stand. It is a pantheistic religion, idolatry, ascribing to matter an attribute that belongs to God alone. Evolutionary reasoning is a denial of the God of the Bible. It is not possible to assent to evolution in any of its forms, to assert the eternity of matter, without denying God in the same breath. Evolution is a pagan religion not a scientific hypothesis.

As God inhabits eternity, there can be no thought of God *becoming* anything, changing from one thing to another, or changing His mind about anything. There can be no succession of moments either in God's existence or His consciousness, so that we cannot speak of God as thinking one thought after another, *or having to wait and see what will transpire before knowing about them and acting appropriately*. He is aware of all that was and is, both actual and possible — and we cannot even say that He does this in an instant or even all the time. He does not even have to wait for us to believe in Christ in order to know that we shall do so. This would make Him dependent upon that which He has Himself created, time and human action. This cannot be. Scripture teaching on matters such as predestination, election, history, the fulfilment of prophecy, present a difficulty only to those whose own minds are bound by an overwhelming sense of the temporal, who imagine God to be even such as they are themselves and so bound by time.

God's relationship to space, or His omnipresence, cannot mean that He is nowhere or is static. He is in all His being present everywhere. Whilst remaining distinct from all He created at the same time, *"Do not I fill the heaven and earth? saith the Lord"* (Jeremiah 23:24). God is not included in space, yet He is not absent from it, above it yet He is present in all of it. There is no less of God present in one place than another. His omnipresence is both intensive and extensive: yet in a real sense these terms seem inappropriate ones to use of God. *"The heaven and heaven of heavens cannot contain thee"* (1 Kings 8:27). In the New Testament it is the Lord Jesus who created, sustains, and fills the universe.

When we think of God with respect to this world of time and space, all things exist, continue to exist, and are held together by Him, *"by him all things consist"* (Colossians 1:17). All that happens on earth is a replication of the internal activity of God. In other words, nothing happens, nothing can happen, outside that which has first gone on within the heart and mind of God Himself. His eternal purpose is perfectly replicated in all that takes place on earth, nothing exists outside it. He is the self-contained source of all that occurs on earth.

The *immutability* of God gives us a distinctly Christian view of history. All that happens, past, present, and future does so because it exists as an externalisation in the created world of the internal workings of the self-sufficient Creator of the world. The events of history do not happen in and of themselves, but they are determined by the unchanging personal will of the eternal God Himself. When He created the world, when the Son became incarnate, nothing changed within God Himself. All *change* in the *temporal* world occurs according to the *unchangeable* plan of the *eternal* God. The world changes, but God does not. If we say certain events that occur on earth are not dependent upon God, if we try to give to man ultimate powers within himself such as those God alone possesses in order to determine events independently of God's eternal purposes, then we have already fallen into the trap of pantheism making creation to be as god. We have given to that which is not God, powers that belong only to Him. We have removed the distinction between God and all that He has made. We have given to creation powers of self-determination, such as belong only to God. Change in creation can only take place because there is *no* change in God. Sequential events are possible only based on the eternal plan of an unchanging God. There is only one other possibility, that history is itself in some sense ultimate and that God is Himself subject to events of which He has no previous knowledge and over which He has no control and this contradicts all that we know of God in Scripture.

## A perfect revelation of the eternal purpose of God

Contrary to the assumptions of the unregenerate mind we have no ultimate control over the details of history, but neither are they determined by fickle fortune. We cannot *"make one hair white or black"* (Matthew 5:36). Who then does? A sparrow does not fall on the ground without God (Matthew 10:29). There is not the tiniest detail life on earth with which He is not intimately and personally involved. He not only knows all things, but He is *active*. *"The very hairs of your head are numbered"* (Matthew 10:30). God takes an active interest in sparrows, how much more an active interest in us, who are made in His image. *"In him we live, and move, and have our being"* (Acts 17:28). How much more in that Word He has given! We may argue about and discuss the manuscripts of the Bible until we are blue in the face, going round and round in circles — in some ways this can prove to be a never-ending distraction — but there is one fact above all others that is a guarantee to us that what we hold in our hands is word for word the Word of God and it is this: that God Himself is day by day actively engaged in the preservation of that which He has revealed and inspired. If He counts and preserves the hairs on our head that may one day rot in the grave, then how much more will He preserve every jot and tittle of that Word which is eternal and is alone able to make us wise unto salvation? It is inconceivable that He should do anything other than preserve His Word commensurate with His being, in a perfect and infallible condition, authoritative, *"profitable for doctrine, for reproof, for correction, for instruction in righteousness"*. After all, above every other purpose for mankind, it is His will surely, *"that the man of God may be perfect"*. Can we be *that* from a word that is itself less than perfect, less than it needs to be? *"...thoroughly furnished unto all good works"* — everything is there in God's Word that needs to be there, it is not an imperfect Word, to the end that in us may be found works pleasing to Him (2 Timothy 3: 16-17).

As with the individual hairs on the head, no less, Scripture must be tied down to actual words given and preserved to our day by God, conveying with precision His eternal thoughts. If we no longer have the words He gave, then we have no authentic Word of God. It will not do to say this was confined to the original manuscripts of the writers and as these no longer exist the possibility of reconstructing them is gone. We share the conviction of the puritan, John Owen, that preserved by God within those manuscripts currently to hand are the very words God gave. Numbers of manuscripts were tampered with and altered at various times by apostates; these are easily identified and they must be discounted. Then as now there were those who would tell us what God *ought* to have said. We have still today the Word of God as originally given. Why would God take such care in giving the Scriptures by verbal inspiration in the first place only for them to be later lost to us? This makes no sense and is contrary to what Scripture itself teaches about God and His work in this world. It is totally inconceivable that God would not take anything but the greatest care to see that His Word comes to us in a form that precisely replicates in our hearts, through the medium of language, what are His deepest thoughts and express will.

> *As God providentially directs all history, it is therefore inconceivable that He should do anything other than preserve His Word in a manner commensurate with His being, in a perfect and infallible condition.*

The God who cannot guarantee us a Bible free of error cannot guarantee us a perfect Saviour, cannot guarantee us a sure salvation, cannot guarantee us anything at all. Such a God whose divine providence does not extend to the personal supervision of the preservation and translation of the precious Word He Himself inspired surely has no control over anything at all. God determines all things, or He determines nothing. God is *sovereign*, with Him rests ultimate power. What He has planned and purposed for this world will and must prevail; no one can overthrow it. *"But our God is in the heavens: he hath done whatsoever he hath pleased"* (Psalm 115:3). Having purposed all things, having made all things, having determined beforehand the glorious consummation of all things, God knows all there is to know about everything and brings all to pass.

God does not tell us everything; in fact, we shall never know or understand all things. This would make us infinite as God. Many things God initially keeps to Himself. What is often referred to as the *'secret will'* of God is not secret because we cannot know it, for when it occurs then we know it. It is secret because *we do not know it in advance*, whereas we do know the *'revealed will'* of God beforehand. Nevertheless, we do know the secret will of God in general terms. We know that He will ultimately triumph and all history leads to this. God's will is the source of all things created and of all events in the created world. He it is *"who worketh all things after the counsel of his own will"* (Ephesians 1:11). There is no way in which the secret will of God can be thought of as in any way conditional. All we can say is that we will not know it until it comes to fruition in time and space.

God's revealed will is given to man today through Scripture so that we may live as He would wish us to live. What God reveals to us affects what we are to do, whereas the hidden or secret will of God deals primarily with what God will do, with or without the instrumentality of men. These two aspects of the one will of God will not, indeed cannot, contradict each other. This means that God will not surprise us by doing something that is contradiction to that which He has revealed in Scripture. Much of history, if not most of it, is realised utterly through His secret will, that is, we are given no advance notice of what God will do specifically, nor how He will bring it about. There could only be a contradiction between what God reveals as His will and what actually occurs as a result of His secret will, were there some equal power over which He had no control.

The meaning and the interpretation of all things go before their realisation in the world of time and space. God controls the future because His interpretation of it precedes its fulfilment. This is why prophecy cannot fail. This is why the promises of God cannot fail. We eagerly await the end of our salvation and the fulfilment of prophecy. We know they cannot fail because we accept the interpretation God has created with them.

## Unity in diversity

Whilst God is one, at the same time He is three persons. He is one in essence, in three persons. He exists in a tri-unity, a tri-personality. This lies at the heart of our Christian belief. Three co-substantial persons, none of which derives from either or both of the others, three distinct persons, yet one. When we speak of the Lord Jesus, we speak of God; when we speak of the Holy Spirit, we speak of that same God; when we speak of the Father, we also speak of that one God. Whilst we can make a distinction between these three, as indeed we do of the individual attributes of God, yet each is exhaustive of divinity itself. Unity and plurality are equally ultimate in God. He is one conscious being, yet also tri-conscious. The doctrine of the tri-unity of God is found in the Old Testament, but it is found most clearly in the New. Father, Son and Holy Spirit are equally one God, and the indivisible divine essence with all its perfections and prerogatives belong to each person to the same degree and in the same way. These are not the names of the same person in different manifestations or relations. God, indeed, can only exist in a triune fashion. Our triune God exists distinct from the world He created, self-sustaining, dependent on nothing outside Himself, in an equal ultimacy of unity and plurality.

As we look about us we find a world full of many varied and different things. If we believe these things to have been somehow thrown up by a purposeless procedure of contingent evolution, it is going to be difficult, if not impossible, to uncover any unifying thread of meaning or purpose. What meaning can one thing have relative to another, if there is no underlying purpose of God behind all things. This is a problem for unbelievers, it is their problem not ours. In the triune God of Scripture diversity and unity are equally ultimate. The Father is not more than the Son nor the Son than the Spirit, all and each are equally ultimate. There is perfect unity in the diversity. What God is will be evident in what He has made. Unity in a diverse world is only possible because there is first this perfect unity and diversity in God. Subordinationism, making one member of the trinity less than the others, is heresy and produces defective theology; it also distorts our view of the created world.

It is only because of the unfathomable triune being of God, in whom unity and diversity are equally ultimate, that we can interpret the world around us. To attempt to explain the doctrine of the trinity to the satisfaction of the human mind is to seek to reduce it to an irrationality it does not actually possess. As long as men retain the notion of the ultimacy of the human mind, there can be no common exploration of the mysteries of the Godhead. The unbeliever looks at the world as existing in an uninterpreted, even irrational form. The believer knows that, although he may not know all the answers, he can turn to what God has given in His Word and pray for a more complete understanding, because with God as Creator nothing exists without meaning.

## *The purpose of God is one*

What is it that gives meaning to our world? Why did God make it? What is the unifying thread of all existence? What about evil? What does God have in mind overall? To uncover the answers to these questions, we need to turn to the Scriptures to what God has said. Were we writing the Bible, we would perhaps have placed our reasons for writing in a foreword at the beginning. For one of the clearest statements about the purpose of God in creation we turn not to the first, but to the last book of the Bible. It is in the book of Revelation that we read of the total destruction of sin and all that came with it and of how that which God *had always purposed in His heart* for creation is fully realised. For God the end is as certain as the beginning and the future as sure as the past.

> "The four and twenty elders fall down before him that sat on the throne, and worship him that liveth for ever and ever, and cast their crowns before the throne, saying, Thou art worthy, O Lord, to receive glory and honour and power: for thou hast created all things, and for thy pleasure they are and were created." (Revelation 4:10-11)

The descriptions in Revelation make clear that, despite the ruin that came to the world by sin, the purpose of creation, namely the praise, glory, and pleasure of God, will ultimately prevail. *The whole of human history is steadily and irreversibly, day by day, moving towards this end.* If we miss this, we understand nothing. Nothing and no one can halt its steady progress.

> **Right at the heart of human history is redemption by the death of God's Son of that which was ruined by sin to the end that God may be glorified in the consummation of His eternal purpose with respect to the creation of the world and of mankind.**

We must see all things in this light. *"God was in Christ, reconciling the world unto himself"* (2 Corinthians 5:19). To us is given *a ministry* of reconciliation (v.18), to us is committed *a word* of reconciliation. In the midst of desolation...

> "...we are ambassadors for Christ, as though God did beseech you by us: we pray you in Christ's stead, be ye reconciled to God." (2 Corinthians 5:20)

If we fail to understand and follow through with these things, we understand and shall achieve nothing. We shall not understand what we are doing here, or where we are going, or the reason for anything that exists or happens on earth.

> "...having made peace through the blood of his cross, by him to reconcile all things unto himself; by him, I say, whether they be things in earth, or things in heaven."
> (Colossians 1:20)

Many portray salvation as some kind of damage-limitation exercise; a salvage operation after the devil has done his worst. This is a caricature of the truth and seems rather like God making the best of a mishap.

> **God is not involved in a haphazard rescue mission to save at least something of this world before all is lost, but in the realisation of His eternal purpose for the world He created.**

A sovereign God cannot be defeated; His purposes in Christ Jesus are yea and amen. All things shall be reconciled unto God. He has ordained

> "That at the name of Jesus every knee should bow, of things in heaven, and things in earth, and things under the earth; And that every tongue should confess that Jesus Christ is Lord, to the glory of God the Father." (Philippians 2:10-11)

*Let us remember that the Scriptures are themselves a vital part of the unfolding purpose of God.* The words of Scripture are that God so loved the world that God gave His only begotten Son, Christ came not to condemn the world but that *the world* through Him might be saved (John 3). The veracity of these words of Scripture depends upon the ability of God to fulfil His eternal purpose to the letter. As this eternal purpose cannot fail and the Bible is a transcript of that same purpose, consequently not one letter of it can fail. We must get this the right way round.

*All that is yet to come to pass, revealed or hidden, all prophecy as yet unfulfilled, is as sure as though it had already happened.* Whilst the world will be saved and there will be a regeneration of all things, we cannot make this to mean, as do universalists, that all men without exception will be saved. Nevertheless, we must insist that the call of the Gospel is sincere and genuine; all are invited to come. Those who refuse will be lost and for this have only themselves to blame. No one can say God did not elect them to salvation therefore they are lost, *because He invites them now to believe!* If they will, they may come. The refusal of the Gospel by godless men cannot be interpreted as a frustration of God's eternal plan. Such a thing is unthinkable, as unthinkable as the Scriptures themselves being unreliable. The purposes of God are fulfilled in Christ, so that those remaining by choice outside of Christ fall short as individuals of that which God in eternity intends for men as a whole. The end of the wicked, who wilfully and deliberately refuse salvation, is equally enclosed within the plan of God as is the salvation of those who believe. The certainty of salvation for those who trust Christ for salvation is as sure as the certainty of damnation for those who refuse Him. If we believe those now in Christ cannot be lost, we must also believe those presently outside Him will most certainly be lost. Only because His plan cannot fail can there be any certainty in the promise that *"whosoever believeth in him should not perish, but have everlasting life"* (John 3:16). Let no man be deceived, those who refuse Christ shall not escape.

Whilst it is true that the godless will perish in hell as part of God's eternal purpose, it cannot be sufficiently emphasised that the responsibility for their own downfall is borne by those who refuse God's remedy of faith in His Son. The invitation of the Gospel is made to all men. We know that in New Testament times the return of the Lord Jesus had a prominent place in Gospel preaching, otherwise there would not have been those who mocked,

> "Where is the promise of his coming? For since the fathers fell asleep, all things continue as they were from the beginning of the creation." (2 Peter 3:4)

To which the apostle Peter replies,

> "The Lord is not slack concerning his promise, as some men count slackness; but is longsuffering to us-ward, not willing that any should perish, but that all should come to repentance. But the day of the Lord will come as a thief in the night; in the which the heavens shall pass away with a great noise, and the elements shall melt with fervent heat, the earth also and the works that are therein shall be burned up. ... Nevertheless we, according to his promise, look for new heavens and a new earth, wherein dwelleth righteousness." (2 Peter 3:9, 10, 13)

The godless confuse the longsuffering of the Lord towards all men with slackness, with a failure to fulfil the promise of His coming. If the Lord delays His coming, it is not because He is unable to carry through all He has purposed, but because He is longsuffering towards sinners, extending the day of opportunity to the end that none should perish but come to repentance and believe. There is little point in doing this unless the offer of salvation is genuine. It is difficult to see how any other understanding of this text than this can avoid some distortion of the plain meaning. Salvation is not of right, but of grace, and this He demonstrates to all men by delaying His coming to judge the world. The wicked man will die in his sins, but this is not to say that God takes any great delight in seeing men made in His own image perish, quite the contrary. Men perish willingly, despite the goodness, forbearance and long-suffering God shows towards them.

> "Or despisest thou the riches of his goodness and forbearance and long-suffering; not knowing that the goodness of God leadeth thee to repentance? But after thy hardness and impenitent heart treasurest up unto thyself wrath against the day of wrath and the revelation of the righteous judgement of God; Who will render to every man according to his deeds." (Romans 2:4-6)

God did not create man simply to feed the fires of hell, but those who share Satan's cause shall share his end. When men so perish, as individuals they fall short of God's design for them and for all men. They need not have perished had they believed.

> "As I live, saith the Lord God, I have no pleasure in the death of the wicked; but that the wicked turn from his way and live." (Ezekiel 33:11)

This was never God's desire in creating man, and there is no reason to this day why any should perish, other than that because they remain obdurate and are unwilling to repent and believe the Gospel. This is His revealed will for the world.

> "For God so loved the world, that he gave his only begotten Son, that whosoever believeth in him should not perish, but have everlasting life." (John 3:16)

"And he is the propitiation for our sins: and not for our's only, but also for the sins of the whole world." (1 John 2:2)

Creation and the re-creation of that which has been ruined by sin both find their place in the eternal purposes of God. God in restoring that which is fractured is not interfering in a self-sustaining, independently existent natural world in a mechanical way, setting to right that which has unpredictably gone wrong as though He were mending a motor car that has suddenly broken down of its own accord. Sin and misery remain only because in the end they are made to serve God's purposes and the remedy is already to hand. We receive good at God's hand, so we also receive evil. We can then say with Job, *"But he knoweth the way that I take: when he bath tried me, I shall come forth as gold."* (Job 23:10) Re-creation is not repairing something broken, any more than regeneration is a restoration of the sinner to his original state of righteousness. This is not what the Bible teaches. On that glorious day, we shall see our risen and exalted Saviour, *"when he shall appear, we shall be like him"* (1 John 3:2), *"we shall all be changed, In a moment, in the twinkling of an eye"* (1 Corinthians 15:51-52).

"For our conversation is in heaven; from whence also we look for the Saviour, the Lord Jesus Christ: Who shall change our vile body, that it may be fashioned like unto his glorious body, according to the working whereby be is able even to subdue all things unto himself." (Philippians 3:20-21)

Our end in Christ is to know something far beyond that which was ever known in Eden, that which God *always had in mind for all His creatures.* We are not to be repaired, not even replaced, but *changed,* having a body fashioned after that of our blessed Redeemer! This is not the body of Adam before the fall, but something only yet seen in Christ. O, come quickly, Lord Jesus!

If we see the disturbance of creation and the destructive violence of sin as being something that caught God unawares because some events can occur that are beyond and outside Him either to foreknow or to determine, there can then be no guarantee that God will succeed seeing that adverse events are not entirely in His hands to prevent. Who then is to say that something new will not appear to upset things all over again and undo His good work, something once more God cannot prevent? This would mean that there can be no certain hope for the Christian, no assurance that God's remedy in Christ is truly effective, the hope of salvation is always under threat. There can only be certainty that the conflict is already won, *because all things from beginning to end are in God's hands.* There is *one* plan and *one* purpose, and the revelation of it is *one* and this is what we have revealed in Scripture! No detail of existence is excluded.

Creation as it now appears even after the fall is what it is because of the eternal counsel of God. What happens does so entirely because God has determined for reasons within Himself that it should be so. Creation has not run out of control, has not slipped through the fingers of God! The intervention of sin must be reacted against and creation brought to God's glorious purpose for it, but all go out from that same unshakeable counsel of God. We look forward to the "restitution of all things" (Acts 3:21).

> "Because the creature itself also shall be delivered from the bondage of corruption into the glorious liberty of the children of God. For we know that the whole creation groaneth and travaileth in pain together until now."
> (Romans 8:21-22)

Men believe it is possible for them to change the course of history God has planned, to thwart His plans and rob Him of victory. They imagine that the life of man exists outside the plan of God and that men are beyond the ability of God to control – God can help, but not control. God can stand on the sidelines and shout words of encouragement, or so we are told, but little else. He is certainly unable to determine the outcome of the race. God starts the race, removes the obstacles in the course perhaps, and then hands out the prizes. The final end of time is determined by the actions of men not God. The will of man, not God is said to prevail. *This picture is a travesty.* The truth is that man is a creature in a created world governed at all times by God.

Meaning can only be expressed as purpose in relation to the unfolding plan of God conceived in eternity. Meaning can only exist when behind the words and sentences there stands the interpretation given by God's revelation of His purpose. It is *this* that provides the content of truth in *any* statement. It includes the actions of all men and all events. My significance as an individual within God's world derives from my own place in the overall plan and purpose of God. I can otherwise have no meaning. True freedom as against the false rebellious freedom of the sinner, who is a prisoner to his sinful nature, is found in becoming a willing prisoner of God, submitting to the authority of the sovereign God of Scripture.

CHAPTER 4

# One People, One Book

*"Neither pray I for these alone, but for them also which shall believe on me through their word; That they all may be one; as thou, Father, art in me, and I in thee, that they also may be one in us: that the world may believe that thou hast sent me."* (John 17:19-20)

When we are looking at the reason why God has given us the Scriptures, we see a logical activity whereby the knowledge of God enters the consciousness of regenerated humanity by means of the inspired written Word of God. This one whole deposit of truth is given to one *whole* body of regenerated humanity. We can quite rightly sing, "Jesus loves me this I know" – nothing is more precious than that, but we find in Scripture that God's love has first a much wider reference than being directed towards individual persons. Those who see Christ dying for a random aggregate of individuals surely miss the point. Perhaps the most well known verse in the Bible can come to our assistance here.

"For God so loved the world, that he gave his only begotten Son, that whosoever believeth in him should not perish, but have everlasting life." (John 3:16)

God's love is directed here towards humanity as *a whole*. This love moved God to give His only begotten Son. God loved the *world*; nevertheless, the possession of everlasting life presumes faith on the part of the *individual*. Let us be more specific, the scope revealed in Scripture for the death of our Saviour is this,

"And he is the propitiation for our sins: and not for our's only, but also for the sins of the whole world." (1 John 2:2)

We may draw at least two conclusions from this verse. First, the sacrifice of Christ is the only shield from the wrath of God for any sinner; only in Christ can he survive unscathed. It alone meets God's righteous demands and can save us from His anger. Second, the intention behind the death of Christ is the salvation of *the world*, that whole world which presently *"lieth in wickedness"* (1 John 5:19). The purpose for the preaching of the Gospel encompasses the *whole* world. The death of Christ is even intended for those who refuse it, but those who refuse it do so willingly and thereby *eliminate themselves* from the grand design of God for the world that is His, to save it through the death of His Son. Those who believe do so only by the grace of God.

Paul speaks of a mystery not previously revealed, hidden in God, but now the manifold wisdom of God is known by the Church, *"according to the eternal purpose which he purposed in Christ Jesus our Lord"* (Ephesians 3:11). Before the Garden of Eden, before there was a first man, there was a plan of glorifying God by the Church in a Second Man, Jesus our Lord. The apostleship of Paul was *"in hope of eternal life, which God, that cannot lie, promised before the world began"* (Titus 1:2). Paul reminds us that God

"...hath saved us, and called us with an holy calling, not according to our works, but according to his own purpose and grace, which was given us in Christ Jesus before the world began." (2 Timothy 1:9)

All that we now have in Christ was always with God, but is now manifested to and in us in time and space.

"...is now made manifest by the appearing of our Saviour Jesus Christ, who hath abolished death, and hath brought life and immortality to light through the gospel" (v.10)

Until the point of the invasion of this world by the kingdom at the *first* coming of Christ – not that this rule was yet established over the kingdoms of this world – Gentiles could know the blessings of salvation only by a relationship with Israel. The refusal by Israel of both the kingdom and its King meant that now a new people, namely the Church, became the centre of its manifestation and life. Only within the Church of Christ can the blessings of redemption be known today. Israel can know the blessings promised to her for this dispensation *only* through the Church. This will remain so *"until the fullness of the Gentiles be come in"* and until *"shall come out of Sion the Deliverer, and shall turn away ungodliness from Jacob"* (Romans 11:25-26), that is, not before Christ comes again. The Church, however, is not the kingdom, and the two must not be confused. The kingdom creates the Church and in this dispensation works through her in the world. We may preach the kingdom, but we do not build it. There will be those who receive it and those who reject it.

The Bible teaches there is but *one* blood-bought people of God.
> "And other sheep I have, which are not of this fold: them also I must bring, and they shall hear my voice; and there shall be one fold, and one shepherd." (John 10:16)

This does not mean that we can speak of Old Testament saints as being part of the Church nor should we speak of 'the Church' in the Old Testament. The Church comprises all who have been baptised into one body by the Spirit of God and that baptising began first at Pentecost. The saints of the Old Testament were not saved by the Law and those of the New by the blood of Christ – *"For it is not possible that the blood of bulls and of goats should take away sins"* (Hebrews 10:4). There is one sacrifice for sin for all men for all time, that of Christ Himself. *"But this man, after he had offered one sacrifice for sins for ever, sat down on the right hand of God"* (Hebrews 10:12). There is consequently, one name given, one way for all men for all time.

> "Neither is there salvation in any other: for there is no other name under heaven given among men, whereby we must be saved." (Acts 4:12)

We look back in retrospect to that which our Saviour accomplished for us on the cross, the Old Testament saints looked forward to it not having seen it, but all receive it by faith.

> "For what saith the scripture? Abraham believed God, and it was counted unto him for righteousness." (Romans 4:3)

None of any of this sets aside those promises made by God specifically to Israel as a nation and yet to be fulfilled. Nevertheless, when speaking of Israel and the Church, we speak of *one people of God.* Paul makes this abundantly clear in Romans 11. There is one olive tree. In Old Testament times, this centred in Israel. Some of the natural branches through unbelief have been broken off, although not all, for *"at this present time there is a remnant according to the election of grace"* (v.5). The majority of Jews today do not believe the Gospel and are lost, broken off. Today, those who are not natural branches but wild branches, not Jews but Gentiles, have been grafted into the one tree. The hardening of Israel is a temporary phenomenon. God will again turn once more to the natural branches and *"the vail shall be taken away"*(2 Corinthians 3:16); *"and so all Israel shall be saved"* (v.26). The kingdom of God currently bringing salvation to us the Church, the new people of God, will finally bring it to Israel. Meanwhile, the conflict between the kingdom of light and the kingdom of darkness continues unabated. The Church is at the centre of this battle. Under the rule of Christ, His Church is His instrument today in the preaching of the Gospel and opposition to the powers of darkness.

The Scriptures do not permit us to see the Church as an afterthought on God's part, as something he instated when other methods of salvation failed. When we speak of the electing love of God, if we would remain within the framework of Scriptural emphasis, God does not abandon the human race to eternal loss and damnation, merely to snatch away a few select individuals on the way, uniting these in Christ. God's purpose is to save *humanity*, He redeems the *race* of men He set upon earth. Those individuals who will not believe will be lost. Those responding to the Gospel are not to be thought of as part of some indiscriminate casting about to see who will receive Christ, here one and there another, all added one to another to make up the Church. No, those who respond to the Gospel are part of God's eternal plan to have a people for Himself by giving His Son to save them, *a plan existing always in the heart of God.* The whole body of the Church was elect in Christ, down to every single member, before each one believed, even before the foundation of the world.

> "Blessed be the God and Father of our Lord Jesus Christ, who hath blessed us with all spiritual blessings in heavenly places in Christ: according as he hath chosen us in him before the foundation of the world, that we should be holy and without blame before him in love: having predestinated us unto the adoption of children by Jesus Christ to himself, according to the good pleasure of his will, to the praise of the glory of his grace, wherein he hath made us accepted in the beloved." (Ephesians 1:3-6)

Many things are made clear in these verses. All the spiritual blessings that are in Christ and to whom they should come was something determined before God created the world. The purpose of God's electing grace being directed towards us is that we should be holy, stand before Him without blame in love. By loving us God is loving Himself as we are made in His image. There is nothing otherwise in us, or coming from us, to induce God to choose us. This is impossible with God as it would make His actions dependent upon something outside Himself, but all His actions towards us are simply *"according to the good pleasure of his will"*, otherwise grace cannot be grace. All is to the end that God may be glorified. The motives for God's actions lie within Himself and are not determined by anything found in us, all these things *"he hath purposed in himself"* (1:9). The Gospel was a mystery kept secret from the beginning of the world but was now revealed to the apostles. All are part of His eternal counsel, this one purpose. To the end…

> "That in the dispensation of the fulness of times he might gather together in one all things in Christ, both which are in heaven, and which are on earth; even in him: in whom also we have obtained an inheritance, being predestinated according to the purpose of him who worketh all things after the counsel of his own will." (Ephesians 1:10-11)

Whilst it is true we must each and everyone believe or be lost, we need to avoid the excessive individualism that loses sight of our unity and oneness in Christ. In the end, we convince ourselves that we are saved for our own sake rather than to glorify God, so that we become self-obsessed and excessively subjective. We convince ourselves that God is there for us, to do our bidding rather than we to do His. Certainly, we retain an individual identity, but at the same time we are inseparable from all other believers. Paul makes clear that there cannot be one without the other,

> "For as the body is one, and hath many members, and all the members of that one body, being many, are one body: so also is Christ." (1 Corinthians 12:12)

We cannot be what we are in Christ without each and every other believer. This is very clear from the functioning of the Church right now in the present dispensation. Here the individual and the whole, the one and the many, meet. We need each other to grow together in grace and in the knowledge of Christ as one ministers to another using the individual gifts that Christ has bestowed *"to profit withal"*. The link between us is so close that when one suffers, all suffer; when one is honoured, all rejoice.

We are individual believers, but equally we are a chosen *race*, or to use the New Testament word, *'generation'*.

> "But ye are a chosen generation, a royal priesthood, an holy nation, a peculiar people; that ye should shew forth the praises of him who hath called you out of darkness into his marvellous light: Which in time past were not a people, but are now the people of God: which had not obtained mercy, but now have obtained mercy."
>
> (1 Peter 2:9-10; cf. Romans 9:25)

Please note the collective nouns: a chosen generation (or race), a priesthood, a nation, a people. Also, please note the use of the plural 'ye' and 'you' rather than the singular, 'thou' and thee', a meaning lost in the inaccuracy of modern translations.

God is today taking out *"a **people** for his name"* (Acts 15:14). We ought not to understand this as being saved *out* of humanity itself — only in the sense that we leave behind all that we were as sons and daughters of Adam — *but as those who now constitute the true humanity.* Those who will not believe, who refuse Christ, remain part of the first creation that is to be done away with, so that they will suffer everlasting loss. They are blotted out of the book of life. They have no part in the new creation.

> "He that overcometh, the same shall be clothed in white raiment; and I will not blot out his name out of the book of life." (Revelation 3:5)

In that last and dreadful day when the dead, small and great, stand before God, the books will be opened. One of those books opened will be the book of life.

> "And whosoever was not found written in the book of life was cast into the lake of fire." (Revelation 20:15)

There is no unity in hell, no oneness, no organic whole, but isolation in terrible loneliness and darkness. In glory it is quite the opposite, there is no aggregate of individuals, but one "body of Christ", one organic whole of which we are each an essential part, *without which the whole would not be complete*. It is this last point that makes the whole number of the redeemed more than an indeterminate collection of individuals. We are saved not for our own individual end, but that we might be many members of one body and bring glory to God in Christ. The original organism of humanity that sprang from Adam, now irrevocably ruined by sin, must end in death. The new humanity in Christ, the second man, the last Adam, occupying that place in the human race originally occupied by Adam, is destined to life. *"For as in Adam all die, even so in Christ shall all be made alive"* (1 Corinthians 15:22). All in Adam die, all in Christ live.

Believers are brought by God into a wholly new state in Christ, the second Man, the last Adam.

> "The first man Adam was made a living soul; the last Adam was made a quickening spirit. ...The first man is of the earth, earthy: the second man is the Lord from heaven. As is the earthy, such are they also that are earthy: and as is the heavenly, such are they also that are heavenly. And as we have borne the image of the earthy, we shall also bear the image of the heavenly." (1 Corinthians 15:45, 47-49)

The first creation has been irreparably ruined, it cannot be repaired or reestablished, but all that belongs to it must be changed. A new heavens, a new earth is to be the abode of a new race of men, at its Head is the last Adam, as the first Adam stands at the head of the first. All about us that is of the first Adam, that constitutes the old man, is done away with completely in the death of Christ.

> "Knowing this, that our old man is crucified with him, that the body of sin might be destroyed, that henceforth we should not serve sin." (Romans 6:6)

The Lord Jesus is indeed *"the Lamb of God, which taketh away the sin of the world"* (John 1:29) — *not* sins as so often cited incorrectly. We read, *"...he appeared to put away sin by the sacrifice of himself"* (Hebrews 9:26). *"For in that he died, he died unto sin once: but in that he liveth, he liveth unto God"* (Romans 6:10). Our sinless Saviour lived as a Man without sin, He knew no sin, but lived over and above it. Tempted and tried, He was *"obedient unto death, even the death of the cross"* (Philippians 2:8). Satan tried in vain to introduce sin into the Saviour. In dying, the Man who had no sin died to sin.

> "For he hath made him to be sin for us, who knew no sin; that we might be made the righteousness of God in him."
> (2 Corinthians 5:21)

In dying, He who could not die died. Here was a Man who likewise took part of flesh and blood as we, as part of the first creation, *"that through death he might destroy him that had the power of death, that is, the devil"* (Hebrews 2:14). In rising from the dead he rose to another condition of human life, a glorified one, a new humanity, *"and become the firstfruits of them that slept"* (1 Corinthians 15:20). Jesus, by the grace of God, was to *"taste death for every man"* to bring *"many sons unto glory"* (Hebrews 2:9-10). Not only did our Saviour accomplish all that was necessary to deal with our sin as sons of Adam by His death, but He perfectly glorified God in so doing.

> "Now is the Son of man glorified, and God is glorified in him. If God be glorified in him, God shall also glorify him in himself, and shall straightway glorify him." (John 13:31-32)

Our Lord Jesus has the perfect place of acceptance with God and we in Him.

We are *a new race of men* whose Head is Christ. We walk now through this earthly scene as dead men, even as Christ our Head died.

> "But God forbid that I should glory, save in the cross of our Lord Jesus Christ, by whom the world is crucified unto me, and I unto the world." (Galatians 6:14)

We are dead to all the old state of existence, but in Christ alive, for in that Christ liveth, He liveth unto God and we in Him. We are not of the world, even as Christ Jesus is not of the world. *"As he is, so are we in this world"* (1 John 4:17). If we are in Christ, we are no longer of the old world, but are strangers and pilgrims awaiting not death, but the realisation of the final element of our salvation, *"the redemption of our body"* (Romans 8:23) at our Lord's coming. Conformity to the ways and habits of this present evil world is due first and foremost to a failure to realise that if we are 'in Christ', we are no longer 'in Adam'. This failure may well be due to the fact that so many who claim to be Christian are still very much in Adam, still very much part of this world as their way of life shows all too clearly, and that they may not in fact be in Christ at all. We are in Christ or we remain in Adam.

Christ, once risen and ascended, sent down the Holy Spirit uniting us to Him. We know by the indwelling of His Spirit that we are in Him and He is in us. Not only do we share the benefits of His death in the forgiveness of our sins, in the condemnation of sin, in being dead to this present evil world, but we are risen with Him, have ascended with Him and sit with Him in heavenly places. The question of our guilt before God has been resolved there, but we are baptised into His death and risen with Him to live in newness of life, His life, our new Head.

> "I am crucified with Christ: nevertheless I live; yet not I, but Christ liveth in me: and the life which I now live in the flesh..."

At present, I am housed in a body that awaits a glorious change, the moment *"when this corruptible shall have put on incorruption"* (1 Corinthians 15:54), and this vile body shall *"be fashioned like unto his glorious body"* (Philippians 3:21). Until then

> "... I live by the faith of the Son of God, who loved me, and gave himself for me." (Galatians 2:20)

As far as all that is of this first creation is concerned, we are dead to it, its innate sin, its misery, its temptations, all that belongs to it. It is there, it may surround us on every hand, it may seek to entice us, or to persuade us otherwise, but we are not part of it and it has no ultimate power over us. This how we must see ourselves. *"For ye are dead, and your life is hid with Christ in God"* (Colossians 3:3). Christ lives in us and we in Him. The purpose and plan of God for His people is plainly and clearly revealed in Scripture.

> "But God, who is rich in mercy, for his great love wherewith he loved us, Even when we were dead in sins...

(when we were not in any position to do anything for ourselves)

> "...hath quickened us together with Christ, (by grace ye are saved;) And hath raised us up together, and made us to sit together in heavenly places in Christ Jesus: That in the ages to come he might shew the exceeding riches of his grace in his kindness toward us through Christ Jesus."
> (Ephesians 2:4-7)

We see things as Christ sees them; we are as He is in this world, dead to it, above and over it.

> "But ye are not in the flesh, but in the Spirit, if so be that the Spirit of God dwell in you. Now if any man have not the Spirit of Christ, he is none of his." (Romans 8:9)

However we may see ourselves, if we are true believers, this is our *actual* standing in Christ: having died and risen with Him, we are seated with Him in heavenly places unto whom all power is given in heaven and in earth. *"And if Christ be not raised, your faith is vain; ye are yet in your sins"* (1 Corinthians 15:17). If Christ be not raised and we in Him, we are still in our sins and we have believed for nothing. The standing and life of the Christian rests in this. This was ever the purpose of God for us to give us sonship with His Son, adoption and glory in righteousness and holiness.

The whole state of those in Christ has been changed, although not yet in the body, nonetheless, still in reality a new life. We are as completely separated from the old as is anyone who is dead and buried is separated from this present life. Even our relation with other men has already changed. We have died to our former state and condition and live now with Christ who is risen. Our place before God is as Christ stands before Him, not as in Adam in the flesh, which is condemned.

> "Wherefore henceforth know we no man after the flesh: yea, though we have known Christ after the flesh, yet now henceforth we know him no more. Therefore if any man be in Christ, he is a new creature: old things are passed away; behold, all things are become new." (2 Corinthians 5:16-17)

We are there by virtue of what the death and resurrection of our Saviour has wrought. All our sins are put away, all that we were in the first Adam, atoned for, gone, totally gone. In Christ we are now fit for the presence and sight of God.

The redemptive work of our Saviour with respect to sin has a much wider reference than a purely individual one. The whole regeneration of the universe is founded on it. God's dealings with this world must be on the basis that sin is still there and this will be finally dealt with when

> "...the heavens shall pass away with a great noise, and the elements shall melt with fervent heat, the earth also and the works that are therein shall be burned up." (2 Peter 3:10)

The earth and the heavens are to be *changed*.

> "And, Thou, Lord, in the beginning hast laid the foundation of the earth; and the heavens are the works of thine hands: They shall perish; but thou remainest; and they all shall wax old as doth a garment; And as a vesture shalt thou fold them

up, and they shall be changed: but thou art the same, and thy years shall not fail." (Hebrews 1:10-12)

Also those who have chosen to remain where they are as part of the first creation will likewise perish in their sins.

"For, behold, the day cometh, that shall burn as an oven; and all the proud, yea, and all that do wickedly, shall be stubble: and the day that cometh shall burn them up, saith the Lord of hosts, that it shall leave them neither root nor branch." (Malachi 4:1)

## *There is only one Word of God and it is one Word*

The body of believers is *one organic whole* chosen in Christ Jesus *"before the foundation of the world"* (Ephesians 1:4), not only at any one given point of time on earth, but reaching down through the centuries from the inception of the Church until that moment when *"we which are alive and remain shall be caught up together with them in the clouds, the meet the Lord in the air"* (1 Thessalonians 4:17). The Church is *one whole* even although some members of that body now are in the presence of Christ. Equally, there is *one whole deposit of truth* in Scripture given to this *one body* throughout this time. We are at a disadvantage because our perception of these things is coloured by our experience of time and its passing, but to God there is no distinction to be drawn. Both the Church and the deposit of truth in Scripture given to her were conceived and laid down before the foundation of the world. There can therefore be no changes made to Scripture nor can it now be supplemented as it perfectly matches the one eternal purpose of God being itself part of it. There is not more of God's Word given to us now than was in the possession of the Church when the apostle John penned his last word on Patmos. We have *one* Word given to *one* body of believers throughout this dispensation. The one was meant for the other. As nothing will be added to the Church other than that which from eternity belongs to her, so that which is necessary for her to know will not be supplemented. As the same Word is given to those who went before and those who follow, nothing will be added now which was not accessible to those who went before. We need no more than those gone before, we can make do with no less. It will not increase nor diminish.

Peter tells us *"no prophecy of the scripture is of any private interpretation"* (2 Peter 1:20). This tells us a number of things. It tells us that the Word of God has one meaning, which is the same meaning for one believer as it is for another. What is true for me, is true for you; what is authoritative for one, another can find no excuse to ignore. This verse also tells us, Scripture is given to the whole body of believers and ought not to be interpreted in isolation from that which has been understood by genuine believers down the centuries and across the world. Upon becoming believers we enter into communion with others holding a body of belief or doctrine, called in Scripture 'the faith' – we share a common consciousness of the truth mediated through Scripture. We ought not to despise the insights of other believers on the Word of God, also those alive in previous times, even although all the statements of men must themselves be subjected to a searching of the Scriptures, *"whether those things were so"* (Acts 17:11). As C. H. Spurgeon put it, we must not assume that all the light we have will come to us through a cracked tile in our own roof. For the same reason we attend the preaching of the Word – that we may apprehend *"the faith which was once delivered unto the saints"* (Jude 3). The word is, 'once delivered' by the apostles and prophets whose words we now have, by God's good grace, infallibly recorded in the Bible we hold in our hands today. A body of teaching *once* delivered will not be added to. We are only able to grow in the faith as we draw from this communion with other believers centred in the Word of God that life-giving sap needed for our spiritual development. In isolation we shrivel and die. We share this same confession with the millions who even now enjoy the presence of the Lord Jesus. Those who come with some new teaching, some new 'revelation', some new insight never before found among the people of God, are certain to be apostates, bringers of false doctrine. The Scriptures are emphatically *not* given to us each one of us separately but access to them is intrinsic to being a member of the body of Christ. We have access to the teaching of Scripture by being made members of the one body of Christ, sharing the same Spirit.

Apart from the God of the Bible, there is no God. Outside the eternal purposes of this same God, nothing exists and nothing happens. Outside the body of those redeemed by Christ there is no salvation, no hope. Outside the Scriptures there is no shared body of truth, only falsehood. Christ is the true trunk of our regenerate humanity, and all that is not grafted into this tree falls away as a rotten branch. After the manifestation of the mystery *"concerning Christ and the Church"* (Ephesians 5:32), no individual obtains a part in salvation except as a member of the organic whole. Are we in Christ, then we one in Him with all other believers. Revelation is completed because salvation is completed and there remains nothing more to be said to mankind than that which God has said in His Son and is revealed to us in His Word.

> *How firm a foundation, ye saints of the Lord,*
> *Is laid for your faith in His excellent Word;*
> *What more can He say than to you He hath said,*
> *You who unto Jesus for refuge have fled.*

Old Testament saints, Noah, Moses, Samuel, David all received separate revelations because at that time the completed revelation was not yet available, nor could it be.

Christ had not yet come, all was not yet said, salvation was yet to be completed, therefore revelation must remain incomplete. A revelation that is incomplete infers a salvation that is incomplete. Once the revelation was completed, the need for all individual and separate revelation fell away. Mysticism which to this day pretends to receive such separate personal revelation thereby frustrates the organic ministration of the Lord. There is no other way for men to come to a knowledge of salvation in our day except through union with this one revelation held in trust by the communion of believers. As there is no salvation outside the true body of Christ, there is no salvation outside that one revelation of the truth committed to her, which we have in Scripture.

> *God is one and One is God; the people of God are one; the purpose of God is one — and there is therefore only one Word of God which is in itself one.*

What we know of God comes to us as a direct act of God employing existing elements in the world, men, language, writing, created by Him for this purpose. God caused prophets and apostles to receive and write under the inspiration of the Holy Spirit so that His thoughts have been transcribed into human language. In Scripture He has conveyed to us all that we need to know in an infallible and inalterable written form so that His truth continues to be available from generation to generation. In His goodness God has preserved that Word which He originally gave intact, so that all is there. Equally, He permits nothing to be added. Godly men were called to translate that same Word into English, without which those not knowing the original languages can have no direct access to the knowledge of salvation. As no detail of human life comes to pass apart from Him, God again so protected His Word in our *Authorised*

*Version* so that it was impossible that anything should be lost in translation or that it should contain errors to mislead us. God has poured out that same Holy Spirit who inspired the human writers of Scripture that through His illuminating work the meaning is made clear to us today as we read. We need no more, we need no less, to live on earth to His glory finding eternal hope in His Son.

The Scriptures leave out nothing that God does not want us to know and there is nothing in it, but that which is essential for us to know. The Word of God is perfect in the sense that nothing is missing that needs to be there and nothing is there that ought not to be there. As long as the writing of Scripture was still underway, it gave an *incomplete* picture. Scripture constitutes a whole where each part must be understood in relation to the sum of the other parts. It follows that those living in those times when Scriptures were still being written were not in possession of the complete picture. To the prophets were even revealed things the significance of which escaped them, but which are now made known to us.

> "Of which salvation the prophets have enquired and searched diligently, who prophesied of the grace that should come unto you: Searching what, or what manner of time the Spirit of Christ which was in them did signify, when it testified beforehand the sufferings of Christ, and the glory that should follow. Unto whom it was revealed, that not unto themselves, but unto us they did minister the things, which are now reported unto you by them that have preached the gospel unto you with the Holy Ghost sent down from heaven; which things the angels desire to look into." (1 Peter 1:10-12)

Paul writes similarly to the Ephesians.

> "How that by revelation he made known unto me the mystery; (as I wrote afore in few words, whereby, when ye read, ye may understand my knowledge in the mystery of Christ) which in other ages was not made known unto the

sons of men, as it is now revealed unto his holy apostles and prophets by the Spirit; that the Gentiles should be fellowheirs, and of the same body, and partakers of his promise in Christ by the gospel." (Ephesians 3:3-6)

With the completion of the Old Testament the final Word was yet to come. Only with the coming into the world of the Son of God could the Scriptures be completed.

"God, who at sundry times and in divers manners spake in time past unto the fathers by the prophets, hath in these last days spoken unto us by his Son." (Hebrews 1:1-2)

All that God has to say to mankind He has said in Christ and all there is to know of Christ is found in God's Word. God has nothing more to say than He has said in Christ, He has nothing more to give than He has already given in Christ. There can be therefore nothing more for us to know than the revelation of Christ in the completed canon of Scripture. The whole body of that which God intended to reveal to us existed in God before one page of Scripture was committed to writing. That which God thought to reveal along with its actual physical manifestation as a book constitutes a complete revelation of God to the sinner.

There are very many these days who object to the very idea of God speaking to man by communicating His thoughts solely in a once-for-all time verbal revelation. Some regard such a notion as what they term 'bibliolatry'. Despite this, the Bible itself claims to be the only authoritative verbal revelation to men. As there is no other authoritative revelation, its denial, rather than opening up to God other avenues of revelation, in reality lets in human authority and the doctrines of devils by the back door. Those who do not accept the *sole* authority of Scripture do not accept its authority at all, but establish their own in its place. Such people will only accept an authority to which they consent and they will acknowledge no authority that places their own 'right' to make a final choice or decision in jeopardy. The claims of authority Scripture makes for itself are offensive to the natural man. The authority of the omnipotent God is not established by man, but all men must stoop to recognise it.

Many today falsely claim that there are still revelations coming directly to believers through the Holy Spirit. They see no reason to suppose that God should suddenly have stopped revealing Himself to individuals. This flies in the face of Jude 3 and passages such as this one in Galatians, which are to be interpreted in the light of the *whole* teaching of Scripture on the subject.

> "But though we, or an angel from heaven, preach any other gospel unto you than that which we have preached unto you, let him be accursed. As we said before, so say I now again, If any man preach any other gospel unto you than that ye have received, let him be accursed." (Galatians 1:8-9)

There are several things to note here. If even an angel came in order to add to that which had been given by the apostles, he should be accursed. If this statement is to make any sense, it must rest on the assumption that what had come through the apostles was complete and nothing more was to be expected. It also meant that the Galatians in the apostolic Gospel possessed an infallible criterion by which to judge those who sought to introduce new teachings. This test is thus set aside by those who indulge in mystic 'revelations'. No non-apostolic writing or teaching can be set alongside the authority of the apostle Paul, but they are all to be tested by *it*.

Another common variation of this type of mysticism is the assertion that the Scriptures speak only in very general terms and individual Christians need a word from God to meet individual circumstances. There being only one deposit of truth given to the Church, Christians today stand only in need of the illuminating work of God's Spirit as they read the Bible. All that the Christian needs is to be found in its pages. The promise of God is that the Holy Spirit will lead the individual believer within the corporate Church into an ever-deepening understanding of the meaning of Scripture. Those who ignore the Scriptures God has given cannot expect Him then to make a special revelation just for them. What many earnest and well-meaning people understand by 'guidance' often amounts to a mistaken understanding of revelation. Many claim to receive details of daily life directly from God rather than from Scripture. At best this is self-delusion, at worst it can have an occult element.

All the various sects, whether it be Roman Catholicism, Russellism, Mormonism, Spiritism, Pentecostalism, all without exception in their own way undermine the sufficiency of Scripture by adding to it, claiming continuing revelation. Continuing revelation within the Roman Catholic Church is accompanied by the blasphemy of the continual sacrificial offering up of Christ in the mass and consequently no finished or certain salvation. Very often, such groups feign reliance and trust in Scripture. Against this we must maintain that Scripture is sufficient of itself, perspicuous, authoritative and necessary. We stand in need of no other revelations. The way we interpret individual portion of Scripture must be subordinated to the 'big picture', the teaching of Scripture as a whole. Those passages not immediately clear must be interpreted in the light of those that are clearer. It is inadequate to instruct believers only in certain parts of the Bible, even memorising verses of Scripture can be counterproductive, if it is not done with the whole of Scripture in view. Only in this way can we avoid going astray.

There is but *one* Word and that Word is one, it is a unity in itself. Unless we see Scripture as an *organic and unified whole* we shall become one-sided and unbalanced. It is not sufficient to 'know our Bible' in the sense of hanging one truth up after another like washing on a line. We need to be found preaching the counsel of God *as a whole*. The 'one-text' approach to a proclamation of the truth is inadequate. We may find one text teaching eternal punishment, but an opponent will search around until he finds one that seems to teach annihilation. One truth does not depend upon one or two verses, but has an indispensable place within the context of the whole sweep of divine revelation, as part of the 'big picture'. Remove it and all the others will be affected, just as a building will be rendered insecure and even dangerous if bricks are removed here and there from its walls. Wrong in one place can so easily mean wrong in all places.

In a message preached in February of 1872, the saintly George Müller said this, *"We cannot pick and choose, it is the whole that constitutes the Word of God"*. It is simply not possible to grasp the individual meanings of biblical 'truths' in isolation without an insight into the comprehensive coherence of all the different aspects of biblical revelation, or *truth*. We ought really to speak of *truth* rather than 'truths'. For this reason we speak of the *Word* of God rather than the words of God when referring to Scripture. Individual aspects of biblical truth reveal their meaning only within this total picture. The meaning of the whole is expressed within the individual structure, guaranteeing the individual meaning. It cannot be torn from the whole without losing its individual significance at the same time. The meaning of a single 'truth' has a dependent reference to the meaning of all other 'truths'. The Christian Gospel is to be presented on the basis that every part is to be preached in dependence upon its place in the *whole* teaching of Scripture. The incarnation, life, death, and resurrection of Christ cannot be understood unless we see these things in the context of the whole of Scripture. They are otherwise quite meaningless.

Events that happen by chance, human actions, decisions and thoughts that originate from within an individual can have no meaning whatever, because they are not related to the whole, to the big picture. Life can have no meaning apart from a comprehensive plan and purpose of God for the world He has created, this is the sole unifying factor between the particular individual facts that make up our universe. Cut loose from this plan and the actions of men are not free, but senseless. The overriding characteristic of modern life is that there is no reason why anything should happen as it does, everything is thought of as being completely arbitrary and thus, without the guiding hand of God providentially bringing all things to pass, descends into unintelligibility. There can otherwise be no valid reason why one should take one course of action rather than another.

## Modern mysticism and the one Word of God

Those of us who believe and rely upon the Scriptures alone do not deny the working of the Holy Spirit within individuals, but in and of itself it will not lead us to a knowledge of God. Where there has been an inspiration which brings with it a knowledge of God, it is not general but exceptional, and then only within the period from Paradise to Patmos, and not for the prime benefit of individuals but *organically* for the good of the whole body of believers. It will be part of Scripture. We do not know about God by adding together what God has revealed to the first person to that of a second then a third. This is not the way Scriptures were put together. The revelation and inspiration of Holy writ was not part of some in-shining of God's Spirit that endlessly repeats itself. It was limited to a definite period and subject to specific conditions. That which was thus given is not to be thought of as one piece being joined to another, any more than we think of the Church as an aggregate of saved individuals, but as forming *one whole*. The Scripture is not a collection of writings made up of one revelation stitched together with another side by side like a patchwork quilt, but is the one thought, the one Word of God.

Inspiration is that direct work of God's Spirit upon the heart and mind of the Scripture writers by which the will and thoughts of God are made known to them verbally. These God-breathed words were given to the prophets and apostles who then infallibly recorded the Word of God on paper. This is one Word given to men. Mystics down through the ages have held a different view. They believe that God, wishing to make Himself known to sinners, communicates separately to individual men, making His will and thoughts know to each one. Each man sits in his own 'cell' and receives a 'visit' from God, who has something particular to say to him. God is said to make Himself known in this way first to one then to another, each individual not necessarily being known to the other. What God has 'revealed' to one may not be known by another. This is supposed to go on, year in year out, in one land and another.

Mysticism has infected different elements of the professing and the apostate Church. It is found in the neo-orthodoxy of Barth and Brunner, 'the bible is God's word when it speaks to me' brigade. Mysticism dominates Pentecostalism and the charismatic movement with its 'tongues', 'revelations', 'visions', and other even more frantic fabrications. False mysticism, to some degree or other, has often infected evangelical thinking in general and 'holiness' teaching in particular. Mystics are in essence obsessive and largely self-centred individualists. They see God as speaking, not to the people of God as a whole, even as with all his gifts to the Church *'to profit withal'*, but to every person on his own, but especially for him. Mysticism is a characteristic of the Roman Church. In medieval times, it flourished in the cold dark cells of Roman monkery. The Roman Church believes inspiration and revelation to be an on-going phenomenon continuing in the church today and in the Pope *ex cathedra loquente*. The content is supplemented and interpreted absolutely by the Roman church. Inspiration continuing in the Roman Church is placed on the same level as that of Moses, David, or Paul.

The Bible, though often apparently in a central position, is in fact sidelined in all mysticism; it has no final authority. Scripture is in reality set aside, and its authority denied. The notion that God has spoken to His people *as a whole* in a book, that we all may know all that God has to say, is not accepted. The Word of God is, in truth, the same to one as it is to every man. Only then can it be authoritative to all men with equal force. God does not need to speak individually to anyone.

> *As everything we need is found in Christ, so everything we need to know about Him is found in Scripture.*

God must, it is thought, speak separately to each individual soul that it may enjoy a secret walk with God. Such an 'inner light' is worse than useless, simply because it is a lie and a deception often put to destructive use by the emissaries of Satan. Were it a true light, people in receipt of such inspiration would speak as the prophets and apostles of old. Each would confirm the word of the other, when, in fact, such modern day 'prophecies' usually contradict each other. Year in year out, from age to age, so it is said, God speaks. Were it true that God imparted privately knowledge of Himself to individuals one by one, such mystically inspired persons ought then to speak as the prophets and apostles, and the witness of one should confirm that of another. There could in such circumstances also be no received and authoritative body of truth intended for all men, no Bible in the form that we have it.

The Holy Spirit does not work in this way now that we have a completed deposit of truth in Scripture. Rather He points us to the truth revealed in the Bible, He explains and applies this truth to the individual heart according to particular need. He quickens the soul to a living knowledge of the truth, but never in any way as to increase the content. For mystics, Scripture is insufficient. They would enlarge the prophet's mantle, draw it tightly around themselves! Such fake prophecies often serve to compel others to subject themselves to the prophet himself, to regulate their lives according to his or her orders. They soar paracletically above the revelation of Scriptures, eventually to leave the Scriptures behind with only the solitary authoritative voice of the prophet remaining.

Once inspiration ended, we have the whole picture; we have all that God has given for us to know about Himself as one unified, coherent whole. There remains nothing more for Him to reveal by direct inspiration. Since the completion of Scripture, there is no other direct Word from God to man that bypasses Scripture going out to the human consciousness of God's elect. There is one table spread for all. The Word of God to all is the Word of God to each one. Here the same message is offered, the same teaching, the same exhortation, the same content to all, not one by one, but in one central revelation, so that each elect child of God may draw upon it under the illumination of God's Spirit. It is from this *one* revelation given for all, which neither repeats itself nor continues to unfold, that the people of God in all places and times have to draw the knowledge of the eternal God. That which God planned in eternity to bring to our race, that knowledge of Him, has been brought within our reach. The individual and organic working of the Holy Spirit is now to lead His people in their work of seeking to understand the meaning of what He has given us. The Scriptures only rise to their full significance when complete. We are privileged in our dispensation to be in possession of the 'big picture'. In the time between Paradise and Patmos and the progressive revelation of God, the people of God stood in a somewhat different relation to Scripture for they did not yet have the whole picture. The Scriptures are validated as such only on completion. A tree begins as a sapling, grows a little each year until the gardener is able to harvest its fruit.

# CHAPTER 5

# Human Consciousness and Divine Communication

*"And the LORD God formed man of the dust of the ground, and breathed into his nostrils the breath of life; and man became a living soul."* (Genesis 2:7)

Newly born babies always seem to the uninitiated to be very much the same, screwed-up faces and lots of crying, food in at one end and a dreadful mess at the other. As the weeks pass and features become more clearly defined, physical similarities with those of the parents become increasingly discernible, ears that stick out or are flat, a round nose or a long one, dark hair or blonde. It takes a brave man or a foolhardy relative to really throw a rattle into the works by suggesting which side of the family this amazing bundle of new life resembles most. Our offspring resemble us. Look at the children see the parents.

Our children resemble us in more ways than we sometimes care to be reminded, but where can we find that which resembles God? The Scriptures tell us that everything God created declares his glory. As there is nothing outside that which He created, all things tell us something about what God is like. *God Himself is the measure of all that He has made.*

"The heavens declare the glory of God; and the firmament sheweth his handywork. Day unto day uttereth speech, and night unto night sheweth knowledge. There is no speech nor language, where their voice is not heard. Their line is gone out through all the earth, and their words to the end of the world." (Psalm 19:1-4)

"The heavens declare his righteousness, and all the people see his glory." (Psalm 97:6)

"For the invisible things of him from the creation of the world are clearly seen, being understood by the things that are made, even his eternal power and Godhead; so that they are without excuse." (Romans 1:20)

What cannot normally be seen of the nature and being of God because it is invisible is made accessible to our senses through that which He has made. *The crown of God's creation is man himself, for he is a finite replica of God, made in His image.* All that goes into making us what we are as living souls is found first in God. Indeed, by looking within ourselves we find there an unmistakable finite revelation of what God is like.

"Because that which may be known of God is manifest in them; for God hath shewed it unto them." (Romans 1:19)

Whether we are aware of it or not, whether we like or accept it or not, to be a human being with human attributes is to be a finite copy of God, albeit now marred and maimed by sin. To deny God is to write off our own humanity, it is to degrade ourselves to something less than human, less than God made us to be. When godless Nietzsche mocked, "Ring a little bell, God is dead", he struck a deadly blow against humanity and led the march to nihilism!

God has no material body, which is why we read with the coming of the Son of God into the world:

"Wherefore when he cometh into the world, he saith, Sacrifice and offering thou wouldest not, but a body hast thou prepared me." (Hebrews 10:5)

He is God *manifest* in the flesh. Man is *made* in the image of God, the Lord Jesus by contrast is *"the brightness of his glory,* and the express image of His person" (Hebrews 1:3). There never could be a greater revelation of God within the material created world than *the express image* of God Himself in the person of the Lord Jesus taking on human flesh. *"Great is the mystery of godliness: God was manifest in the flesh"* (1 Timothy 3:16). It is in this area that false teaching first crept into the early Church. This heresy corrupted early texts of the New Testament so soon after the departure of the apostles. The person of Christ is generally the first line of attack by false teachers and false religions to this day. This is why we are warned...

> "For many deceivers are entered into the world, who confess not that Jesus Christ is come in the flesh. This is a deceiver and an antichrist." (2 John 7)

Some will say Jesus is God but not man, others that He is man but not God. The Bible says He is one person, distinctly and without mixture both truly God and truly man.

Although the world did not and does not recognise the fact, the Lord Jesus, eternal Son of God, crossed the line between the uncreated and the created in the opposite direction to that aspired to by Satan: *"He was in the world, and the world was made by him"* (John 1:10). He became everything that we are in order to secure our deliverance.

> "Forasmuch then as the children are partakers of flesh and blood, he also himself likewise took part of the same; that through death he might destroy him that had the power of death, that is, the devil." (Hebrews 2:14)

In one significant way the Lord Jesus did not become like us, He did not share our *sinful nature*. Although *"in all points tempted like as we are"*, He was *"without sin"* (Hebrews 4:15).

Today it is our purpose as the regenerate children of God on earth to manifest what God is like — *"Glorify God in your body, and in your spirit, which are God's"* (1 Corinthians 6:20). As those born of God we have a *"treasure in earthen vessels"*, namely, the light that

> "...hath shined in our hearts, to give light of the knowledge of the glory of God in the face of Jesus Christ."
>
> (2 Corinthians 4:6)

Whatever our experience of life, it will be to the end *"that the life also of Jesus might be made manifest in our mortal flesh"* (4:11). God made the world to glorify Himself, to demonstrate the majesty of His perfections. This creation still does so, despite the fall. It does it the more so in those who through His grace have been made

> "...partakers of the divine nature, having escaped the corruption that is in the world through lust." (2 Peter 1:4)

---

*Sinners cannot contemplate themselves without seeing an instantaneous picture of God – indeed, if they deny Him, they must ultimately deny themselves because they are like him, for if God does not exist neither can that which is made in His image.*

---

Even as the reflected image in a mirror indicates the existence of the reality behind the image, in a similar way no one can avoid Him whose image is reflected within his own personality. The resemblance of the human psyche and human consciousness to God is so close that to admit its existence is to recognize the existence of God at the same time, it is unavoidable. One way in which rebellious sinners will try to erase this inescapable image of God that confronts them and strikes their consciences day by day is to attempt to rid the human constitution of all that is not material and physical. To admit anything else would be to allow the return of a God whom they desperately need to remove from their lives. Emphasis is placed exclusively on the physical aspect of man because it finds no direct counterpart in God's essential being and is thus less of an immediate reminder of Him. There is no other reason for this on their part, no scientific proof, nothing more than an unsubstantiated assumption that there can be nothing beyond that received through the five physical senses.

Those godless systems of thought still holding on to a non-physical aspect to human personality will set God to one side, should they still accept His existence in some form or other, by also ascribing to the human heart those attributes which belong exclusively to God. The distinction between God and man is erased, both are said to be essentially on the same level 'spiritually'. They see the human heart as itself determinative and not as having been made after the image of any other being, so it cannot be derivative or dependent in any way. They place their own heart at the centre of the universe in the place of God; just as Satan did before them they set their *"heart as the heart of God"* (Ezekiel 28:2). *"Keep thy heart with all diligence; for out of it are the issues of life"* (Proverbs 4:23). To go astray here will affect everything we do.

## God has made us in some aspects like He is

God alone exists in and of Himself with no need of anything other than Himself. Man can exist only because God first exists in the way He does. The Bible tells us, *"God created man in his own image, in the image of God created he him"* (Genesis 1:27). God has given to man a being similar to His own, a finite replica, without participating in the divine *being*. There must be ways therefore in which man is like God and God is like man. The glory of man is that he reflects, even in a fallen state, something of what God is like. He bears the image of God.

First, God is a *Spirit* and man faintly reflects this. Second, God has attributes of *understanding*, which man also replicates if he would have true knowledge, albeit always within the constraints of his finite humanity. Third, there are God's *moral* attributes, for want of a better term. These make His being determinative for us in all ethical and moral matters. Finally, there remain His attributes of *sovereignty*, His will, His power. We express all these characteristics within the limitations of our own finitude and creatureliness, whereas God reveals Himself in them in infinitude and deity. It is in these particular attributes of His being that God is known to us, that He is immanent, near us.

We are something more than flesh and blood, more than a complex system of chemical reactions and electrical impulses. This is because we reflect in finite form God's own spirituality. Materialists deny that man is in anyway spiritual or non-material. They maintain that our mind is to be explained in purely physical terms, as are all other intangible elements of the human personality. Such considerations dominate the behaviourist system of psychology and the Marxist view of human consciousness. Once all things are reduced to the material and nothing else, God goes, but man disappears as well.

Our God-created spirit makes us individuals, distinguishes from each other. We are each created as an individual according to the purpose God has for us in particular from eternity. Without being spirit, we can be nothing more than just one more human being that has simply popped up on the planet from nowhere with no real individual significance, living a life that can have no meaning. We are then little more than a hunk of flesh, born to live and die, and then to rot in the grave or be cremated to ashes — to turn into 'social waste', as some minor hospital manager here in the UK recently so indelicately expressed it. Thus in the first instance it is a refusal of Bible teaching about *God* rather than man that makes one man treat another with contempt, disrespect, and dishonour. Materialistic philosophies degrade men and hold human life as disposable and cheap.

To realise that God is a Spirit is the first step in understanding what it is to worship God. What the Bible teaches is very clear.

> "God is a Spirit: and they that worship him must worship him in spirit and in truth." (John 4:24)

Only spirit can worship a Spirit. When speaking of spirituality we do not mean some single generic concept of which God is one example and man another. God's spirituality is not another aspect of the universe. We need to be very careful when we hear people talking about 'spiritual values'. All that many of these people mean is that beyond the visible and physical there is another intangible aspect of the created universe that is spiritual. It is still thought of as being part of the universe and at best makes God to be just another aspect of a spiritual-material universe. Idealist philosophers understand spirituality in this way, so placing the spirituality of God and man on the same level, all part of the one world in which we all live. Their 'values' have thus originated from within the created universe.

God is an absolute and self-contained Spirit. It was not necessary for God to create the material universe in order to show by contrast that He is a Spirit. Man being created in God's image is spirit, though not *a* spirit, being both physical *and* spiritual. God is *a* Spirit; God is immortal and invisible. In the words of the well-known hymn:

> *Immortal, invisible, God only Wise,*
> *In light inaccessible hid from our eyes*

The Lord Jesus told us,

> "No man hath seen God at any time; the only begotten Son, which is in the bosom of the Father, he hath declared him?" (John 1:18)

Any 'seeing' of God is a spiritual not a physical seeing. It is quite impossible for us to physically see anything of God other than in an expression through His creation and especially through human beings. To see the Lord Jesus remains the only way to see God directly and physically.

> "Who only hath immortality, dwelling in the light which no man can approach unto; whom no man hath seen nor can see: to whom be honour and power everlasting. Amen."
> (1 Timothy 6:16)

The Lord Jesus is presently in heaven and will remain there until His coming again, so that no one alive today can claim to have seen God physically. Anyone making such a claim is deceived or a deceiver.

Contrary to the false teaching of some, we shall not be lifted out of our natural limitations as creatures in the hereafter in order to facilitate a greater insight into the being of God, even when then without sin. God will remain eternally incomprehensible, to be other than that He would cease to be God. Although the issue of separation through sin has been fully resolved in Christ, we remain finite creatures and God remains infinite Creator. Contrary to the promises made by Satan, we can never cross this divide. God can be seen by us ever only in the context of our being creatures. The understanding and impressions of God in the human consciousness will always be finite.

> "All things are delivered unto me of my Father: and no man knoweth the Son, but the Father; neither knoweth any man the Father, save the Son, and he to whomsoever the Son will reveal him." (Matthew 11:27)

Despite our likeness to God, the distinction between Creator and creature must ever remain in place.

All that we have said thus far about God indicates to us that we worship a personal God. The Bible speaks to us of a God who is a self-conscious and moral being, who in all that He is and does is dependent upon nothing and no one beyond Himself. There is no idea of the good, of truth, of beauty over and above Him after which He fashioned His creation. Rather, all things display the excellencies of His majesty. Truth, goodness, beauty are all defined by *the being of God* from whom all such notions derive.

All these attributes are personal not simply abstract universal principles and they exist only in a personal form, first in God, but then thereby also in us. Nature and human thought are not simply God becoming self-conscious. *History is not God becoming self-conscious through human activity.* God is eternally conscious of all that He is, as we have seen, and needs nothing outside Himself through which to *become* what He already is. Like God, we are self-conscious personalities and *our consciousness too is not dependent upon things around us,* but is there because we are made in the image of God and He sustains and keeps us. There is no question here of a Hegelian impersonal Absolute Spirit thinking out its thoughts using human minds. Nor does God only become aware of Himself in an object in which His own self is reflected. God and the man He has created are both self-conscious persons between whom there is a communication of thoughts from one to the other. In God's case, we are talking about a tri-unity of persons in one being between whom there is also communication.

Every human being replicates elements of what God is like within the parameters of his finitude. Our mind will be after the pattern of His mind. To think according to the truth we must think as He does both in pattern and content. God is a rational being and the world that God has created will express that self-same rationality. The mind of man being finitely reflective of God's mind is thus capable of receiving the thoughts that God would reveal to us. The human mind has now become polluted with sin and needs the cleansing of the blood of Christ, it needs the regeneration of God's Spirit. The ability to think may be hindered by sin, but the human mind remains inherently suited to think the thoughts of God. This is denied by theologians such as Karl Barth. If God were 'totally other' in the way that many theologians have suggested, the possibility of a verbal communication in the way the Bible teaches it becomes impossible.

God is revealed in Scripture as the light and as living in light. It is this light in God from which the light of our own self-consciousness is lit within our souls. At the same time, nothing within our consciousness exists but that God knows it altogether.

> "For there is not a word in my tongue, but, lo, O Lord, thou knowest it altogether." (Psalm 139:4)

We also read, *"for the righteous God trieth the hearts and reins"* (Psalm 7:9). Reins are the deepest roots of our soul life. Such complete transparency of pure, clear consciousness is also a characteristic of the being of God. As our consciousness is a created replica of that found in God, it is perfectly possible for God to know our thoughts completely and for us to share the thoughts of God. He first thought as He does before creating a similar capacity within us in a finite form. We must ever maintain this distinction:

> "For my thoughts are not your thoughts, neither are your ways my ways, saith the LORD. For as the heavens are higher than the earth, so are my ways higher than your ways, and my thoughts than your thoughts."
> (Isaiah 55:8-9)

Nevertheless, we must also say that God is able to cast His thoughts in a form able to be assimilated by our human consciousness. For this reason God can and does communicate with men in this day and age through Scripture.

Our knowledge is 'in part' and will one day pass away to make room for something higher.

> "For we know in part, and we prophesy in part. But when that which is perfect is come, then that which is in part shall be done away." (1 Corinthians 13:9-10)

Those who deny the existence of self-consciousness necessarily deny the possibility of knowing anything more than that which we now possess. One day, I shall know myself as God knows me.

> "For now we see through a glass, darkly; but then face to face: now I know in part; but then shall I know even as also I am known." (1 Corinthians 13:12)

Whilst one day we shall know many things that are today a mystery to us, even in heaven, we shall not know all things. Some things would require us to be God to understand them.

The work of God's self-revelation is not completed until that which is in the heart and mind of God becomes alive in our own consciousness. What we now need to consider is to what extent the soul of man is suitable ground in which the seed of God's Word can germinate, take root, and grow. How is it possible for man to receive the Word of God into his consciousness?

## A shared consciousness

For there to be communication between God and man there must also be some common factor in both God and man that makes this possible. God and man must have some common ground of consciousness. The Word of God can enter our hearts and minds only because we are made in His image; only because there is some counterpart of God in us able to receive it and then only when the light of the Gospel has shined in our hearts. We can think the thoughts of God, even if not in identical fullness, only because our mind is made to some degree like His. We can share His feelings, feel as He does about things in measure, only because we are made in His image. Our human wills can operate as they do, making meaningful and responsible decisions, only because all that we are is analogous of that which is found in God. We share a common consciousness with all men, a consciousness made after that found in God, so that we are able not only to share thoughts with each other, but we can also receive that which God would reveal to us all. It means that *God has access to the hearts and minds of all men.* God is inescapable. This common human consciousness enables first, communication between men; and second, communication with God.

There is also an organic unity between us and the rest of creation, between our consciousness and all that we observe around us. The receptivity of our subjective consciousness to impressions of the objective world 'out there' is made possible because we are all part of the one creation. Our physical senses give us a window on the physical world. Through this means, that which is observable to us makes an impression upon our consciousness within our mental faculties. If what we are observing is material then the lines of communication will also be material. Before we actually become aware of things beyond ourselves, there must be the conditions within us ready to receive them.

Unbelievers maintain that man's connection with the rest of the universe is purely accidental, governed by chance occurrence from which no meaning can be culled, no purpose threads together a disparate jumble of incidental facts. Were the whole world nothing but a total accident, the product of evolutionary contingency, it is difficult to see how there can be a common link between ourselves and everything else beyond us; we would be unlikely to have any facility within ourselves to receive into our consciousness what we observe and make any sense of it. There could be no connecting link between anything. That with which we have contact outside ourselves does not exist in a chaotic disorder but is a cosmos, a *universe*. Our thought, our mind has been so created as part of this one universe that it is able to recognise the relationships existing between one thing and another. If this were not the case, we could have no thoughts about what we see around us.

Although the world and everything in it, our lives and all we experience, may seem complex at times and beyond our grasp, there is, because of the eternal plan of God, a system, and so a meaning in everything. That which is beyond us, outside us, will fit our inner world like a glove because we are predisposed to receive it. God has made us that way. Because God understands it, our minds, being a finite replica of His mind, are also able to receive it within our finite capacities. He who made the world out there also made the world within us after His own image.

It is in the interest of the unbelief of many theologians and philosophers to deny the existence of a personal self-conscious God along with human self-consciousness as a non-material entity. They make human-consciousness entirely dependent upon the phenomena arising in the material and physical world. Yet the truth is, we cannot retain a human consciousness without at the same time retaining a God-consciousness. To be rid of an innate consciousness of God, godless thinkers must dispose too of human consciousness, which continually testifies to them of the presence of God.

In his early writings, Karl Marx described consciousness of any kind as an illusion (cf. *The German Ideology*). Such 'phantoms' are formed in the human brain by an ever-changing environment. Conceiving, thinking, language, rather than emanating from the unseen human soul, are the direct consequence of the external 'material behaviour' of men. *"Life is not determined by consciousness, but consciousness by life,"* he wrote. Self-consciousness is an illusion created within us by being aware of others round about and the environment in which we live. Were there no one and nothing out there to create this self-consciousness in us, we could not be aware of ourselves. Human consciousness is dependent upon the material and physical world and man's interaction with it.

We should note carefully that this concept is at the heart of all forms of socialism and it exposes too the link between Marxism and modern 'environmentalism'. The nature of our existence is said to be determined by others around us and our environment. Are these bad, we shall be bad. In this way, personal guilt and responsibility for sin can be eradicated. We can blame our parents, our upbringing, social conditions, but there is no need for us to feel guilty and punishment for wrongdoing is inappropriate. Who could Adam blame but his wife and beyond? Eden was a perfect environment and he had no parents. To improve the environment, to improve the condition of men and their relationship one to another, is to improve the nature of man himself. We are told that improvement of the human lot is achievable only through social and environmental means.

> *A denial of the self-conscious immaterial human soul is the first step down the road to ignorance, stupidity, and all kinds of evil.*

The fact that every human being is a *conscious* being, conscious of his or her own existence and that of things around them, presents ungodly people with real difficulty and we have no reason to let them off the hook lightly. The denial of a non-material human soul reduces men to a purely physical machine functioning alone by chemical reactions and electrical impulses. The illusion of self-consciousness formed in the human brain is but a dream, little more than a fairy story, something from *Alice in Wonderland.*

> In a Wonderland they lie,
> Dreaming as the days go by,
> Dreaming as the summers die:
> Ever drifting down the stream -
> Lingering in the golden gleam –
> Life, what is it but a dream?

The king is dreaming about Alice, so Tweedledee exclaims,
> "And if he left off dreaming about you, where do you suppose you'd be?"
> 'Where I am now, of course," said Alice.
> "Not you!" Tweedledee retorted contemptuously. "You'd be nowhere. Why, you're only a sort of thing in his dream!"
> "If that there King was to wake," added Tweedledum", you'd go out — bang! — just like a candle!"
> "I shouldn't" Alice exclaimed indignantly. "Besides, if I'm only a sort of thing in his dream, what are *you*, I should like to know?"
> "Ditto," said Tweedledum.
> "Ditto, ditto!" cried Tweedledee.
> (from *Through the Looking Glass*)

Behavioural psychologist, John Watson, claimed that 'consciousness' was neither a definite nor usable concept, the *"belief in the existence of consciousness goes back to the ancient days of superstition and magic".*

We may speak of a common human consciousness, but cannot do so whilst at the same time completely setting to one side the difference between the regenerate and unregenerate mind. The unregenerate mind of the sinner ...

> "...receiveth not the things of the Spirit of God: for they are foolishness unto him: neither can he know them, because they are spiritually discerned."
>
> (1 Corinthians 2:14)

Whilst the unbeliever has a consciousness within him able to receive what God has to say to him and is thus always accessible to God, because he sits in darkness and is blinded by the god of this world, until God shines in that heart, he will see nothing coming to him from God. The Word of God without such illumination remains a closed book. The problem is not one of language to be cured by ever new and modern translations more readily accessible to the men of our day, but it is a matter of spiritual darkness. The sinner sees nothing because he is spiritually blind and does not even realise it. He thinks he is rich, he thinks he can see, but in truth is *"wretched, and miserable, and poor, and blind, and naked"* (Revelation 3:17). The blind beggar does not see the rags in which he is clad. To those who have enlightened eyes to see it, the sinner's awful condition is very apparent, but the man still sitting in his sin sees nothing of it. *"Professing themselves to be wise, they became fools"* (Romans 1:22). Furthermore, God holds the blinded sinner entirely responsible for continuing to remain in this sad condition.

The Bible teaches that we are made in the image of God and that to know the truth about anything means to be dependent upon Him and what He knows and reveals to us. Unbelievers maintain man can discover what there is to be known on their own. The Bible teaches that the mind of man at the fall became fatally twisted, depraved and now stands in need of regeneration. Unbelievers say that there is nothing wrong and the human mind is perfectly normal. The truth is that the fall affected every human faculty. What Adam knew, even before the fall, was derivative and limited. He did not, nor could he know everything. The unbelieving mind imagines it can access everything independently of God, and what *it* cannot know no one else can. The unbeliever has no option but to seek for meaning, not outside the physical world within the eternal counsel of God, but within creation itself. He thinks that if he examines what is about him for long enough, he will come up with all the answers he needs. That godless men discover anything is due to the grace and mercy of the very Person whom they despise and deny, who is good to all men to the end that they should repent. Nevertheless, those without God in the world can have no *true* understanding of anything, whether of salvation or science. Truth will always be mixed with error in everything. Those born again of the Spirit of God operate on a different level even than Adam before the fall. Regeneration is more than a restoration of paradise; we are taken beyond it for *"we have the mind of Christ"*. The remnants of sin currently still with us prevent us from realising the full potential of what is ours in Christ. We have been restored to a position where we recognise where lies the source of true understanding and knowledge and can now live and act accordingly.

> "For who hath known the mind of the Lord, that he may instruct him? But we have the mind of Christ."
> (1 Corinthians 2:16)

Those reconciled and regenerated are committed to the task of taking up into their consciousness that which God has revealed to us of His thoughts. Such who do not share this life, who are not part of this regenerate race, cannot enter into this, such things *"are spiritually discerned."* Without being born again of the Spirit of God, there is no way by which we can receive a revelation of God's thoughts into our consciousness. Left to himself, even without sin, no one could discern what is in the heart of God, not even towards himself.

> "Eye hath not seen, nor ear heard, neither hath entered into the heart of man, the things which God hath prepared for them that love him." (1 Corinthians 2:9)

This was ever so, even from the beginning, even *before* the fall.

> "For since the beginning of the world men have not heard, nor perceived by the ear, neither hath the eye seen, O God, beside thee, what he hath prepared for him that waiteth for him." (Isaiah 64:4)

This is not simply a matter of being a sinner, it is also a matter of being a finite being dependent upon God to reveal what is on His heart, to replicate within his heart and mind that which abides first with Him. This can only occur when God reveals this and what is revealed is opened to our inward being by the Spirit of God. Without a work of God's Spirit, though we have an inordinate amount of human intellectual ability, we shall remain ignorant of *"the things which God hath prepared for them that love him"*. We are speaking here of that which is eternally with God, His purposes in the Gospel, His eternal irrevocable plan, His knowledge of all things — these are the things God hath prepared.

> "But we speak the wisdom of God in a mystery, even the hidden wisdom, which God ordained before the world unto our glory? (1 Corinthians 2:7)

Only the Spirit of God knows what is in God's heart, only the Spirit of God can reveal these things.

> "But God hath revealed them unto us by his Spirit: for the Spirit searcheth all things, yea, the deep things of God."
> (v.10)

It is the spirit of man that knows what he knows of those things that relate to himself, even as the Spirit of God knows the things of God and is the bridge between us and God.

> "For what man knoweth the things of a man, save the spirit of man which is in him? even so the things of God knoweth no man, but the Spirit of God. Now we have received not the spirit of the world, but the spirit which is of God; that we might know the things that are freely given to us of God." (vv. 11-12)

We see a very sharp divide between the world, *"which by wisdom knew not God"* (1:21) and the spirit which is of God. The wisdom of the world is a contrary wisdom that regards the wisdom of God as foolishness. Talk of the resurrection of the dead, of the second coming of Christ, of heaven and hell? It is all impossible nonsense! Relying only on his natural capacities and without the spiritual enlightenment of God's Spirit, man cannot receive the things of the Spirit of God, *"for they are foolishness unto him: neither can he know them, because they are spiritually discerned."* Those without the Spirit of God, unbelievers, men of the world, they cannot receive *"the things of the Spirit of God...the things which God hath prepared for them that love him"*. Paul's testimony was of the things *"freely given us of God ... Which things also we speak"*. Those things given to the apostles did not come clothed in words originating from within man, it was not even a partnership between God and man, they came *"..not in the words which man's wisdom teacheth, but which the Holy Ghost teacheth; comparing spiritual things with spiritual"* (v.13), imparting the spiritual things of God to spiritual men. Knowledge of what is in the mind of God can be imparted only by the Spirit of God *in words God Himself chooses.*

---

**What God revealed to the apostles came, not as some unclothed content, some vague 'meaning', but in words themselves chosen and given by God. When we read our Bible, we read words given by God.**

---

We have a Bible inspired word for word, word for word given of God, otherwise we cannot know the mind of God! Inasmuch as we are indwelt by the Holy Spirit, we may know and experience His enlightenment as we read that which God has revealed, so that we can in that measure think and know as He does. Unbelievers resent deeply any suggestion that there are things believers can know that they cannot.

# CHAPTER 6

# Faith, Language, and Consciousness

*"Now faith is the substance of things hoped for, the evidence of things not seen"* (Hebrews 11:1)

By God's grace a shared human consciousness, even in a fallen world, enables us to communicate and understand each other. Without this common consciousness, communication between men would be impossible and life on earth would come quickly to a standstill. Through memory and language, thoughts can be made to overcome even those obstacles imposed upon them by time and space. Human consciousness spans the generations, enabling us to benefit from the knowledge of previous generations but also to pass on the knowledge that we have acquired to those succeeding us.

## All men live by faith in something

Faith is often set against reason as though each belong to a different world. Faith is said to deal with things spiritual, reason with human knowledge. A common assumption is that we use reason for those things we can prove, and faith for the things we cannot. This is not so. There is a real sense in which faith of some kind is a part of everyday life for everyone. Faith is a function of the soul by which it obtains certainty of any kind. Faith cleaves, holds fast, leans on, and trusts implicitly. Faith is the starting point for all knowledge.

> *Faith is an act by which our consciousness is compelled to hold something as being true so that we can then think and live in the light of it.*

Faith ends all uncertainty. The Bible says, faith is itself our link to the reality on which we build; it is itself the evidence we need in order to move forward. We do not arrive at faith *after* examining the evidence; everyone *starts* with faith. Through faith the soul obtains certainty, *directly and without demonstration. All men live by faith in something.* Life would otherwise be impossible. Faith will rest on the truth or it will rest on a lie. We are all committed to one or to the other.

In order to learn, we must first see ourselves as something distinct from that which we want to learn about. To do this we must *believe in ourselves* in the sense of acknowledging our own self-conscious existence, man as made in the image of God. Those who deny self-consciousness are really telling us that we have not the wherewithal to *know* anything. It is only faith that can give us certainty of the existence of the living human soul and of God who created it. Such faith comes to us through the Word of God. Belief in the God of the Bible and belief in ourselves are not unfounded assumptions. They accord perfectly with the way things really are, and therefore with what God has *revealed to us in Scripture*. This is where we begin not where we end. Faith is no leap into a great unknown to discover what is on the other side. We believe at the outset in these realities because through faith we know, we know because we believe! By faith we have a firm conviction of those things we hold to be true, but this does not come about by 'proofs', observation, or demonstration, – anymore than it does in anything, even for those who oppose the truth, despite what they tell us.

Faith of some kind precedes every thought, every conclusion. No conclusion of any kind can be arrived at without investigation and reasoning that has *already begun with faith*. Faith is not the *outcome* of investigation and demonstration, but the prerequisite for them. We do not believe because we first prove, we demonstrate the truth based on *what we already believe*. All men function in this way, they seek to prove what they already assume or believe to be true. We do not first *prove* the reliability and authenticity of the Bible we use and *then* believe in it. We believe and demonstrate the authenticity and truth of that of which we are already totally convinced. The only other position from which we can begin is one of doubt in God's Word. Building on doubt can never lead to a structure of faith. We *know* God, we *trust* His Word, we *believe* in ourselves as God made us. Faith is no unfounded assumption in need of demonstration, but is the instrument of its own certainty. We need the certainty of faith in the personal self-conscious God of Scripture before we begin, but also of the reality of our own self-conscious human souls. Communication is from consciousness to consciousness.

In the end, all the certainties of life come to us by faith, they are based on trust all along the line. What chaos would ensue were we all obliged to accept our parentage only after it had been proved to us, lingering doubts would still remain! DNA clinics would surely be onto a good thing. Even those things 'proved' to us we accept by faith in the methodology used to demonstrate the assumption. Some kind of faith is the starting point for all aspects of knowledge. All perception takes place through the senses, either directly or assisted by some kind of technical apparatus such as a telescope or microscope. Where our senses are weakened we will use spectacles to assist our sight, or use some device to aid impaired hearing. We believe that these instruments are reliable and are not conveying to us a distorted view of reality. We rely on this being so, and do not question it until some contradiction forces us to do otherwise. In a similar way, we need to have complete faith in the Bible as God's infallible Word at the outset. It is vital that we are convinced that the book we hold in our hands is a completely reliable instrument of divine communication and is not open to question.

Impressions gained by our physical senses travel through the nervous system to the brain and from there to our consciousness. Knowledge of the things around us does not rest entirely upon the action of our senses. Knowledge does not stop with our senses, but we must also ask ourselves how our consciousness is certain of the reality of that which we perceive. The result of these sensations and impressions consists of forms, images, and shapes. Things have an existence in the mind *apart* from our perceptions, in dreams and in our imagination. Perception can be of value only when we know that what our senses have given us are from real objects and that changes are due to real changes. We believe in our senses, we trust them. It is then, by a *faith* or trust in our senses that we are able to distinguish between dream, fantasy, and reality. When someone comes into the room, we ought not feel the need to punch them on the nose to elicit some response in order to verify this beyond the initial impressions of our senses alone. The whole of our life is founded on this kind of assurance. Whether we are watching our children playing in the back garden with spectacles perched on our nose or whether examining something under a microscope, effectively both are the same. The one observation is not 'ordinary everyday life' because we use spectacles and the other 'science' because we use a microscope! We begin with a faith in the reliability and accuracy of our own senses. Real science only begins once observation is finished. We can be deceived or mistaken, taking as real that which is only an appearance. Conjurors entertain us with such deceptions. Deception does not rob us of faith, it just makes us more careful next time! Our convictions with respect to the real world are based on something we can only really describe as a kind of faith. Can we really believe our eyes? We try to check and double check, but even then we are dependent in the physical world on one or more of our physical senses and we can only check one against the other. We all behave like this every day of our lives.

All this is equally true in the world of reasoning and thought. Unless we have some conviction already, an axiom, or fixed truth accepted before everything else, we shall be going nowhere and be unable to begin thinking about anything. The question is from where we obtain these. Do we base them on the revealed Word of God or do we look for them elsewhere? All arguments begin without a consideration of proof or demonstration. The certainty is with faith. This is perfectly in tune with what Scripture tells us.

> "Through faith we understand that the worlds were framed by the word of God, so that things which are seen were not made of things which do appear."
> (Hebrews 11:3)

*Not observation but revelation* is important in all these things. No one was there to witness the world come into being save God alone. Those who disallow faith in God must place their 'faith' somewhere else would they know how the world began.

Someone introduces himself, we believe him. A judge in court must rely on testimony and so perjury is a serious offence. My father and mother reveal to me who I am, I trust what they tell me. It is quite wrong to suppose that science establishes facts, and faith is only called for when there is uncertainty. Faith is the last link between the object of our knowledge and our knowing consciousness. It is by faith that we are certain of anything. This is true in matters of salvation even as it is with respect to everything else concerning our lives. At rock bottom, in the difference between believers and unbelievers we are, almost by definition, dealing *with two different faiths.*

> **Unbelievers who imagine that their knowledge and understanding of what they observe rests exclusively on their physical senses are deceiving themselves.**

Their understanding is directed by previously accepted axioms that determine what can and cannot be true, all of which are a matter of 'faith' and not of proof. They take a gigantic leap without being able to justify it.

According to the Scriptures, faith in Christ is a gift of God. It is not something we produce ourselves. Although God does not believe on our behalf, at the same time, the desire and the strength to lay hold of Christ for our salvation is worked in us by the Holy Spirit.

> "For by grace are ye saved through faith; and that not of yourselves: it is the gift of God: not of works, lest any man should boast. For we are his workmanship, created in Christ Jesus unto good works, which God hath before ordained that we should walk in them." (Ephesians 2:8-10)

The conviction that we should trust in Christ comes to us through hearing the Word of God. Without the Scriptures, without those to preach God's pure Word, men will not find Christ. *"So then faith cometh by hearing, and hearing by the word of God"* (Romans 10:17). Without the faith that God gives we will not believe.

The believer works from axioms, fixed principles, *truth* drawn directly from the Word of God. The very first verse of the Bible is such an axiom: *"In the beginning God created the heaven and the earth"* (Genesis 1:1) — our understanding of what we observe of the universe will be built on this. *"Man became a living soul"* (2:7) is another such axiom and it will direct our understanding of the human psyche as will *"for all have sinned, and come short of the glory of God"* (Romans 3:23). The unbeliever will have his own such 'truths' upon which he will build his own understanding of things and interpret what he observes through his physical senses. The certainty of these axioms is provided in all cases by faith. The axioms, if they are false, will lead to a false understanding. Understanding begins when observation is ended, when we make sense of what we see as we begin to interpret it according to our faith — whatever that faith is. *All men begin not with proof but with faith.* In every area of life faith remains the final link by which what is revealed to us interpreted to us by Scripture is taken up as truth by our consciousness.

Many truths, or axioms, are to a limited extent intuitive within the constitution of sinful men. All men know some of these things by virtue of being made in God's image. According to the first two chapters of Romans, we know ourselves to be God's creatures and sinners by nature. Such knowledge man can never completely eradicate, try as he will. Even in his fallen condition, Adam was still able to recognise the voice of the Lord God walking in the garden. The opportunity for Gospel preaching is that sinful men will still recognise the authoritative voice of God in Scripture for what it is. Our souls, were it not for sin, would appropriate the truth of Scripture without question, but because of sin a 're-programming' is necessary, something undertaken by the Holy Spirit in regeneration.

We must not imagine that the unbeliever knows nothing of God. It is not even enough to say that the godless man knows only that God *exists* but knows nothing about what kind of a God He is. According to the apostle Paul, they see His *"eternal power and Godhead"* (Romans 1:20). They know themselves to be sinners and accountable to Him *"their conscience also bearing witness"* (2:15). We need to remember this whole matter of us being made in God's image, of being in some ways like God ourselves, means that our own consciousness will impress upon us a constant and inescapable confrontation with God. The point is that because of sin sinners refuse it, suppress it, do *"not like to retain God in their knowledge"* (1:28). They will do whatever they can to be rid of what is blatantly obvious to them. Massive intellectual exertion is used in an attempt to replace creation, to dispense with all knowledge of God – all to evade the wages of sin. No God, no sin, no hell — to this end they construct a world of their own devoid of God. Of course, God does not just disappear on their say so! The godless man lives in a confusion of truth and error: truth from which he is trying desperately to escape; and error, which he hopes to slip into place as truth. Men, in a restricted sense, know God.

All this only serves to underline the truth that we can know nothing of God unless He reveals Himself to us, unless He touches us at the very heart of our being. *"In thy light shall we see light"* (Psalm 36:9). Freely and independently He reveals Himself to us in a way suited the constitution He gave us. We are able to receive God's revelation of Himself to us because we are made in His image, otherwise it would be impossible for us to know Him. To try to construe God from the subject by projecting ourselves ethically, or from the object naturalistically, will fall short of giving us any genuine conception of God. God reveals Himself to us, only thus can

He be known, and faith is the only means of appropriating what He has so revealed.

> "All things are delivered unto me of my Father: and no man knoweth the Son, but the Father; neither knoweth any man the Father, save the Son, and he to whomsoever the Son will reveal him." (Matthew 11:27)

We know ourselves, we know God, by faith and through His written Word.

There cannot be two different and equally valid ways of thinking. One way will be according to the truth, the other according to the lie. The activities and aims of these two will run in opposite directions because their starting points cancel each other out. These two builders are not at work on the same house, but each is building his own. Those who build on creation create a different structure than the one who builds on evolution. He who builds on the perfectibility of human nature erects a different structure than he who knows man to be a fallen creature in need of the new birth. For the one to acknowledge the validity of the other, he would be first obliged to forsake his own standpoint and accept that of the other. Each contradicts what the other asserts as being true. No polemics between these two serves any purpose without one or the other first giving up his own starting point. No agreement is otherwise possible. The unbeliever's knowledge is science "falsely so called". It may be said of them when confronted by the truth that which was said of the Jews of His day by the Lord Jesus in response to His parables.

> "And in them is fulfilled the prophecy of Esaias, which saith, By hearing ye shall hear, and shall not understand; and seeing ye shall see, and shall not perceive."
> (Matthew 13:14)

## The effects of sin on the human mind

The Bible teaches creation, it also teaches that man fell into sin. Being created in the image of God's holiness and righteousness, Adam would have known instinctively how he ought to live. Following his own nature would have led him in the ways of righteousness. In addition to this, God communicated verbally with him, giving specific commandments and instructions. An example of this is found in the commandment not to eat of the tree of the knowledge of good and evil, a test to see whether he would indeed live according to the will of God.

We usually accept that our senses provide us with an accurate picture of reality. Had human development proceeded without the interruption of sin, our thought life would have been perfect, but now as a result of sin a disturbance has been introduced between ourselves and that which we perceive with our senses. Sin cannot be restricted to the spheres of ethics and morality; its effect is felt throughout the totality of our being.

> "This I say therefore, and testify in the Lord, that ye henceforth walk not as other Gentiles walk, in the vanity of their mind, having the understanding darkened, being alienated from the life of God through the ignorance that is in them, because of the blindness of their heart."
>
> (Ephesians 4:17-18)

In these verses, Paul speaks of the vanity of the mind, a darkened understanding, of ignorance, of alienation from the life of God and blindness of the heart. The natural man in a state of sin cannot see within his consciousness that which comes from God. Sin has radically affected the human mind so that it no longer works as it did at creation.

Sinning in essence was an attempt to do without God, to strike out on an independent course. Man would determine his own righteousness, his own truth, his own goodness, away from and beyond God. Looking within him or to some aspect of the created universe, he would seek understanding without reference to the God of Scripture. He would seek to know as God knows; nothing was now beyond his comprehension. To attain this kind of knowledge, to reach beyond the limitations his finitude imposed upon him would make any knowledge of God or reference to Him unnecessary. This does not mean that he always denied the existence of God, or all sense of God's transcendence. He would, however, always imply that God was less than self-sufficient and self-contained and that knowledge, truth, righteousness, goodness, all have an existence of their own apart from God. Ultimately man cannot cut himself off from God because, even in his sin, man remains dependent upon that which he denies so fervently.

Even as we begin to reflect upon ourselves, we ought to acknowledge that in reality we hardly know ourselves, still less those around us. Indeed, without the Word of God we would not begin to understand the sinfulness of our own hearts and minds. God alone knows the true motivation of our hearts; He knows about everything we undertake in life.

> "O LORD, thou hast searched me, and known *me*. Thou knowest my downsitting and mine uprising, thou understandest my thought afar off. Thou compassest my path and my lying down, and art acquainted *with* all my ways. For *there is* not a word in my tongue, *but*, lo, O LORD, thou knowest it altogether. Thou hast beset me behind and before, and laid thine hand upon me."
> (Psalm 139:1-5)

A false assessment of ourselves will affect our thought processes.

Sin has reached to every part of man. This means that there is a very definite effect of sin on the workings of the mind. It now has a tendency both to devising and accepting that which is *false*. It is necessary to check and double check that the information we are receiving is true. Even *unintentional mistakes* must be attributed to the inward effects of sin. We will err in our observation and perception because our senses have been weakened by sin. The memory and thought processes are imperfect too. We are subject to *self-delusion* and *self-deception,* and sometimes we may convince ourselves that error is truth. Our self-consciousness may not be able to always distinguish what has come from outside and what is the product of *our own imagination,* and may well produce images that then dominate our thoughts. We may have acquired from infancy things that have been generated by *the imagination of someone else*, through our schooling, in everyday speech, sayings and widely accepted axioms. We may have thus become ensnared and misled by numerous deceptions.

Clearly, our own *physical condition* will be far from perfect, this too will affect our mental disposition. We may be prone to rashness, suffer from depression generated by indisposition, or physical weakness may cloud our thoughts and prevent us from thinking properly. Our thinking can also be directed by *disorganised human relationships* due to sin, upbringing, social circumstances, and poverty. Given their early life, the non-existence of a proper family life, the constant presence of extreme examples of sinfulness, some children have a very poor start to life and it is little wonder that many enter adult life already soaked in sin. This will all affect the way people think. No one lives completely to himself, *that which is in the heart and soul of others,* falsehoods and inaccuracies will be mixed in with our own to form what is the complexity of our own outlook on the world.

Nevertheless, a *darkening of the understanding* will not eradicate logical thinking completely. It will, however, weaken the power of thought and send it off in the wrong direction. It will produce conclusions that appear to be logical only to those who live in darkness. To think straight, to think with the maximum effectiveness possible in this dispensation, we need the enlightening of the Spirit of God which comes by regeneration. Before the fall Adam had a certain affinity and harmony with his environment that is now lost to us. Harmony within us and between each other, and above all with God, has been disrupted by sin. Our thought life is thus marked by discord.

We may *in good faith make a mistake*; we may say something that is inaccurate. An unconscious mistake will ultimately have sin as its cause, in a lie there is a deliberate attempt to mislead. Satan's *lie* is a hidden impelling power at work within the world that makes the whole of his domain false. It is an unholy principle, a distorted perspective, and travesty of the truth. This *lie* is no mistake. This *lie* injuriously affects the functioning of the consciousness of man. It propagates fantasy as reality, fiction as history, fairytales as science. It *intentionally* brings into our minds representations of existing things that are contrary to the way they really are. Satan's aim is to replace the truth with his *lie*. As long as there was no sin, there could be no necessity to defend the truth. Satan first lied; he is the father of it. This marks the beginning of the conflict *for* the truth. Satan began by making God out to be the liar and himself the speaker of the truth, itself a lie.

We do not all fall into complete insanity because we are sinners, although it does cause us to accept a false premise, to reason illogically, and to draw false conclusions. The original harmony that existed between man and God's world is disturbed although obviously not entirely broken off. There is a lack of harmony, of real love, between fellow human beings. There is also a disharmony within ourselves, we are not now naturally at peace within ourselves, and everything seems disconnected and unrelated. If we have no true knowledge of ourselves, if there is a disturbance of sin within our self-consciousness, the same will be true of our consciousness of God. This too will be perverted and disjointed. When the bond within us that draws us towards a knowledge and love of God is weakened by sin, then the basis for all true knowledge is in a very poor state indeed. Such a knowledge of God may be all but unrecognisable or perverted into all kinds of false religion, feelings and emotions, and even turn into a real hatred of God

## Consciousness and language

Our consciousness operates in a twofold manner: first, through images; second, through concepts. At the same time, no mental image or concept can be communicated to others, or retained in a permanent form, without some physical means of doing this. An image can be captured in a picture or photograph, a concept in spoken or written language. Without language, the human race would disintegrate because of an inability to communicate. A common language externalises our shared consciousness, our shared way of thinking. A common language binds people together in a way nothing else can, which is why the confusion of tongues at Babel so effectively dispersed the people. Language and imagery provide necessary outward and physical expressions of what is going on within us. *"Out of the abundance of the heart the mouth speaketh"*(Matthew 12:34).

We not only use language in communicating with others, it enables us also to communicate with ourselves. We cannot know ourselves without language. Thinking is, as Martin

Luther expressed it, speaking within ourselves. Language turns the contents of our own consciousness, of our own thought life, into our own property. Indeed, without language the mind could not function fully, *it could not communicate with itself, we could not think and develop thoughts*. It is difficult to see how it is possible without language for my consciousness to know itself or to recognise any difference between itself and the external world.

A good command of words and syntax enhances our ability to think. In order to know about anything, we take up a position of subject over against the object about which we intend to reflect and draw conclusions. Grammar reflects the various thought-patterns of this subject-object relationship; if we think and know at all, we will do so grammatically. The decline of the teaching of grammar in schools reflects once more the godless view of human consciousness ruling modern education and explains why so many leave school incapable of much intelligent thought, still less of expressing themselves in any coherent manner.

> *Language is the vehicle of human consciousness.*

Thought takes place in an ordered and verbal way and we communicate our thoughts to others in words arranged in an appropriate order. It is by means of language that that which is not physical, but exists in our consciousness, bursts forth into the physical world by means of sounds we produce physically. This is then received physically, we hear the words of others, and this is transmitted to our non-physical consciousness. God spoke to Adam in words. God speaks to us today in words. He uses language, itself a part of creation. It is vitally important to bear in mind that language is in the first instance the *spoken* word. This is clear when we read in the Bible of how God communicated with the prophets and apostles.

> "My servant Moses is not so, who is faithful in all mine house. With him will I speak mouth to mouth, even apparently, and not in dark speeches; and the similitude of the Lord shall he behold." (Numbers 12:7-8)

God reveals Himself to men in various ways but His communication with men is *verbal*. In most languages, the *written* word is a codified record of the sounds of words that are spoken. This is of significance and cannot be sufficiently stressed, if we are to understand anything about the Scriptures and how they come down to us in an accurate form in our own language.

The word (Greek *lógos)* has primarily to do with speaking; it is a word uttered that embodies a concept or idea. Our minds inevitably turn to John's Gospel, *"the Word was God"* (1:1), *"the Word was made flesh"* (1:14). Jesus did not become less God for taking on human flesh, nor was He less than human for being God. In the same way, the thought of God does not become something less than it is for being clothed in human language. The *logeîon* in ancient Greece was what we would call the speaker's platform. The *theologeîon* is the place on the platform from where those men spoke who represented the gods as speaking. The word 'theology' is not a combination of *theós* + *lógos*. *Lógos* has the idea of speaking rather than of thought. It could also indicate the action of a *theológos*, one who speaks about or from God as well as thinking about Him. Only later on did the idea of utterance slip into the background causing that of thought, knowledge, to come to the fore.

Only through language can communication of thought take place between persons. What we know of each other's thoughts must be mediated through the physical world; we cannot transfer thoughts mind to mind without language and a physical expression of it. Concepts are tied to language and thereby to the faculties of speech and hearing. Images are also physical, related to the faculty of sight. The combination of visual images and language as speech, which we call writing, constitutes the most complete means of communication possible between one person and another. This is why Jesus could say,

> "For this people's heart is waxed gross, and their ears are dull of hearing, and their eyes they have closed; lest at any time they should see with their eyes, and hear with their ears, and should understand with their heart, and should be converted, and I should heal them." (Matthew 13:15)

Nothing at all had got through to the hearts of these people, nothing of what He had been saying had penetrated their consciousness, either visually through their eyes of what they had witnessed of Him or through their ears of what they had heard Him utter. Whether in the form of images of Him impressed upon their minds or of concepts communicated by words, they were both blind and deaf to both. Something needed to happen to them if this were to change. To His disciples Jesus said, *"But blessed are your eyes, for they see: and your ears, for they hear"* (Matthew 13:16). Because sin has worked its way into every corner of our human frame, thought and language have been affected by it. The new birth works its way through the various parts of our constitution, including our thought processes, but it does not affect our physical attributes substantially or constitutionally, for this we await a new and glorious body like that of our risen and ascended Saviour.

Communication of thought can be effectively transmitted in this way from the consciousness of one person to that of another. When we add to this the perfect working of God, we see that using means He has Himself created for the purpose, the transmission of His thoughts to us by the use of language would be perfect, infallible, and faultless. Even as the aim of communication is to replicate in the consciousness of another what has arisen in our own, in the case of God, using His inspired Word, He is able to faultlessly reproduce in our minds that which was first in His own.

Language on its own would be able to accomplish its task only to a limited degree, for a brief period and to few people, were there no means of perpetuating and preserving it. We cannot store anything in our minds without the means to do so. Using memory and language in a written form, knowledge is made to span the ages and spread from person to person. Writing through the art of printing is preserved in a wider and more permanent form. Both writing and printing find their primary and highest end in making God's Word accessible to individuals of every nation on the earth. So it was that God in His gracious providence watched over the introduction of writing and, much later, printing from moveable types. That the divine commission should be fulfilled, that the apostolic testimony to the Gospel of Christ should reach *"the uttermost part of the earth"* (Acts 1:8), it was necessary first that God's Word should be committed to writing and then in due time printed.

The Word of God conceived in the heart and consciousness of God creates a body for itself in human language, even as the living Word, the Son of God, took upon Himself a body of human flesh.

> *The thoughts of God and the words that serve as its body together constitute the Word of God, even as the physical body of Christ is veritably Christ Himself.*

This is important because many these days try to drive a wedge between meaning and the words that carry it, suggesting that whilst the meaning may be inspired of God the words are not. Such a suggestion makes no sense whatever. The meaning cannot be divorced from the words that carry it. Change the words, change the grammar, change the meaning.

The 'word' in Scripture does not refer only to the letters by which we recognise it; these are but a 'body' carrying the word. Letters are a written code for the sounds uttered, which in turn express the concept. None of these distinct elements can be pulled apart from the other and still retain its significance. Without a concept, the sounds of words degenerate into an empty babble. The 'word' *manifests* itself in sounds and letters. Even as the Lord Jesus is the Word, God manifest in the flesh, so the eternal counsel of God, His Word, is manifest as words on a page in Scripture. Letters on their own do not make a word, the combination of letters we call a word must have an agreed substance or signification. Thoughts need words as words need letters for there to be written language. Those reading what is written decode it, return it to spoken words, silently or audibly, this in turn produces thoughts in our consciousness. We must not confuse these different elements; each requires the other. If we see only that which is written down, the letters, or hear only the sounds of language, we still have not reached the word, the object of which these things are the vehicle. It is perfectly possible to reproduce the sounds of an unknown language without having grasped anything else, but they will be meaningless to us. This is precisely the point being made by the apostle Paul with reference to speaking in an unknown tongue in 1 Corinthians 14. Those who perceive man only as a physical being see only the shell and miss the essential nature of our humanity. Yet without a body to see we can know nothing of anyone, they are dead to us and we to them. If Scripture is reduced simply to dead letters on a page, it can have no meaning for us. The Word of God incorporates *all* of these distinct elements from the consciousness of God to the printed page. Its purpose cannot said to be complete until it is received into our minds and hearts, where it is to dwell *"richly in all wisdom"* (Colossians 3:16).

Taking this route, our thoughts, which are expressed in words, take on a physical form as sounds or as combinations of letters in the place of those sounds. It is only when words pass through the physical and material world that we are able to receive the thoughts of others. The analogy in the Lord Jesus taking upon Himself human physical flesh is again inescapable. Those who see Jesus only in terms of His physical human manifestation, *and not as God* manifest in the flesh, simply do not know Him; they have not comprehended Him (John 1:5). To ensure that God's thoughts are perfectly replicated in human minds, it is essential that that which was communicated to the writers of Scripture by God in words and arrangements of words, should take on the physical form of words as letters, the jot and tittle, and that these are then all perfectly reproduced and preserved on paper. This God accomplished by an extraordinary work of His Holy Spirit within those who wrote. This is what we understand essentially by the verbal inspiration of the Bible.

The Lord Jesus is the Word of God because in Him is expressed God's essential being in a physical sign.

> "And the Word was made flesh, and dwelt among us, (and we beheld his glory, the glory as of the only begotten of the Father,) full of grace and truth." (John 1:14)
> "God, who at sundry times and in divers manners spake in time past unto the fathers by the prophets, hath in these last days spoken unto us by his Son, whom he hath

appointed heir of all things, by whom also he made the worlds; Who being the brightness of his glory, and the express image of his person, and upholding all things by the word of his power, when he had by himself purged our sins, sat down on the right hand of the Majesty on high." (Hebrews 1:1-3)

Even as the Lord Jesus as the Word of God cannot be separated from the essential being of God Himself, neither can the word given to created things be pulled apart from the essential nature of the things named.

To create, God spoke, *"And God said, Let there be light: and there was light"* (Genesis 1:3). That which was not became that which was. That which existed previously only within the mind and consciousness of God now found a distinct *physical* expression and form. According to the above verses in Hebrews, all things continue to exist by the *"word of his power"*. The meaning of any word is inseparably linked to a belief in the biblical doctrine of the creation by God of all things out of nothing and thus to His eternal plan for the world.

*Once we forsake biblical creation, we lose all basis for the meaning of individual words, for their function in connected speech and their relationships in the sentence, which we call syntax.*

A name is more than a label attached for purposes of recognition, it classifies, it becomes one with the essential character of that which is named. We ought not to try to separate the name from the essential nature of the object named. True science will continue today what Adam began, naming that which we uncover in God's world, whether they are objects or phenomena. In Eden Adam exercised dominion over all that God had made, naming all the creatures that God brought before him.

> "And out of the ground the Lord formed every beast of the field, and every fowl of the air; and brought them unto Adam to see what he would call them: and whatsoever Adam called every living creature, that was the name thereof." (Genesis 2:19)

As the thinking subject Adam stood over and above that which he was naming, clearly a position he could only take towards creation and not towards God, who can be known only as He *reveals* Himself to us. On seeing the creature before him, Adam would have instantly recognised and understood what it was and named it accordingly. Since the fall, our intellectual and physical powers being much diminished, only after diligent and wearisome investigation and study is it possible for us to attain but a vague understanding of the world in which God has placed us.

We do not give God names. He reveals Himself to us and tells us how we are to address Him. God's names all reveal something to us of His nature. *'El* or *'Elohim* signifies that God is the first and of absolute power. Generally appearing in the plural it presumes the doctrine of the tri-unity of God. *Adonai* indicates that God is ruler. *'El-Shadai* points to God possessing all power in heaven and on earth. The name *Yahweh* gradually replaced the earlier names and is that of the covenant God. In the New Testament *Theos* takes the place of *'Elohim. Kurios,* Lord, refers to God and Christ and continues the idea of *Yahweh.*

Names in Scripture, both of places and people, have a meaning inseparable from that which is thereby signified. A change of name meant a change in the nature of the place, object, or person receiving the new name. Our mind turns immediately to Abraham and to the apostle Paul. There are examples of this throughout the whole of Scripture too numerous to mention here. Sometimes God did the naming, sometimes man.

> "And he called the name of that place Beth-el [house of God]: but the name of that city was called Luz at the first." (Genesis 28:19)
>
> "And God said unto him, Thy name is Jacob: thy name shall not be called any more Jacob, but Israel shall be thy name: and he called his name Israel." (Genesis 35:10)
>
> "And she said unto them, Call me not Naomi [pleasant], call me Mara [bitter]: for the Almighty hath dealt very bitterly with me." (Ruth 1:20)
>
> "And Jesus answered and said unto him, Blessed art thou, Simon Bar-jona ... And I say unto thee, That thou art Peter..." (Matthew 16:17-18)
>
> "To him that overcometh will I give to eat of the hidden manna, and will give him a white stone, and in the stone a new name written, which no man knoweth saving he that receiveth it." (Revelation 2:17)

*'Take the Name of Jesus with you'* is more than a sentimental song, we are expressing our faith in our Saviour, our love to Him in all that He is and has accomplished on our behalf — this is all encapsulated in the name that *God* has given Him. To Joseph the angel said,

> "Thou shalt call his name JESUS: for he shall save his people from their sins." (Matthew 1:21)

God is saying, this is who Jesus, my Son, is!

> "Wherefore God also hath highly exalted him and given him a name which is above every name: that at the name of Jesus every knee should bow, of things in heaven, and things in earth, and things under the earth; and that every tongue should confess that Jesus Christ is Lord, to the glory of God the Father." (Philippians 2:9-11)

His Name cannot be separated from all that He is and all that He has done.

## The deconstruction of language and the disappearance of meaning

In naming something we utter something about the essential nature of that thing, but we also classify, show the connection one thing has to another within the creative purpose of God. Reject this purpose and another source of meaning must be sought from within the created universe itself. "Language, like consciousness," says Marx, "only arises from the need, the necessity of intercourse with other men." This was no new idea, but it appeared earlier in the writings of Rousseau. Language is not then a gift of God to men, it is not an innate capability placed creatively within us to be developed. Instead, language is said to have been invented by necessity as men encountered other men. In Rousseau's mythical 'state of nature', where there was no property or marriage, but everyone came and went as they would, there was no need of language. Only as relationships between human beings and 'societies' began to develop were communication and language needed! As human concourse became more complex so too did language. As with consciousness, language was never a gift of God, but socially and environmentally originated, dependent, and determined. An isolated individual living in a void could have no self-consciousness nor could he speak or even think anything; he would be totally without meaning. Self-consciousness is said to be relative and socially determined, but so too is language.

The natural man believes the world to be constantly producing that of itself which is entirely new and therefore it cannot be subject to a sovereign God who exists apart from these same processes. God is Himself part of the ever-moving machine and subject to it. It necessarily follows that there must be things that God does not know, and so the God who is in a position to speak to us authoritatively and finally cannot exist. As there is nothing stable about what there is to be known, there is also nothing stable about language, nothing is fixed. There can be no final meaning to anything. As the relations between men, and within their environment change, so new 'meanings', 'ideas', 'values' are generated, which in turn give rise to language. We need to 'modernise', whether this be our bible, our worship, or our politics! Meaning and language are inherently unstable. Truth unchanged and unchanging is an illusion. Clearly, anyone giving the least credence to this view of language cannot at the same time believe the Bible to be the unchanging Word of God to man. In this context revelation and inspiration in a biblical sense are abolished and must be redefined.

The father of modern linguistics was the Swiss linguist, Ferdinand de Saussure. The book for which he is best known, *Course in General Linguistics,* was put together by his students and colleagues after his death in 1913. Although little-known outside academic circles, his influence in the field of linguistics can be likened to the work of his contemporaries, Emile Durkheim in sociology, Charles Darwin in biology, Karl Marx in economic and political thought, and Sigmund Freud in psychology. The effect of his work was just as devastating as these other men and just as godless. Saussure explicitly denies what the Bible affirms and then sets off in the opposite direction. He vandalises our understanding of language. Were his theories remotely akin to the truth, real communication between men would be impossible, and the possibility of God's Word reaching human hearts a pious dream – which is precisely the point! Having implicitly denied the existence of the non-physical human soul and its inherent self-consciousness, Saussure must, and does deny any place for pre-existing concepts or of anything having a non-material essential nature, being expressed physically through language. Immediately, all grounds of meaning disappear for in this scheme of things there can be no place for an all-embracing plan and purpose of God.

According to Saussure, language is to be thought of as a system of signs. A sign has two parts: the *signifier*, the form that signifies; and the *signified*, the idea signified. The Bible view of language is 'logocentric' (from *logos*, word). Before the advent of modern linguistics, this view was widely held by linguists. In a logocentric view of language, sounds are a representation of meanings present in the consciousness of the speaker. The 'signifier' is then the representation through which one has to go in order to reach the 'signified', that which is in the mind of the speaker. Phonemes, units of significant sound, and letters, are devices which, when used in combination, represent the *essence* of that which is thereby signified. The written word stands in the place of the sound sequence, which in turn represents the thought. Whilst recognising these various distinctions, if language is to function at all, there will be an unbreakable bond between them in the mind of the speaker of that language, they will not be separated out. Interpretation of what is written or spoken can be defined as a recovery of those concepts present within the consciousness of the original speaker or writer.

Saussure attempted to escape from this view of language. Meaning, he thought, is not something to be recovered, but something *we each create for ourselves* and interpretation does not recover the past but should *transform* the world today. Recovery of that which was in the mind of another is impossible. This means that God cannot speak to us today from a book with meanings locked into words written nigh on 2000 years or more ago. Verbal inspiration is an irrelevance. If God speaks to us at all, it is in a 'dynamic' way using the words on the page as clues or stimuli to produce a fresh and immediate meaning for us today in the world in which we now live. God's 'word' is that which comes to me at that moment when I am reading; it is not something once given, revealed, inspired, and preserved in a book which an unchanging, stable and permanent signification of eternal truth, such things do not exist. All a book such as the Bible can do is present us with physical marks from which we, or the Spirit of God, can produce thought and meaning. This is very far from what the Bible claims for itself, or teaches us about the nature of language.

We must recognise that because of the effects of sin upon our mind, our imperfect ability to express ourselves, or because of some external interference, the thoughts of others may not come to us in a precise and accurate way. However, when we take the Bible in our hands, we are not dealing with any ordinary human book. The God who revealed and inspired its contents, who preserves and watches over it, also interprets to our hearts the meaning within it by His Spirit that we may perfectly understand what He would have us know. Despite this, again because of the effects of sin, we may fail to grasp what it is that God wants to say to us in Scripture and this gives rise at times to misunderstanding and explains, even when agreed upon most things, why different points of view can exist among genuine believers.

For Saussure, the reality of signs is not located in the signified, an intangible and irrecoverable concept, but in the material marks, which can then be interpreted in an autonomous, even anarchistic way. It all rather smacks of an *Alice in Wonderland* world. Language has become something surreal and inherently unstable. No divine plan or purpose gives meaning to what Saussure saw as a complex and chaotic universe. Objects are to be defined by their relations one with another. *Meaning is to be found within the material world and the relations between the things in it, not in anything beyond it.* Things are what they are, not because God made them what they are, but because they are what everything else is not when placed alongside them. 'Red' is a colour relative to all other colours. Take all the other colours away and we are not left with red, but with no colour at all. Without all the other colours, there could be no such thing as red. Things are not defined by what they are in and of themselves, but by the differences existing between them. We learn what red is by looking at every other colour. All the other colours give red its meaning. Red is red because it is shown to be different from green, or blue, or any other colour. Red carries traces of all the other colours within it, because without them it cannot be defined. Presumably, red could turn yellow one day or some colour yet unknown to us! But of course, where meaning is intrinsic, a totally red world would still be red, and the word would still retain its meaning permanently. Such thinking is not confined to linguistics, but has permeated virtually every other academic discipline. The painter, Georges Braque, made this statement, "I do not believe in things; I believe in relationships". The philosopher, Alfred North Whitehead, provides a general summary:

> "The misconception which has haunted philosophic literature throughout the centuries is the notion of 'independent existence'. There is no such mode of existence; every entity is to be understood in terms of the way it is interwoven with the rest of the universe."

Following this same line, another philosopher, Ernst Cassirer, claimed that the world is no longer essentially a collection of independent entities, of autonomous objects, but a series of relational systems.

Meaning is derived from oppositions and differences rather than existing in positive terms. We ought not to think of the presence in our consciousness of a single idea, or signified, but of a whole network of differences. Every sign carries within it traces of all the others as entities that define it. Words similarly, written or spoken, are not linguistic units in themselves, but are purely arbitrary. Any one word is to be recognised by its differences with every other word in the dictionary. Language is a system of differences in which all its various components are defined solely by their relations one with another.

In Scripture we see that the name and the essence of that signified by it are inextricably linked. Saussure drives a wedge between thoughts or concepts, (the signified), and the physical expression (the signifier). His basic principle was that there can be no inevitable formal link between signified and signifier. There can be a natural connection between signifier and signified *only* if the sign, as the Bible teaches, has an essential meaning unaffected by time. We see that the eternal purposes of God bring to language a stability it could not otherwise possess. The sign would otherwise be, exactly as Saussure suggests, contingent and subject to the continual change of human relations. There would be no abiding word. The relevant relation within the material world necessary for meaning could obtain only at one particular time, it would then move on to something else. To divide meanings from the words that carry them is to break language apart and render it virtually useless and, if such a thing were possible, would destroy the unchanging integrity of God's Word. The only meaning for the modern linguist is the immediate one. That which gives meaning to language continually changes so that the link between a word and its meaning will also change – it is a contingent and arbitrary link only. The ability to look at an object from a God-like perspective from above, such as was given to Adam, is not possible as objects are defined by their ever-changing relations with each other. Language can have nothing to do with systematic naming of objects, as described in Genesis.

What we are given in the place of genuine and permanent meaning is the product of a complex network of ever changing socially determined linguistic dialectics. No meaning is ever quite the same twice. The social relativism used by Karl Marx to define consciousness we now see applied to linguistics by Saussure. The similarity is inescapable.

> "...in all cases, then, we discover not *ideas* given in advance but *values* emanating from the system. When we say that these values correspond to concepts, it is understood that these concepts are purely differential, not positively defined by their content but negatively defined. by their relations with other terms of the system. Their most precise characteristic is that they are what the others are not." (*Course in General Linguistics*)

Before moving on we need to recognise that 'values' is a word much loved and bandied-about today by the educational establishment and the chattering classes. Teaching children 'values' has nothing whatever to do with passing on to them virtuous moral or spiritual principles. This is doubtless what we are intended to think. We must not be deceived; the use of the word 'values' is given here a very specific meaning that is deliberately hidden from the uninitiated. Here is a specific example of the way in which language can be manipulated, where most readers see a surface meaning in the text, but others are reading a hidden subtext. 'Value' in the above extract replaces 'idea' and is the product of defining social oppositions. To state the matter simply, a 'value' or 'idea' is arrived at in the same way that we arrived at a definition of the colour red: by not being anything else when placed alongside all other colours. Translated into ethical terms this thinking has also produced the relativistic moral morass that characterises modern western lands.

Modern bible translations have been largely guided by the linguistics of Ferdinand de Saussure. This is ground enough in and of itself, apart from other considerations, to reject them out of hand. In Eugene A. Nida's book on bible translation *Toward a Science of Translating* published in 1963, the work of Saussure in the field of structural linguistics heads the list as having had an unequalled effect on the science of translating. Second in this same list as most significant in the application of these methods are the members of the Summer School of Linguistics, otherwise known as the Wycliffe Bible Translators. The modern linguistic theories of Saussure are a source of the 'dynamic equivalence' translating methodology behind the *New International Version*. Let us be very clear in our own minds that in using or sanctioning the use of translations guided by Nida's theories, whether the foreign translations of the *Wycliffe Bible Translators,* or those in English such as the *New International Version,* we are supping with Satan.

---

**Underlying these texts is the theorising of godless men, a modern view of language that destroys all possibility of God's Word reaching human hearts.**

---

If you can live with this, fine, remember, however, what you are reading is not the inspired Word of God, but something else.

# CHAPTER 7

# Revelation

*"The secret things belong unto the Lord our God: but those things which are revealed belong unto us and to our children for ever, that we may do all the words of this law."* (Deuteronomy 29:29)

The films of comedian Karl Vallentin are still enjoyed by television audiences in his native Germany, particularly in Bavaria, but also in neighbouring Austria. For one of his sketches, the stage is in almost total darkness. A solitary street lamp sheds its dim and forlorn light in a narrow circle on the floor. Vallentin paces round and round and round within the circle of light constantly looking at the ground with a long face and a worried look. A policeman approaches and asks him what he has lost. In a very matter-of-fact way, he tells the officer that he has lost his house key and so cannot get into his house. The policeman dutifully assists in what proves to be a fruitless search. "Did you really lose your key just here?" the policeman asks. "Oh, no," replies Vallentin, "I lost it over there" and points to a dark corner of the stage. "Why then," asks the exasperated policeman, "are we looking over here?" To which there comes the reply from Vallentin, "There's no light over there!" There is little point in looking for something where there is no light. Equally, it makes no sense to use the light we have in a search that will yield nothing and condemn us to walking round and round in circles. Looking in the wrong place will reveal nothing, however good the light. Yet, this is precisely the modern dilemma of godless men. What they need is shrouded in darkness, what they see yields them nothing. No true knowledge of God is possible until He first imparts life where death once reigned and sheds light where darkness prevailed. *"For with thee is the fountain of life: in thy light shall we see light"* (Psalm 36:9). Where there is no life there will be no light.

God has made all men able to receive knowledge of Himself. He is the original of which we are the image, a finite human reflection of what He is like. Were this not so, He could not touch us and we could not know Him. There is little point in God disclosing Himself to a creature who cannot receive revelation. Were man not able to receive God's revelation such a revelation would be evident only to God. A revelation that does not reveal anything to anyone is not a revelation. Objective divine revelation must be transposed into subjective conscious knowledge within us to be of use to us. That which began in the mind of God must find its way into our minds and there blossom to create in us a replica of God's thoughts. Such a process can only take place when carried through by the active involvement of God at every stage. Yet sadly, because of innate sin, the human soul with its potential for being flooded with light of God is, in its present natural state, overcome with darkness. We have said that there are two kinds of people, those who are born again of the Spirit of God and those who are not, those within the Kingdom of God and those outside it. Anyone who has experienced the new birth is united to Christ who is 'Head of the body', and the relation between his or her consciousness and the Holy Scripture is born from this. If we are not bound in this way to Christ as head of the new humanity, we cannot kneel before Him in worship, neither can the Bible be to us a *Holy* Bible.

All knowledge is one and not a collection of unrelated 'facts', because God is Creator of them all. The Bible is not an accumulation of unconnected utterances about God, who He is and what He does. The Bible gives us the 'big picture' and is concerned with the whole of life. We hold in our hands a very special book that is as it is by His divine and supernatural working and for this reason Scripture cannot be examined in the same way as any other ancient text. Yet, this is precisely what most 'scholars' attempt. They forget or deny that its origins and its preservation are in the hands of omnipotent God. Its written words are no less authoritative than the audible words spoken to the prophets or those that fell from the lips of the Lord Jesus. A genuine believer will not question the words of his Master. Those who argue that the veracity and trustworthiness of Scripture is dependent upon evidence subject to reason place themselves above Scripture as do those who seek to answer sceptics and doubters on the same basis. In doing this, the Bible loses its authority for us; our reason becomes the final court of appeal in its place. We thereby lose the ground upon which the whole of our faith rests. The acceptance of Scripture in the end rests upon one thing: the testimony of that faith worked in us by the Holy Spirit.

Even as the glitter of a precious diamond is proven only by itself, so the divine majesty of Scripture can only shine forth from the Word itself. To derive as we do the proofs of Scripture for its divine character from within itself is devoid of force with its opponents who have elevated fallible human reason in its place. What use is it if we show a diamond to those who refuse to look or are unable for some reason to appreciate its beauty? Miracles and the fulfilment of prophecy have no power of proof with anyone who has already ruled out such possibilities without a valid reason. The divine character of Scripture, the majestic style, the unity of its contents, the effectiveness to lead to salvation, the blood of martyrs, all these things make sense only to those *who already believe*. Those with a veil over their eyes will see nothing. Only genuine believers will see the beauty of Scripture, even as only they see the beauty of Christ.

## The darkness clouding the human mind

At creation, the human thought processes were unaffected by sin. We conclude from this that Adam by nature would have viewed all around him as it truly was. The conclusions he drew from what he observed and the interpretation he gave it would all have been accurate. His knowledge, although finite, was true. Adam would have been able to reason from nature and arrive at nature's God. Today, because of the distorting affect of sin upon the human mind, this is no longer possible — all that will be gained is a distorted view of God. Adam in paradise was 'normal'; we are not. Sin has brought darkness and ruin in its wake. Adam would not have thought of himself at the first as the ultimate judge of right and wrong, truth and error. What he knew, he knew in submission to God. *"The fear of the Lord is the beginning of knowledge: but fools despise wisdom and instruction."* (Proverbs 1:7).

Adam saw himself as a creature made in God's image and dependent upon God. He would not have begun with himself, independently of God. He did not set himself the impossible goal of trying to know all there is to know about everything and fall into irreversible despair because he could not do so. He recognised his human consciousness was not ultimate and determinative, but created and therefore derivative, designed to receive the Word of God. Men cannot take a route independent of God and still be right! Adam recognised at the first that he could not make up his mind all on his own, but all he studied and observed he related without question to what God had revealed to him directly.

In Eden, Adam received revelation from God in addition to that which was accessible to him in nature and within himself. Without such special revelation, he could have known nothing about the origin of creation itself or anything of God's purposes for all He had made. God spoke directly and audibly to Adam. God gave him, for example, immediate instructions with respect to the tree in the midst of the garden. Upon the entry of sin, however, a barrier arose to separate God and man. Such revelation now had to work *exclusively from without* to the inside rather than being something ever-present within and without. Sin had bolted the door of the human heart tightly shut, the light went out, and man was left sitting in a darkened room where previously there had been a clear manifestation of God.

How did God reveal Himself to man before the fall? His whole life within and without would have been flooded with a revelation of the glory of the Lord. The revelation of God within the soul was still unclouded. Things changed drastically when sin entered. When God called to Adam, *"Where art thou?"* (Genesis 3:9), it could not have been that the omniscient God did not know where Adam had hidden himself. There are many aspects to these fearful words, but at heart they recognise the estrangement and distance that now separated God and man. From now on God's revelation of Himself no longer appeared unclouded to Adam's spiritual vision. *From now on God would approach men from a point outside themselves.* Adam and Eve now perceived the presence of God approaching them from outside, *"they heard the voice of the Lord God walking in the garden in the cool of the day"* (Genesis 3:8). The speaking of God directly to the soul of man was now no longer possible because of sin. All that man would gain in knowledge of God came in a direction from the external to the internal.

There was also a change materially. The revelation in nature and within man himself now became *antipathetic,* God revealing Himself in anger. Special revelation, more particularly in Scripture, is essentially *sympathetic,* demonstrating God's pitying grace. When God appeared to Adam and Eve after their disobedience, *"Adam and his wife hid themselves from the presence of the Lord amongst the trees of the garden"* (Genesis 3:8). Sinners today still use creation to cover up their sin. After the fall, man's faith is redirected to something within himself or within creation and away from God in support of his rebellion against God. The sinner now needs to direct his faith to an external and physical revelation, God manifest in the flesh, faith in Christ.

Something else happened, God *ceased to speak and reveal His thoughts directly to each and every man.* Instead, He spoke only to selected individuals, so that they would then pass on to others what it was necessary for them to know. God spoke to the patriarchs, and then with Moses He spoke *"face to face, as a man speaketh unto his friend"* (Exodus 33:11). God revealed Himself to the prophets. *"God, who at sundry times and in divers manners spake in time past unto the fathers by the prophets."* (Hebrews 1:1) In Old Testament times, if anyone wanted to know something from God or they wanted God to do something for them, they turned to a prophet. Samuel fulfilled this role, as did Elijah and Elisha later on. The communication with God enjoyed by the prophets was a privilege of the few. This continued throughout the period from paradise to Patmos and until completion of Scripture. Scripture now being complete, there can no longer any need for any other direct word from God. Today, God speaking in Scripture has the same authority as God's direct word to Adam in Eden.

Those today, and they are many, who think they hear more than is now given in Scripture, either within themselves or without, suffer from spiritual delusions. Such a route is now closed to us. Once among the prophets himself, King Saul had been forsaken by the Lord and was faced with the terrifying prospect of confronting the Philistines in battle. Receiving no word from the Lord ". . . *neither by dreams, nor by Urim, nor by prophets*" (1 Samuel 28:6), he sought a word from God outside the given way by seeking out a woman with a familiar spirit at Endor, something strictly forbidden. At one time, he had himself put many of these same people to death. Those who find no word from God in Scripture will find nothing to their spiritual benefit by looking outside them. Those seeking an additional word from God outside the Scriptures step in the footsteps of King Saul and will reap the same reward. The link between extra-biblical 'revelations' and the occult is a very real one. To forsake the Bible as the sole authentic voice of God is to forsake Him who gave it. If the will of God is no longer clear to us in His Word, if a veil covers our minds, then He must surely have abandoned us.

Before Moses and beginning of the Scripture record, the godly and the ungodly alike will have received what God told Adam passed on from one generation to the next by word of mouth, perhaps even by written fragments (cf. Deuteronomy 32:7-8). The heart of man being degenerate, this 'tradition' then became increasingly debased into myths and legends such as those that developed in Babylon. Ideas of eternal punishment and blood redemption are found to this day in perverted forms in heathen religions. The truth was obscured through sin, hence the need for a reliable and authoritative Word from God. Even as in paradise man needed more than nature to reveal what was in the heart of God, so in a world of sinners this is much more the case. Such revelation now comes to us through Scripture. After falling into sin and spiritual darkness, man could no longer interpret aright and so became even more dependent on the Word of God. Above all, if men are to find a remedy for their spiritual affliction, they need to know of their soul's lost condition and God's solution; this they will learn only from Scripture.

Light floods the soul at the new birth. As long as the sinner remains in his darkness, his mind will be out of kilter with divine purposes. When the light once shines within, there is at least then a beginning within his consciousness that enables the appropriation and mental processing of that revealed content which faith receives. This does not necessarily mean that enlightened souls gain more acuteness of thought, but rather that by divine illumination they are enabled to apprehend what is revealed, whereas those still in darkness cannot even see these things. Acuteness of thought is another matter and varies from person to person, being dependent on other factors. The regenerate mind of the believer will show a radically different attitude to revelation than the alienated mind of the unbeliever. The believer feels the need for it and recognizes his dependence upon it and need to live by it. The natural mind refuses it as a vexatious nuisance.

Spiritual understanding can only come from within that circle where divine illumination shines. This includes not only individual believers but also groups of believers, indeed the whole of the body of believers. Apart from the illumination of the content of revelation to the individual believer, there is need to recognise how illumination works with respect to the wider understanding of the body of Christ as a whole, and how this in turn serves and enriches personal knowledge. It is the Holy Spirit who is the 'teacher of the Church' interpreting the contents of revelation to all believers, working in us a saving and sanctifying knowledge of God, not by suppressing our heart and mind but taking hold of them, stimulating and employing them as His tools. This work of the Holy Spirit reproduces in us that which was originally found in the mind of God as understanding, first generally in the body of believers, but then also within individuals.

No single believer is able on his own to think his way through to a full understanding of the whole of the content of divine revelation. This is done together by all believers down the years. This task continues. In Scripture, we explore an inexhaustible mine of infinite riches. It would seem that throughout the history of the Lord's people since New Testament times, some doctrines have gained more prominence at times than others; perhaps they were recovered after being long forgotten. At the time of the Reformation, justification by faith was necessarily central, whereas prophecy was largely neglected. On the point of setting sail for the New World, the pilgrims were reminded by their pastor that God has yet more light to shed forth from His Holy Word. Can any generation ever claim to have exhausted the riches stored in sacred writ? Nevertheless, according to his own needs and the measure of his gifts, the individual believer will be able to understand all that is necessary initially for salvation and then for the development of his own Christian testimony in those circumstances allotted to him by God.

## Seeking God where He may be found

The very idea of revelation assumes that there is One who reveals Himself, there is one to whom God reveals Himself, and that there is a possibility of contact between these two. When thinking of revelation we must not imagine that we are faced with two equals communicating with each other. God is man's Creator and He maintains and governs him and his affairs moment by moment. Furthermore, the lines of communication are not ones that just happen to be there, but they were put in place by God to meet His ends for the salvation of the world. Revelation is not a collection of bits and pieces that have come from God at different times, but it is an organic whole given to the whole human race.

Let us be ever mindful that revelation is *not* given ultimately for our benefit. To interpret God's revelation of Himself in this way is to misunderstand and deform it. Nevertheless, God takes infinite pleasure in being known of His creatures. All of creation is a glorious revelation of God. "*...for thou hast created all things, and for thy pleasure they are and were created.*" (Revelation 4:11) God is not motivated to create or reveal Himself in or to us because of any considerations outside Himself. This would imply need and imperfection in God. God cannot be glorified by anything coming to Him from outside Himself but only by His own perfections and the reflection of Himself in all He has made. The revelation of God glorifies Him in bringing the whole creation and His creature man to the end that He has beforehand purposed for them. Even those things given for the service of man are to the end that he might serve and glorify his God and Maker. All revelation proceeds from the word *(lógos)* of God and its purpose is not ended until it is reflected back to God in the consciousness of humanity to His praise and glory.

For revelation to have its effect in us, three constituents are necessary. Without *revelation*, nothing can be known; without *faith*, there can be no appropriation of revelation; without the engagement of the human *thought* processes, nothing can be transposed into a subjective knowledge of God. Faith is the link to the original that draws into human hearts that which is received by revelation. Working in the light shed abroad in our souls by the Spirit of God, the knowledge received following the process of thought will then be a reflection of that found in God.

Our knowledge of God springs from the impression that God makes upon our consciousness. This self-revelation of God is central to the Christian faith and did God not *reveal* Himself to us, we could certainly know nothing of Him. Furthermore, without quickened hearts, we could know nothing of Him. We do not come to a knowledge of God from a position of doubt but only one of faith. In the Bible, having 'a knowledge of God' is the same as having eternal life. *"And this is life eternal that they might know thee the only true God, and Jesus Christ, whom thou hast sent."* (John 17:3)

Only someone with faith worked in his heart by God can say with any measure of reality, *"Thy word is a lamp unto my feet, and a light unto my path"* (Psalm 119:105). Blind men see nothing, not even with a lamp in their hand. A light in the hand of a blind man does not help him to see where he is going. To the spiritually blind, what God has revealed of Himself in the Bible and in nature is obscured, even as those privileged to witness the coming of His Son in the flesh knew Him not (John 1:10-11). They ought to see what is plain, but they do not because of their blindness. 'Modernising' the language of the Bible will do nothing to make it more understandable. What spiritually blind men need is the healing touch of the Lord Jesus upon their eyes! Something He is more than willing to perform when they ask Him.

Only God knows God. If we are to know God, He must reveal Himself to us, but then only when and how He will. We know that which is human because we have a human spirit, a human consciousness.

> "For what man knoweth the things of a man, save the spirit of man which is in him? even so the things of God

knoweth no man, but the Spirit of God. Now we have received, not the spirit of the world, but the spirit which is of God; that we might know the things that are freely given to us of God. ...But the natural man receiveth not the things of the Spirit of God: for they are foolishness unto him: neither can he know them, because they are spiritually discerned." (1 Corinthians 2:11-12, 14)

If we are to know God and understand that which He would reveal to us, we needs must be indwelt by the Spirit of God. Spiritual things can only be received spiritually. The spirit of the world can reveal to us nothing of the things given to us of God. Those who are still on the other side, still unchanged from the day when they were born, 'natural men', will find that which God reveals in His Word not just unintelligible but foolishness.

Once man possessed a soul flooded with light, but now he sits imprisoned in darkness. Where once he saw all things in the light of God's revelation, he is now severely restricted and must look at everything in terms only of that which remains to him. God having withdrawn Himself, the sinner can now only interpret all he encounters as it comes to him in terms of the material world and his physical senses, and all devoid of any divine illumination. Nothing exists for the spiritually blind but only that which he thinks he can see! Only that which comes to him through his physical senses is real to him. This is the fatal and misguided assumption that sinners make.

The world and all that is in it has been created by God and it continues by His providence. This means that ungodly men in denying this truth lack a proper starting point and consequently cannot arrive at a true explanation of what they observe around them, or even one that is entirely satisfactory to themselves. Not willing to begin with God, they begin from within creation itself.

"But where shall wisdom be found? And where is the place of understanding? Man knoweth not the price thereof; neither is it found in the land of the living. The depth saith, It is not in me: and the sea saith, It is not with me." (Job 28:12-14)

Apart from 'special revelation', where God breaks into our world in an extraordinary and supernatural way, creation around us, the workings of God in history, and knowledge of ourselves, all show the glory of God. Nevertheless, 'natural revelation' can only make any real sense when God has revealed Himself to us as God through Jesus Christ, by a *subjective inward* work of the Holy Spirit to shed light within and dispel the darkness, coupled with an *outward objective* work in conjunction with the Word of God.

Men *ought*, as Adam before the fall, to be able to see the invisible attributes God in creation,

"For the invisible things of him from the creation of the world are clearly seen, being understood by the things that are made, even his eternal power and Godhead; so that they are without excuse." (Romans 1:20)

That which God has made God 'speaks' to men unmistakeably of Him.

"The heavens declare the glory of God; and the firmament sheweth his handywork. Day unto day uttereth speech, and night unto night sheweth knowledge. There is no speech nor language, where their voice is not heard."
(Psalm 19:1-3)

The reason men arrive at some conclusion other than the truth lies within themselves, it is not because the revelation of God in creation is in any way deficient for this purpose. Made by God, it can do no other than manifest Him. God is equally detectable in His providential working. Those heathen nations outside the promises made to Israel and who were permitted...

"...to walk in their own ways, Nevertheless he left not himself without witness, in that he did good, and gave rain from heaven, and fruitful seasons, filling our hearts with food and gladness." (Acts 14:16-17)

Men ought to recognise from this that God is good towards them. God shows His goodness, but also His wrath "...*the wrath of God is revealed from heaven against all ungodliness and unrighteousness of men...*"(Romans 1:18). An outpouring of God's wrath will surely be most intense where God's glory was most vividly displayed in creation, *upon man.* Because of what they see of God in creation and providence of the goodness and the wrath, all men ought to conclude that somewhere special grace of God is revealed that will enable them to find Him. His providential working is to the end that "*they should seek the Lord, if haply they might feel after him, and find him*" (Acts 17:27).

Despite all this, the unregenerate man remains as blind as a bat as to the true nature of *natural* as well as *spiritual* things and perpetually gets things completely wrong. This is because he does not see *all* things, including the natural world, in their relation to God. There is no artificial separation to be made between understanding heavenly and earthly things. Heavenly teaching is needed even to see earthly truth.

> *The distinction to be made is not that the unregenerate man may know earthly things but not heavenly, but that his view of all things is marred by sin.*

Above all, man ought not to fail to have his thoughts turned God-ward when looking within himself, for he is made in the image of God. He ought to thereby recognise that he derives from God and it is with God he must begin and not with himself. The Cartesian 'I think therefore I am' turns the truth on its head — it is a lie! Nothing is to be found anywhere, not in ourselves, not in the universe, that does not flow from God. Those who scoff and scorn may grin whilst the worm of their own conscience eats them up inside. The indelible impression of God within them continually wells up and there is no escape despite their best efforts at suppression. All men to some extent, Paul tells us, live by the law of God written in their hearts. We see examples of this everyday. Men will allow certain sins, particularly for themselves, but the most blatant of those same sins they will condemn.

All men are without excuse, nature itself reveals sufficient to make them search for Him. Yet instead of bursting forth in praise, the sinner's pride becomes even more inflated the more he learns. Such is the ingratitude, such is the madness of men that they use that which God has evidently made to deny His existence! As soon as man is self-conscious, he actively sins, suppressing that within which he hates, every reminder within himself that God is to be reckoned with. Despite this, the whole of creation rises up to point an accusing finger.

*We cannot know our world, we cannot know ourselves, unless we know God truly.*

Because God made the world, because He keeps it, because He knows and determines its beginning and its end, to know Him and submit to His Word is to follow the pathway of truth. Before the fall when Adam thought of himself, he would at the same time have instinctively thought of God because of the revelation of God within him. He would have thought of God as being Creator and of himself as being a derivative creature. Sinners no longer think like this, but place themselves on a par with God. They see no need of revelation, what God knows they can also know by themselves. Thinking like this, the best 'god' they will find is one like themselves, one who is a part of creation himself and not distinct from it. Yet in truth, God is the original, man the derivative. *"He that planted the ear, shall he not hear? He that formed the eye, shall he not see?"* (Psalm 94:9) Whatever man does, God did before us. Do we think? God had thoughts before us. If this were not so, we could know *nothing*.

Men get into difficulties because they reason with themselves as the ultimate arbiter of truth seeking to know the truth from within the world itself. God is left totally out of the picture. They know this has led them up a blind alley, hence their pessimism and restlessness. Many a scientist claims to have found God in nature, in physics, but this will not be the God of the Bible. They know there is more than their findings have delivered, but they obstinately refuse the only source of truth because their hearts are set against God. If we follow what the Bible says about God and about ourselves, we shall follow the truth. If we are wrong here, we shall be wrong everywhere else.

Man will find no remedy in the natural world for his desperate plight, for this he needs the Bible, a special word from God. Men need Christ; otherwise, they are lost without remedy.

> "Neither is there salvation in any other: for there is none other name under heaven given among men, whereby we must be saved." (Acts 4:12)

Today, we find Christ only in Scripture. Man needs an additional revelation of God over and above that which is found within himself and around him, the revelation of God's grace to be found only in the Bible

Whilst the sinner may feel some guilt before God, may feel uneasy with the innate knowledge of God within him, all of which he will suppress, this is not to say he has any real understanding of his need. The blind beggar may refuse all offers of help because he does not know his need. Even then, sitting in his filthy rags he cannot see his true condition until his eyes have been opened! Men know nothing of what it is to be dead in trespasses and sins and subject to the wrath of God without being told. Left to himself, the sinner can have no idea that Christ came to save him. In his blindness, he will see little relevance in a message warning him to flee from the wrath to come. Not only is the sinner blind to his own need, but also he is deaf to a message that he does not think answers a need of which he is only vaguely aware. Such men need ears to hear and eyes to see.

## Searching where there is no light

God was as He is before He created the world. Whilst God is distinct from all He has made, nevertheless, because the world was made by Him it cannot do other than manifest His glory. The whole world with man in it was created as one magnificent manifestation of God's excellencies. God not only reveals Himself in the natural world, but since the entrance of sin, He has revealed Himself redemptively: actively through *miracles*, verbally through *prophecy*, and physically by *appearing in the world* Himself. The purpose is that, together with redeemed humanity, the whole of creation will one day be filled with God's glory.

There is a very real sense in which all knowledge comes as revelation in one way or another, because *all* creation manifests the glory of God. God has created things for us to discover and given us minds capable of making sense of them. Nothing we find within the physical universe operates outside the providential care of its Creator. No 'laws' operate from within themselves like clockwork, all things are subject to

God's providence. We watch God at work in all nature. There are some things with respect to the created world and God's will for them that we cannot know by simply looking at them. God must give specific instructions with regard to them. *This was true even in the sinless environment of paradise — there was need even there for a word from God.* Simply by looking at the tree of the knowledge of good and evil, there would have been no indication of its particular significance until God gave specific instructions with respect to it.

> "But of the tree of the knowledge of good and evil, thou shalt not eat of it: for in the day that thou eatest of thereof thou shalt surely die." (Genesis 2:17)

Here was something Adam could not have known without God communicating with him directly. We are not expected to study the natural world today on our own without regard to what God has said about it. We need to know the purpose of all things and what they are leading to, and this is only possible when God reveals it to us directly. God has told us in Scripture all we need to know about the physical universe in order to arrive at proper conclusions in our scientific investigation.

God has told us that things were not always as they are now, the present state of things is not 'normal', but sin has brought a terrible curse down upon the physical universe. Before the fall Adam would have known himself to be a creature made in God's image, afterwards men needed to be informed in some detail of this fact. We can learn much about the human body by studying chemistry. Despite this, what we need to remember about man is that although formed of the dust of the ground, God *"...breathed into his nostrils the breath of life; and man became a living soul"* (Genesis 2:7). Together with the soul, the body was created immortal. The unbeliever, assuming the present state of affairs to be normal, will conclude from looking about him that the body is necessarily subject to permanent death and cannot be resurrected. The Christian knows that conclusions about the future of the human body cannot be drawn from observations of the present conditions within the natural world. Here we know from what God has said in the Bible that death came by sin and is consequently *unnatural not natural*. We also know from Scripture that all men shall be raised from the dead, some to eternal perdition, those in Christ to eternal bliss. The facts revealed in Scripture are essential to a true understanding of the human condition, without them we fall into falsehood and error. Outward contemplation of the visible things God has created will tell us little on their own unless knowledge from God comes to us by another route.

The subjective human consciousness can only relate to the objective world out there because we are all part of the one created world. The object we observe through our physical senses is not the chaos godless modern thinkers would have us believe, it is God's ordered cosmos. We being part of that same created universe are predisposed within our minds to recognise it as such. If this were not the case, we could have no thoughts about what we observe. Godless men in reducing everything to disorder and chaos are denying that to which their own constitution bears testimony. Our mind is ready to receive knowledge of the truth because it is predisposed to do so by virtue of being part of the *one* universe God has created.

To grasp with our understanding, we place ourselves as thinking subject over and above the object of our investigation. This approach is possible within creation, that over which God has given us dominion, which includes ourselves and other men, but we can never have dominion over God and so He can never be the passive object of such researches. We have some understanding of what it is to be a man because we are men. That which we know of God in ourselves because we are made in His image is a form of revelation, and this we only begin to understand when God begins to reveal Himself to us in a wider manner. Through Scripture, we interpret that which God has revealed of His glory and power in the natural world, including within ourselves. There is that which we cannot know of God because there is nothing analogous in us.

> "For what man knoweth the things of a man, save the spirit of man which is in him? even so the things of God knoweth no man but the Spirit of God." (1 Corinthians 2:11)

All that God reveals to us of Himself He *wills* that we know it both in content and manner. Contemplation of His glory in visible things is of no value to us without the revelation of Scripture. Unintentional revelation cannot happen with God. We, on the other hand, continually let slip things about ourselves by our words and deeds, despite ourselves, because we are not in complete control of all that happens to us.

We cannot subject God to our researches. Zophar demanded of Job, *"Canst thou by searching find out God? Canst thou find out the Almighty unto perfection?"* (Job 11:7). We cannot investigate the eternal, invisible God by subjecting Him to the 'scientific method'. There is nothing to analyse, no phenomena from which to draw conclusions. Verification is excluded; the very idea of testing the self-revelation of God is nonsense. He is not Himself a part of the world He has made. In our knowledge of Him, we are dependent on His good pleasure as to what and how much He tells us. Apart from this, He cannot be known. What we know of God He has willed to reveal, we can know no more. We stand in awe before God as God. We can receive no knowledge of Him as long as we refuse to receive knowledge of Him in utter dependence and submission.

Knowledge of God is not as other knowledge. Anyone who claims for himself the *right*, to say nothing of the *ability*, to investigate God has completely reversed the order of things. This man has placed himself, a sinful and finite creature, above the almighty sovereign God. He will end up with a false God formed after the musings of his own imagination, for God cannot be the object of man's research. Were God an object to be investigated on the same level as all other areas of human knowledge, then He would be subject to the same principles of understanding. Since God cannot be reduced to a common ground or placed on the same level with all He has made, when it comes to understanding, we stand in a very different relation to God than we do to all other created things around us. The way we know God is very different to all other ways of knowing. With every other area of knowledge we *take* what we know, even then we do so in submission to what God has revealed concerning the natural world. In the case of God, it is the object, God, who must reveal Himself. The flower in the field does nothing but is passive, does not change in the least as it is studied. We cannot actively *take* knowledge of God. God does not allow Himself passively to be examined. Either the sinner must live without knowledge of God, or from God's side there must come an activity to impart knowledge of Himself to us.

Had man not sinned, he would have been able to uncover from creation everything there intended to teach him about God. Even then, this would not have been through empirical research and conclusions thus drawn, but only because they *reveal* God. No conclusions can be drawn about the infinite by beginning with the finite. The pathway from one side to the other is open in one direction only. Our Lord, the living Word, was made flesh, entered the temporal, physical, objective world of men. In the same way, the written Word comes from the consciousness, the very heart of God and enters the temporal physical world. In this way, both become accessible to us. The only way we can know God is through Christ. The only way we can know Christ is through the Bible.

Although God approaches men now externally in objective revelation, without an internal and subjective work of God's Spirit we shall make no sense of it. All revelation will pass through our physical senses at some point. The greatest revelation of all time was the Lord Jesus, *"God was manifest in the flesh"* (1 Timothy 3:16).

> "No man hath seen God at any time; the only begotten Son, which is in the bosom of the Father, he hath declared him." (John 1:18)

None of these things can be properly interpreted without the spiritual eyesight to see them for what they truly are. Demonstrate to an unregenerate man the truth of creation, the reality of Bible miracles and the fulfilment of prophecy; even show him the historicity of the resurrection and he can do nothing other than explain them all in natural terms. Living in a world without God and the illumination of the Spirit of God, everything has to be interpreted without Him. Beginning in darkness the unbeliever ends in darkness.

# CHAPTER 8

# The Presence, the Power, and the Prophets of God

*"For whatsoever things were written aforetime were written for our learning, that we through patience and comfort of the scriptures might have hope."* (Romans 15:4)

We cannot live without the presence of God, this God manifested by *theophany*, by appearing to us. Without His saving power we are ruined, this He demonstrates in *miracle*. We cannot live without the Word of God, this He gives us in *prophecy*. The revelation of God came in both word and deed. In theophany and miracle, they come as deed, but both of these stand in need of God's interpretation, of His Word. Given the perversity of the human heart man would be sure to misinterpret them, providing his own explanation. We must not isolate Scripture, but see it as an integral part of God's complete work of revelation and redemption.

It is a mistake to think of revelation only in terms of knowledge. God reveals Himself by intervention in the affairs of men. He is the God who does things on behalf of men. It is true that we need true information, but knowledge alone is not enough. We need to know, but we also need to change. God needs to work within us, we need to be made new creatures. Conversion is a change of mind that has been brought about through a change of heart. Many change their mind and give the appearance of conversion, conforming outwardly to what would be expected of Christian people. This is insufficient.

> **Sin involves more than believing the wrong thing, it is also being the wrong person.**

Our world suffers from the consequences of sin, from its curse. The perversion in the soul must be righted by a work that God alone can accomplish. It is by miracle that God brings to nothing the power of sin in the soul of man. At the same time miracle reveals to us His redeeming work. God restores the spiritual health of the world by miracle. The greatest of all miracles is the person and work of Christ. Through this work, the human soul is restored to favour with God and freed from all the effects of sin. All the miracles our Saviour performed point to what He came to accomplish for us and in us. Without the one 'miracle' of the new birth no one can be saved.

Miracles, if they are to lead to faith, are to be given that interpretation of them found in Scripture; we are not at liberty to make of them what we will. Indeed, without the verbal revelation of Scripture we shall make no sense whatever of the physical intervention of God in our world by way of miracle. Miracles alone have no power to convince us of the truth, whether we observe them directly or whether we read of them in the Bible. We only see the hand of God in natural and miraculous occurrences when God Himself opens our eyes to see things as they truly are from Scripture, otherwise we will not believe. The protestation of the rich man in hell to Abraham concerning his brothers is in vain, *"if one went unto them from the dead, they will repent"* (Luke 16:30). To which Abraham replies, *"If they hear not Moses and the prophets, neither will they be persuaded, though one rose from the dead"* (v.31). Those who refuse the Scriptures will not be persuaded by a miracle. The unbeliever already excludes the possibility of explaining anything as a miracle even before having examined what has occurred.

How do we bring unbelievers to see and believe the truth. Many assume that if unbelievers see 'healings', 'tongues' and 'prophecies', they will turn to the Lord. This is not what Jesus said. Indeed, in Luke 16, this superstitious belief is only held by those suffering in hell! Just one miracle, that is all it would take to make them believe! All that is needed to persuade people believe is 'Moses and the prophets' – *the written Word.* If they refuse that, then they will refuse every miracle, even were someone come back from the dead to tell them what is beyond the grave. Jesus did many miracles that show Him to be the Son of God, but John writes

> "And many other signs truly did Jesus in the presence of his disciples, which are not written in this book: But these are written, that ye might believe that Jesus is the Christ, the Son of God; and that believing ye might have life through his name." (John 20:30-31)

The *writing down* of these things is the means appointed by God through which we are to come to a knowledge of salvation. If we refuse the written record, we will refuse even if we were to see the miracles with our own eyes.

Use of the Hebrew word *'nabi'* (prophet) ought not to be restricted to meaning one to whom God has revealed what will happen in the future, although it will include this. Furthermore, the *function* of a prophet is not confined to those whose God-given *office* was that of a prophet. Prophecy as prediction is just one particular aspect among many others with respect to the content of what God has revealed. The idea of a prophet is of one who brings to his fellow men that which he has received of God. Prophets do not receive the Word of God just for themselves.

> "Searching what, or what manner of time the Spirit of Christ which was in them did signify, when it testified beforehand the sufferings of Christ, and the glory that should follow. Unto whom it was revealed, that not unto themselves, but unto us they did minister the things, which are now reported unto you by them that have preached the gospel unto you with the Holy Ghost sent down from heaven; which things the angels desire to look into." (1 Peter 1:11-12)

The Spirit of God *in* them speaks *to* them, that they might minister *unto* us. This is true throughout the time of the giving of Scripture. All such are, technically speaking, prophets.

The apostle Paul can be understood in this sense as a prophet. Indeed, we see an overlap between what was the work of a prophet in the Old Testament and the work of an apostle in the New. Although we recognise that the function of a prophet and an apostle is similar, both offices are distinct. Both words have a specific and a more general meaning. Often they are spoken of together (cf. Luke 11:49). Paul being an apostle was clearly also a prophet in the more general sense because God revealed to him that which he then passed on to us.

> "But I certify you, brethren, that the gospel which was preached of me is not after man. For I neither received it of man, neither was I taught it, but by the revelation of Jesus Christ." (Galatians 1:11-12)

The giving of Scripture now being complete, the office and function of a prophet in this sense are now gone. Now we have access to the thoughts of God through that which was revealed to the prophets and apostles and has been infallibly recorded in Scripture. Through reading the Bible, that which was first revealed to them can now become ours.

Ordinarily, we must understand that when we read of God speaking He spoke audibly in a language understood by the hearer. The Scriptures themselves indicate that this was so. God speaking to the child Samuel cannot be understood in any other way as he mistook the voice of God for that of Eli. To understand this speaking of God in anything other than a literal and physical way is simply wrong. There are those who suggest that when the Bible records God speaking, it is some kind of influence on the mind, or an awakening in the human consciousness, or something equally as nonsensical. To say anything else than that God spoke on these occasions in a physical and audible manner undermines the authority of Scripture; it makes the Bible something other than God's *Word,* and removes undermines the basis of biblical inspiration. This is, of course, what those who say such things intend. A written Word presumes a spoken Word.

God speaking presumes that He has a thought that He wants to communicate to man. The communication of thought to men can only take place when that thought is clothed in words. This process takes place in a very concrete way not in some cloudy, pseudo-spiritual non-verbal 'influence' on the mind. To impart His thoughts God clothes them in the words of human language and utters them to men. When God *speaks,* words pass through the physical world and this they can do *only* as an audible sound falling on a physical human ear. This sound is then transmitted to the brain along the nervous system. From the physical world it reaches man's non-material, spiritual consciousness and reappears as a thought existing seconds ago only in the mind of God. What a wonder, what a privilege! Such a thing ought to humble us to the dust and cause us to praise God for His grace.

We have no access to the non-material part of our fellow men without passing through one or more of the five senses. God graciously takes account of human limitations to make His thoughts intelligible to us and does so by clothing them in human language.

> *When God speaks audibly, or at times in some other way, in order to communicate His thoughts to men, this will always involve the use words.*

God knows every language. He created them all, every dialect. God reveals Himself and speaks to whom He will. God is now silent because in Christ Jesus He has said all He has to say and He now speaks only through the Scriptures.

Long before He came into the world, Christ was in the world as the true Prophet through those who came as prophets before Him. Even so, the true Word from God did not begin with those whom God sent as prophets. It came right from the moment sin entered into the world. Without this Word the whole of creation would have collapsed instantly, for even in its sinful state the world and those in it are preserved alive only by the hope of salvation and that in Christ Jesus. Without the hope of salvation, the whole world is lost. Without the revealed Word of God, there can at no time be access to that salvation.

> "...man doth not live by bread only, but by every word that proceedeth out of the mouth of the Lord doth man live." (Deuteronomy 8:3; cf. Matthew 4:4)

A world without a hope of salvation could not last for a second. Salvation and the Word of God cannot be pulled apart. Had there not already been a redemptive purpose beforehand, there could have been no Word. Because there was a previous redemptive purpose there was a Word, a Word without which man cannot survive. The Word spoken by God in promise of salvation was the first verbal revelation of God's redemptive purpose in Christ.

> "And I will put enmity between thee and the woman, and between thy seed and her seed; it shall bruise thy head, and thou shalt bruise his heel." (Genesis 3:15)

God walked and talked with man after the fall. Originally, Adam would have received and made known the thoughts of God. At the fall this changed, Adam began to think his own thoughts. His 'enlightenment' plunged him into darkness. By nature man would no longer naturally make the Word of God the rule of his life in all matters. Above anything else, it is a reversal of this that indicates today a work of God in the soul. All men assume they can do what they will with what God reveals: judge, refuse, or deny it. Those who bow in submission to the Word of God are his 'servants', the rest are his enemies. Servants are receptive, submissive, and obedient. The apostle John begins the last book of the Bible with these words, *"The Revelation of Jesus Christ, which God gave unto him, to shew unto his servants..." (Revelation 1:1).* It is to those who are His servants who receive His Word.

Between paradise and Patmos, God progressively revealed more and more of His redemptive purpose. He chose men as His servants through whom he would make known His revelation to others. There are two main stages to this revelation, that of the Old Testament and that of the New. In Old Testament times, on occasions, God let His will be known by lot or He spoke through the Urim and Thummim. More often, He spoke through dreams and visions, which is why prophets are also known as 'seers'.

> "Beforetime in Israel, when a man went to enquire of God, thus he spake, Come, and let us go to the seer: for he that is now called a Prophet was beforetime called a Seer."
> (1 Samuel 9:9)

God also spoke audibly to them. God speaking was just as much God intervening in the physical world, as when Christ came as God manifest in the flesh, both are the *Word* of God. What took place in the Old Testament period was preparatory to the work of the Lord Jesus, the great Prophet, in whom the Spirit of God dwelt without measure. He was the Word become flesh who *declared* to us the Father. The Old Testament has not been superseded by the New, but is part of that whole body of God's one Word to men. It is part of the revelation of Christ and the part must be interpreted in relation to the whole of which Christ is at the centre.

## Outside Christ no knowledge of God, without Scripture no knowledge of Christ

There is an indissoluble link between the revelation of the glory of God in nature in general, in man, and the revelation of Scripture. They constitute but *one whole* rich revelation. The Bible ought not to be viewed as supplementary or an addition, but as a constituent of all that God wants us to know about Him. What men know of God by virtue of being made in His image needs the enlightenment of the revelation secured in Scripture for it to be seen for what it really is. God did not create one single soul but a whole race of men in a cosmos of self-revelation. Only in this organic unity of the entire human race in the created world does God's self-revelation in creation reach completion. Scriptures tell us *"For all have sinned, and come short of the glory of God"* (Romans 3:23). When one man fell, all others fell with him as part of a total humanity and the world of which he was part was inevitably drawn into the effects of his action. Sin could not have spread in this way were one man simply an isolated repetition of another. The totality of revelation is to a totality of humanity.

Christ Jesus came to be Head of a new humanity. The contrast between the two men could not be clearer, *"For as in Adam all die, even so in Christ shall all be made alive"* (1 Corinthians 15:22). It is through this new humanity whose Head is Christ that God will be revealed in the created world. Thus it shall be that *"...the earth shall be filled with the knowledge of the glory of the Lord, as the waters cover the sea."* (Habakkuk 2:14) The knowledge of the glory of God is the common possession of the redeemed, of all in Christ. Individual knowledge of God and communion with Him is only possible within the body of that new race.

With or without sin, human existence is successive because it is bound by time. The entire human race did not come into existence all at the same time, but successively. Without sin, there would have appeared a progressive development of the knowledge of God. With the coming of sin, the revelation of God in the innermost depths of the human soul has not been completely eradicated any more than the image of God in him has been removed. The sinner remains human even whilst a sinner.

---

*There remains a dreadful manifestation of God at the heart of every sinner, a terror that drove Judas to hang himself.*

---

This terror is sufficient to drive men mad. How often do we learn that someone having committed some particularly wicked deed in perfect sanity of mind has subsequently lost his senses and been committed to an asylum? Had sin been permitted by God to have an absolute effect, there could be no help against it. Had He not already previously intervened on man's behalf, we would all have been irretrievably lost. We cannot exist for an instant, even in a state of sin, apart from God's grace and then to the end that we should be saved in Christ. All men would otherwise have sunk into a darkness that no light of revelation could penetrate.

The effectiveness of the revelation of Scripture presumes an action by God in which the operations of Satan, sin, and death are curbed. Evil predominates, the wheels of sin continue to turn, but praise God, He has a foot on the brake pedal. God restrains day by day the destructive power of sin and creates, as He will, a milieu in which the Gospel as revealed in Scripture can be effective. What a place would this world otherwise be, were God not active in His grace to all men to the end that they might be saved! The special revelation of God in Scripture is intended for the sinner surrounded by God's grace; only under a regime of such 'common grace' is regeneration possible.

God does not just love individuals. Scripture tells us that God so loved the *world*. God gave His Son not *just* for individuals. The purpose of God's electing grace is not simply to save individuals adding one to another and leaving the rest to perdition. God's intention is *to save humanity*. He redeems *our race* of men. If every single human being then is not saved, it is because they who are lost through their unbelief are cut off from the rest. As the original organism of humanity found its unity in Adam, so now Christ occupies the same place in the human race originally occupied by Adam. In this sense it is not something entirely new, but the original humanity is reconciled and regenerated — for it is not possible that sin should triumph on earth.

> *It is within the redeemed body of believers alone that the knowledge of God is reproduced within a regenerated and enlightened consciousness.*

God's revelation of Himself is His only Word to humanity as a whole. Revelation is progressive and historical, even as humanity unfolds itself historically. It is, however, organic, addressed as a whole to humanity as a whole. It can have significance for the individual only in relation to this whole. The primary aim of revelation is the vindication of God in view of the entry of evil into the world. God sent His Son so that *all who believe in Him will be saved* and in this we see how God loved *His* world (cf. John 3:16). It will show that creation even in the face of the entry of sin has been no failure. Revelation aims to achieve actual triumph over sin, guilt, and death. It cannot stop at a plan alone in the mind of God but must be turned into reality by the action of God.

The preparation and preservation of Holy Scripture has reference to the life of the whole body of believers of all times. Whilst prophecy will first be of benefit to those living at the time of its utterance, it is intended also to minister to believers of all times afterwards, this latter being of greater rather than lesser significance. The primary purpose will be its benefit to the whole believing community.

> "For whatsoever things were written aforetime were written for our learning, that we through patience and comfort of the scriptures might have hope." (Romans 15:4)

The Scripture is more than a progressive history of the people of God and their salvation. It is rather the end of all that preceded its completion and the instrument of all that follows.

Knowledge of the Father is only to be obtained through the Son. If we have no knowledge of the Lord Jesus, we have no knowledge of God the Father. Those who reject the Lord Jesus know nothing of the living God. The Father does not speak directly to us, but only through and in Christ as Head of body.

> "For in him dwelleth all the fulness of the Godhead bodily. And ye are complete in him, which is head of all principality and power." (Colossians 2:9-10)

As the subject of restored humanity, it is through the Lord Jesus alone that we can know God. Knowledge of God is complete in Him, it is perfect. *"All things that the Father hath are mine"* (John 16:15). *"As the Father knoweth me, even so know I the Father"* (John 10:15). Christ, *"in whom are hid all the treasures of wisdom and knowledge"* (Colossians 2:3). From Him this descends to individual believers.

> "All things are delivered unto me of my Father: and no man knoweth the Son, but the Father; neither knoweth any man the Father, save the Son, and he to whomsoever the Son will reveal him." (Matthew 11:27)

Christ is our prophet. The knowledge that Christ *as Head of the body,* has of the Father, is not divine self-knowledge, but is a *human knowledge* of God. It is a knowledge that fills the measure of the human capacity for knowledge. Were this divine and so beyond human limitations, it could throw no light into our darkness. The knowledge of God due to His union with the Father was not the result of analysis or investigation but is intuitive.

> "No man hath seen God at any time; the only begotten Son, which is in the bosom of the Father, he hath declared him." (John 1:18)

Christ does not seek to convince us with arguments, He declares the Father. He does not engage in scientific demonstration, but shows Him. He does not analyse, but unveils the truth.

The natural man uses his reason to draw knowledge from the object that is then subject to him as the thinking subject. When I as a believer would know about God, Christ is for me the thinking subject in the restored humanity, in whose common consciousness the *"manifold wisdom of God"* (Ephesians 3:10) is reflected. He *"is made unto us wisdom"* (1 Corinthians 1:30).

> "He shall shall glorify me: for he shall receive of mine, and shall shew it unto you. All things that the Father hath are mine: therefore said I, that he shall take of mine, and shall shew it unto you." (John 16:14-15)

Christ is the way and the life, but also He is the truth (John 14:6). Christ is the truth because He is the Word, the *lógos*. The *lógos* of God is revealed in two ways: first, in the flesh by the *incarnation;* second, in the world of our consciousness through *inscripturation.* It is a revelation in *being* and in *thought.* This is an organic whole in Christ, which shows itself most strongly when Christ as a man utters the oracles of God.

The word *(lógos)* in man reflects the Word of God. There is a causal relationship between these two, because Christ is the subject of the new humanity and not we ourselves. Our *lógos* is the human counterpart in us of the divine *lógos,* working within our thought processes. We can know God only in Christ through the operation of the Holy Spirit. It is still the thinking man who is the subject, but in this case, Christ. Should I attempt this without Christ, as do godless theologians, then I put God on trial. The thought processes by which regenerate humanity turns into knowledge the revelation received by faith begins in Christ. There must be those thought processes by which the individual comes to a personal knowledge of God. Then there is that central complete knowledge of God that the whole body of Christ possesses in Him. This must then be radiated outwards to become the understanding of the new humanity.

Knowledge of Christ is to be sought immediately in Scripture as the *material principle* of knowing. Here God has communicated numerous facts and revelations, which under His supervision became embodied in Scripture. Our Lord as the living Word is no longer with us in the flesh. Until He returns, God has given us all we need to know of Him in Scripture, the written Word. The Head of the new humanity speaks to us there through other human beings to whom He has spoken. Peter says of the prophets: *"holy men of God spake as they were moved by the Holy Ghost"* (2 Peter 1:21). If we would know the Lord Jesus, it is in Scripture that we shall now find Him. We have no other way of appropriating that which is revealed than by faith in that Word, ultimately therefore in Him.

The Lord Jesus made clear to the Jews that they knew nothing of the Father, *"Ye have neither heard his voice at any time, nor seen his shape"* (John 5:37). Indeed, the only physical manifestation of God available to them was standing before them. Evidence that the Word of God had not reached their hearts was that they rejected Him. The way we approach the written Word reflects our attitude to the Lord Jesus.

> "And ye have not his word abiding in you: for whom he hath sent, him ye believe not. Search the scriptures; for in them ye think ye have eternal life: and they are they which testify of me." (John 5:38-39)

To refuse the testimony of Scripture is to refuse Christ Himself and shows we have nothing of God's Word in us, no knowledge of Him.

---

**To alter God's written Word is to take on a changed view of Christ.**

---

The new, deliberately 'modernised' versions of Scripture will necessarily present a changed and 'updated' Christ, another Jesus. A false bible presents a false Christ. Following Saussure and Nida, a 'moderniser's' bible is relevant and necessary only as it speaks for the present moment. Links with the past are by definition irrelevant and unimportant. By contrast, the authentic Scriptures show an organic unity throughout time and with those to whom God spoke in the past.

> "For had ye believed Moses, ye would have believed me: for he wrote of me. But if ye believe not his writings, how shall ye believe my words?" (John 5:46-47)

Once again, we see that God's Word has a perspective that is beyond time.

We do not find in the Bible isolated incoherent thoughts, but a unity of thought antagonistic to the thinking of the natural man. What enters our mind is a mirror image of divine thoughts, all that we need to be saved and to live lives that glorify God. Its words speak to us who know Him, for we hear the voice of our Saviour. *"My sheep hear my voice, and I know them, and they follow me"* (John 10:27). There is a precise correlation between that which Scripture under the influence of God's Spirit creates in our minds and the divine thoughts of God. However, without the life of God within us, the pages of the Bible remain dark. The Bible has something to say to all men, regenerate and unregenerate, God-fearing or God-hating. We hear our Shepherd's voice, others hear the voice of a stranger. We read what no unbeliever reads, His voice consoles and whispers peace to our souls. To the stranger to God it annoys, repels, contradicts him and his world, it is a savour of death. This book is the instrument of the Holy Spirit by which spiritual life comes to dead souls. It works to *quicken* our faith; it causes us to *exercise* faith. It is not a dead letter but a fountain of living water springing up to eternal life.

Our fallen race of men can find no adequate knowledge of God from the natural world around or within them because of sin, so they stand in special need of an auxiliary revelation that places a knowledge of God within their grasp to suit their sinful condition. Nevertheless, this extra-ordinary and special revelation does not have the purpose of restoring that knowledge which Adam lost. All the knowledge we possess in this dispensation shall pass and in its place there is to come the 'seeing face to face'. Then, we shall recognise the divine face as being that of the One whose image we saw darkly here on earth.

Had sin not ruined Adam's race there would have been no need of special revelation of the kind we now experience. *The knowledge that Adam possessed connotatively is now mediated denotatively - from without to within.* Adam would have eventually progressed to knowing face to face. All that are our riches in this life shall pass away. Special revelation is referred to as a glass which renders temporary aid, to receive for us the image and reflect it back again; but that glass too shall one day belong to that which is of the past.

> "For now we see through a glass, darkly; but then face to face: now I know in part; but then shall I know even as I am known." (1 Corinthians 13:12)

Then there shall come an entirely different knowing, *even as we are known.* This knowledge will come to us entirely by the data provided in creation. Nothing, of course, shall be lost of that already revealed of the rich revelation of the mercy of God. The difference between then and now is that we shall then take up this rich gain once more into our normal existence.

The Mediator shall surrender up the kingdom to God, but in a manner that leaves Him still as Head of the body, Head of the human race in glory. This He will forever remain. Adam will never take honour again in that which he lost at the fall through sin. The whole dispensation of special grace will have past and with it special revelation as we now know it. That which is now special will then be natural to us.

*If in the purposes of God, it was His will to give men books and the printed page, then it was that we might receive the one book needful to men, the Bible.*

## One sufficient Saviour, one sufficient Scripture

Yet, we must not think of a book as only printed marks on a page. That which we see travels along our physical visual nerves to transport it to our consciousness, in the case of Scripture it takes us into the sphere of divine thoughts. The process of God's revelation of the thoughts of His heart involves the use of language and words. To make sense of revelation, in whatever form, it needs to pass beyond mere impressions and feelings, observations and perception, and be processed as thought to become genuine understanding. The process of revelation would not be possible without language. The possession of language from the start assumes a thought process that was immediate and as natural as breathing. This means that without a Bible that is infallible and fully and verbally inspired, we have no reliable Word from God interpreting for us the universe and condition in which we find ourselves. Furthermore, if we have no access to God's infallible Word *in a language we can understand,* we have no access to the thoughts of God.

All created reality was brought into being and continues to be determined in every detail by the will of God — *and this therefore, above all, will include the giving of Scripture! The transmission of the sacred Word into languages understood by others beyond the original readers, for whom it is also intended, takes place under the providential eye of God, who preserves His Word in every detail that we too may share His thoughts.* If the hairs of our head are all numbered and no sparrow falls to the ground without our Father, then it is inconceivable that such a watchful Father should pay no regard when His Word passes from one language to another or that He should have made no provision for this. Careful translation of God's Word from one language to another under the guidance of God's Spirit by men designated by Him to undertake the task is one thing, a deliberate attempt at rewriting what God has said according to the godless principles of men like Saussure and Nida is quite another. The one will be a faithful translation as efficacious as the original text; the other will not be God's Word at all.

In God's mind from eternity, there is an exhaustive knowledge of all things. *"Known unto God are all his works from the beginning of the world"* (Acts 15:18). That which is found in the Bible pre-existed its emergence in space and time, before one page was written.

> *That which God beforehand determined to reveal to us in His providence is embodied in Scripture so that the* content *of Scripture pre-existed its revelation and inscripturation.*

What God has given in the Bible was eternally in His heart to give us. It is for this reason that we can be sure *"the Scripture cannot be broken"* (John 10:35). Equally, it was never other than His purpose to give it us *in every form* that He has done so – as a written book in a language we can understand.

When communicating with others our thoughts will run into barriers and limitations as we try to express what we mean. No such limitations exist for God. God is not speaking to another like Himself, but to a creature whom He has made and whom He keeps from moment to moment. God does not communicate with us through an accidental route coincidentally available to Him and with which He has previously had nothing to do, but through *one that He has Himself constructed* to serve His purposes. This includes language and writing, all of which He has given. We are created by God to know Him and with a capacity for all knowledge that He would reveal to us, but also *God created the route by which that knowledge reaches us.*

Not simply the pre-existent knowledge but also that which it has brought forth, the Word and its physical expression both in Christ and in the Bible is the self-revelation of God to the sinner. We only have a complete picture when God has said *all* He has to say. This could only be when Christ had come. He has said all He has to say in Christ, in Him is all we need to know. Special revelation was completed with the coming of Christ.

> "God, who at sundry times and in divers manners spake in time past unto the fathers by the prophets, Hath in these last days spoken unto us by his Son, whom he hath appointed heir of all things." (Hebrews 1:1-2)

> *Only in the living Word is the written Word complete. God has said all He has to say in Christ and will say no more. All we can know of God is manifest in Him.*

There is nothing more for us to know of Christ than is found in the written Word. An attack on the sufficiency of Scripture, implying the need for new revelations of whatever kind, is an attack on the sufficiency of Christ. All that we can know today of God springs from the completed revelation of Christ in Scripture. A finished work of the living Saviour provides the ground of a finished written Word. Those denying the sufficiency of Scripture by claiming additional revelation implicitly deny the sufficiency of Christ and thereby ought not to assume themselves unquestionably to be among the redeemed. Salvation is complete, the revelation is complete, and all in Christ.

We have seen that special revelation bears a universally human character and significance. The working of special revelation is much wider than Scripture itself. The Bible is not identical with it, but is instead entirely a product of it. In special revelation, *fact or deed* and *word* run parallel with each other. All that God wanted us to know could simply have been disclosed for us in a book let down on a cord from heaven or dictated directly from heaven, something on the lines of what is claimed for the Book of Mormon or the Koran. This ignores all those other elements that surround Scripture and render it efficacious. *Special revelation encompasses all those things initiated from God's side that are not part of that which God has revealed of Himself in the natural created world.* Included are: the whole plan of redemption and everything involved in realising this plan; all special leadings, signs, wonders; the entire inspiration and formation of Scripture; the regeneration of believers; all illumination by the Spirit of God.

---

*Special revelation as a principle of knowing has produced not only Scripture, but even now proceeds from Scripture by the present working of the Holy Spirit.*

---

God's Spirit maintains, applies, and vitalises the knowledge of God by the illumination of what is written in the Bible, within the consciousness of individuals as they read, but also by the work of the ministry in the body of Christian believers.

The body of believers, the Church of Christ, is built after the rule of Scripture. Faith in Scripture is supported and maintained by the communion of believers. It is unscriptural to imagine that a believer simply taking the Bible in his hand is left utterly to his own devices and desires, formulating doctrine for himself. On being born into the body of the regenerate one enters a circle in which a confession of *"the faith which was once delivered unto the saints"* (Jude 3) already exists. We share the same faith with believers now alive in every part of the world, with those gone before us, and with those now in the presence of Christ their Lord.

We must always maintain a proper relationship between that which concerns our human race as a whole for all time and the knowledge of God coming to the individual at one particular time. It may be objected that the Scriptures cannot be an instrument of salvation in any absolute sense as many centuries elapsed before it was finally completed and that many found salvation before this time. This argument loses much of its force when we read of the 'great mystery' in the New Testament.

> "Now to him that is able to stablish you according to my gospel, and the preaching of Jesus Christ, according to the revelation of the mystery, which was kept secret since the world began, But now is made manifest, and by the scriptures of the prophets, according to the commandment of the everlasting God, made known to all nations for the obedience of faith." (Romans 16:25-26)
>
> "Whereof I am made a minister, according to the dispensation of God which is given to me for you, to fulfil the word of God; Even the mystery which hath been hid from ages and from generations, but now is made manifest to his saints: To whom God would make known what is the riches of the glory of this mystery among the Gentiles; which is Christ in you, the hope of glory." (Colossians 1:25-27; cf. Ephesians 1:9; 3:9-10; 1 Timothy 3:9; Titus 1:2-3)

It is this mystery that is the key that unlocks our understanding of the course of revelation. The progression of revelation did not unfold atomistically or aphoristically. There is no question here of God making things up as He goes along, responding to unforeseen events along the way, but of all things being planned in advance. We gain the view from Scripture that we have to do with a revelation which proceeds through definite stages and moves along to its final goal. Scripture obtains its full significance only when God's grace and revelation is directed to our race of men as a whole for all time. Then, of course, there is no need for anything to be added to it. Any idea of a need of continuing and supplementary revelations now is seen for the nonsense it is. Even before the completed Scriptures placed God's revelation at the centre of our lost race, men were still saved by faith in the revealed Word of God, written and living.

Nevertheless, Scripture was intended to fulfil its *full task* only from that moment when its last word was written to the end that the saving love of God be extended to the lost world. We must account all preceding this as being preparatory to it. The finality of the sacrifice of the Saviour and the completion of Scripture are linked. The preparatory and temporary nature of all that went before is clear.

> "For then must he often have suffered since the foundation of the world: but now once in the end of the world hath he appeared to put away sin by the sacrifice of himself." (Hebrews 9:26)

There is one Word *(lógos)*, which is Christ by the incarnation and the Scripture by inscripturation, that goes out to humanity for its salvation by God. There is knowledge of God only through the incarnate and the written Word.

Were salvation incomplete this would necessitate further revelation. Hence, those who claim the need for further revelation, by implication deny that the work of salvation is completed. After the unveiling of the mystery, the completion of that which is to be revealed by God and given to humanity as a whole, we must go on to assert that except as a member of the organic whole body of believers there is no salvation for the individual. Noah, Moses, Samuel, and many in the Old Testament received separate individual revelations because humanity did not yet possess its completed revelation. Once the completed whole was received, the need for separate revelations fell away. Those who today pretend to receive individual revelations from God fragment the organic ministry of God's Spirit to the whole body of redeemed humanity. There is now no other way to come to a knowledge of God other than in union with this central revelation, even as there can be no salvation outside the one body, the one Church of Christ. Those who deny or diminish the Scriptures, even by implication, at the same time deny and diminish Christ.

We cannot assert that with the completion of the writing of Scripture therefore the process is at an end, or that this by itself is enough for the individual. A book is not placed in our hands simply for our reason then to make the best it that it can. The Holy Spirit, who is Himself the author of the book, is the One who also must open its contents to our consciousness and apply it to our hearts. Our human consciousness is thus enabled to take up that which stands on the page before us. He it is who leads us to an ever richer understanding of that which is intended for us and is indispensable to us. This work of the Holy Spirit adds no new content to Scripture, no enlargement of the substance of the knowledge of God.

> *Scripture could not be produced until its whole content had been wrought out in life, and redemption objectively accomplished.*

Equally, we cannot say that redemption was accomplished and then recorded for us in a mechanical way in Scripture. The Scripture, which is itself living, was produced progressively and spontaneously and has itself a vital role in God's redemptive purpose. Although redemption precedes

Scripture, the Holy Spirit began to speak with men even in Paradise itself. God's Word always goes before His life, and His thought always precedes redemption. Christ speaks, then works redemption in us. The Holy Spirit always acts through the Word in bringing a soul from death to life.

We must note some differences in the working of God before and after the completion of Scripture. At first, God's Word came to the soul directly or by the words of a prophet. Now these have ceased, that Word comes to us sealed in Scripture, interpreted to us by the Holy Spirit. During the Old Testament period, Scripture being incomplete, whilst there are glimpses of redemption in Christ, especially in the Psalms, there was constant need of the supplement of direct revelation. Now, the Scripture reveals to us the whole counsel of God, and nothing can be added to it or taken from it. Woe betides anyone who attempts to do so! The Bible as God's thoughts made intelligible in human language is to men of all nations and times the instrument of our salvation. It presents a finished salvation in a finished book. The Bible is not merely a paper book; here God speaks to the souls of men. God speaks and in speaking quickens. It is not that the Bible causes life, but is the instrument by which He works faith in our hearts. *"So then faith cometh by hearing, and hearing by the Word of God"* (Romans 10:17).

CHAPTER 9

# The Apostolic Gospel

*"But though we, or an angel from heaven, preach any other gospel unto you than that which we have preached unto you, let him be accursed. As we said before, so say I now again, If any man preach any other gospel unto you than that ye have received, let him be accursed."* (Galatians 1:8-9)

U sing these words, the preacher urges us to fulfil the last command of the Lord Jesus and take the Gospel to the far corners of the earth:

"Then the eleven disciples went away into Galilee, into a mountain where Jesus had appointed them. And when they saw him, they worshipped him: but some doubted. And Jesus came and spake unto them, saying, All power is given unto me in heaven and in earth. Go ye therefore, and teach all nations, baptizing them in the name of the Father, and of the Son, and of the Holy Ghost: Teaching them to observe all things whatsoever I have commanded you: and, lo, I am with you alway, even unto the end of the world. Amen."
(Matthew 28:16-20)

Clearly, the world stands as much in need today of powerful Gospel preaching as it ever did or will. Zeal in Gospel work is to be encouraged not despised, but it must be zeal according to knowledge. In our great desire to see the Gospel preached, we often overlook the fact that the eleven disciples were with the Lord Jesus *on their own* and it was to them that these instructions were given. There is no justification from the text for us to appropriate these words immediately to ourselves.

The task of taking the Gospel to the ends of the earth was here initially committed, *not to the Church local or universal, not to believers then or now, **but to the apostles***. If our preaching of the Gospel is to be with power and according to the truth, we must first accept that the only authority it can have is apostolic authority – only then will it carry the authority of Christ. We cannot simply jump over the apostles, or just regard them as the first Gospel preachers among the many that followed. The apostles enjoy a unique position, one they will never relinquish, not now or in the future.

At a meeting of ministers held in Northampton in 1786, the following incident occurred. Younger ministers were invited to propose a subject for discussion. There being no immediate response, a young minister, William Carey, proposed to discuss *"whether the command given to the apostles, to teach all nations, was not obligatory on all succeeding ministers to the end of the world, seeing that the accompanying promise was of equal extent."* The air at that point could doubtless have been cut with a knife. The chairman could hardly contain himself. Addressing Carey, he rebuked him, *"You are a miserable enthusiast for asking such a question. Certainly nothing can be done before another Pentecost, when an effusion of miraculous gifts, including the gift of tongues, will give effect to the commission of Christ as at the first."* This outburst was typical of the brand of Calvinism prevalent among English Baptists at the time. Such thinking is still widespread today among Pentecostal-charismatics, many Calvinists and neo-puritans, and others who mistakenly await 'a revival to end all revivals'. These views provide a suspiciously comfortable excuse for many to do nothing about bringing the Gospel to the lost. Carey had put his finger on the real nub of the issue with amazing clarity. Of course, it is physically impossible for the apostles to fulfil all aspects of this divine commission on their own.

The commandment to go *"into all the world, and preach the gospel to every creature"* (Mark 16:15) was given to the apostles to execute. It is only *through the apostles* that anyone else has any part in this. The apostles are long since gone, but their testimony remains. That command was nevertheless to be completed by countless servants of Christ carrying forth *the apostolic testimony* to the ends of the earth. Ours is an apostolic task, we only have a message to preach by virtue of the apostles' testimony. This testimony we have before us, infallibly recorded in the Bible and for this reason it is to be placed at the centre of the proclamation of the Gospel of Christ.

As believers, we confess fellowship with the Father and with the Son through the apostles, in the sense that their testimony was not confined to the believers alive at that time and those with whom they came into contact, but also because under divine inspiration they wrote down their testimony for us. As a result, this testimony has gone out to the uttermost part of the earth. It has overcome the limits of time and of space, reaching men of subsequent times all around the earth. Even now in our own day, *the apostles preach the Word of God* every time the Bible is expounded in truth and power.

## Exclusive apostolic authority

The Lord Jesus took steps to ensure the completion of His mission and so He appointed apostles. He attaches to this body of men a definite authority and commissions them with a definite task. First, they are to be witnesses of all that they have seen. Second, they are to proclaim the things that are to come. This double task was given to them not only with respect to those who were then alive and to whom they would preach by word of mouth, but it has a wider reference to 'all nations' and in those nations to all believers, and for those who believe 'unto the end of the world'. We must ask how it is possible for the apostles personally bring the witness to all nations and throughout time. Either they would have to remain alive, or as they all died early on, it would have to be though the instrumentality of writing.

The words of those who preach the authentic biblical Gospel today carry apostolic authority and therefore also the authority of Christ. We do not preach by our own authority, but through that delegated first to the apostles by Christ. This binds us firmly to preaching the Scriptures, which are the apostolic testimony. *Only when we preach the Bible and nothing else, do we preach with the authority of Christ.*

---

*Those who preach anything other than the Bible have no authority from Christ for what they are saying.*

---

The revealed Word of God was and remains the measure of all that men preach and teach.

> "And when they shall say unto you, Seek unto them that have familiar spirits, and unto wizards that peep, and that mutter: should not a people seek unto their God? for the living to the dead? To the law and to the testimony: if they speak not according to this word, it is because there is no light in them." (Isaiah 8:19-20)

Such 'prophets' either speak demonic revelations (cf. 1 Timothy 4:1), or they *"...speak a vision of their own heart, and not out of the mouth of the Lord"* (Jeremiah 23:16).

> "The prophet that hath a dream, let him tell a dream; and he that hath my word, let him speak my word faithfully. What *is* the chaff to the wheat? saith the LORD. Is not my word like as a fire? saith the LORD; and like a hammer that breaketh the rock in pieces?" (Jeremiah 23:28,29)

Two here seem to be prophets: one is false and presents words of his own imagination as the Word of God, chaff instead of wheat; the other faithfully declares the Word of God. How can we tell the true from the false? Today, we have an *objective measure*, the written Word, the authentic Bible. We also have a *subjective measure*, the effect of the true divine Word upon our own hearts and consciences. It comes to us like a fire, like a hammer, in unparalleled light and power. When reading the Scripture, the sinner hears the voice he does not want to hear, the voice of almighty God speaking within. This is why he hates the Bible, he recognises who it is who speaks. Those who make a pretence of religion, but are in reality strangers to God's saving grace, also hate the Word of God. The *Authorised Version* of the Bible comes increasingly under attack, not because it is outmoded or for some reason to do with manuscripts and texts, but because as a true and faithful rendering of God's Word it speaks only too precisely to the sinful heart and must be made to say something else. Godless falsifiers of the Word have God are not interested in an accurate and faithful translation, far from it, they need a false Word to justify their own deeds. Those who love the Lord hide His Word in their heart, they obey it; it abides in them.

> "For this cause also thank we God without ceasing, because, when ye received the word of God which ye heard of us, ye received it not as the word of men, but as it is in truth, the word of God, which effectually worketh also in you that believe." (1 Thessalonians 2:13)

The Word of God shows itself to be such by the effect it has upon those who believe. Those who believe have thereby a far greater testimony to the truth than one based upon the arguments of men. As the man born blind we can say, *"One thing I know, that, whereas I was blind, now I see"* (John 9:25). Though a man be persuaded by argument of the truth of Scripture with out experience of the divine power of God, he does not believe it in faith and in truth. It is the *"engrafted word, which is able to save your souls"* (James 1:21).

> **It is God Himself, who by His Spirit infallibly convinces us of the truth and authority of the Scriptures.**

That the Lord Jesus not only gave to the apostles a call to preach the Gospel to those then alive, but also to be His authoritative witnesses to believers until the end of time is evident from the following passage.

> "Neither pray I for these alone, but for them also which shall believe on me through their word." (John 17:20)

This verse has reference to all believers among all nations to the end of time. This is underlined by the repeated use of 'that' in the verse following

> "That they all may be one; as thou, Father, art in me, and I in thee, that they also may be one in us: that the world may believe that thou hast sent me." (John 17:21)

If these words refer only to those converted in that day through the verbal word of the apostles, then they would contain little comfort for us. When we remember that their word has been perfectly preserved for us in Scripture, and that through this word we have been saved, then we can know that at that moment when our Saviour faced His coming death upon the cross, He was thinking and praying for you and for me and for *all* who through the testimony of the apostles would find salvation. Evidently, the unity of all believers in these verses cannot simply refer to the immediate converts of that time. The world until the end is to receive this witness. In John 17:14 Jesus prays, *"I have given them thy word (lógos)"*. This Word has come first to the apostles and then through them to us and to the world until the end of time.

It follows from all this that the Lord Jesus would have purposed that this apostolic testimony must remain available in *a fixed form after their death.*

> "Go ye therefore, and teach all nations, baptizing them in the name of the Father, and of the Son, and of the Holy Ghost: Teaching them to observe all things whatsoever I have commanded you: and, lo, I am with you alway, even unto the end of the world. Amen." (Matthew 28:19-20)

Here the significance of the apostles and their testimony is extended to all nations until the end of the world. The apostles themselves realised the exceptional significance of their role.

> "That which was from the beginning, which we have heard, which we have seen with our eyes, which we have looked upon, and our hands have handled, of the Word of life; (For the life was manifested, and we have seen it, and bear witness, and shew unto you that eternal life, which was with the Father, and was manifested unto us;) That which we have seen and heard declare we unto you, that ye also may have fellowship with us: and truly our fellowship is with the Father, and with his Son Jesus Christ." (1 John 1:1-3)

John says of himself and his fellow apostles: first, the manifestation received was so real that he even says 'our hands have handled' it; second, that they were called to preach what had been manifested; third, that men can know the Word of life only through fellowship with the apostles. Only through that which the apostles preach can we have fellowship with them and thus with the Father and His Son, the Lord Jesus Christ. Only thus can the oneness Jesus prayed for be achieved.

Remembering that the Scripture was not yet completed, yet we see how this apostolic testimony was to be spread when Paul in writes to Timothy,

> "And the things that thou hast heard of me among many witnesses, the same commit thou to faithful men, who shall be able to teach others also." (2 Timothy 2:2)

The idea behind this verse is again that the apostles have been given something that is fixed for all time and it is this that faithful men would teach to others in a kind of chain or network down through time.

The significance of the apostles is made clear by the Lord Jesus in many places, including the following:

> "These things have I spoken unto you, being yet present with you. But the Comforter, which is the Holy Ghost, whom the Father will send in my name, he shall teach you all things, and bring all things to your remembrance, whatsoever I have said unto you." (John 14:25-26)
>
> "But when the Comforter is come, whom I will send unto you from the Father, even the Spirit of truth, which proceedeth from the Father, he shall testify of me: And ye also shall bear witness, because ye have been with me from the beginning." (John 15:26-27)
>
> "I have yet many things to say unto you, but ye cannot bear them now. Howbeit when he, the Spirit of truth, is come, he will guide you into all truth: for he shall not speak of himself; but whatsoever he shall hear, that shall he speak: and he will shew you things to come. He shall glorify me: for he shall receive of mine, and shall shew it unto you. All things that the Father hath are mine: therefore said I, that he shall take of mine, and shall shew it unto you."
> (John 16:12-15)

As witnesses, the apostles were to record the life and work of the Lord Jesus on earth, but they were also to make known all that which *after His ascension* He would make known to them. This later revelation would come to them in a different way – by the Holy Spirit. Nevertheless, the later revelation would not be different in kind, because the Lord most clearly says that the Holy Spirit 'shall take of mine'. Referring to the Holy Spirit, Jesus says, *"Whatsover he shall hear, that shall he speak: and he will shew you things to come"*. The Lord Jesus is here speaking about definite material, already present in His consciousness, but which He has not yet imparted to them, but which, after His ascension, the Holy Spirit will take from the Lord Jesus – *"he shall take of mine"*– in order by inspiration to communicate it to the apostles. As if to especially emphasise this point, the Lord Jesus repeats it three times: in verse 13, *"he shall not speak of himself, but whatsoever he shall hear"*; in verse 14, *"He shall glorify me: for he shall receive of mine"*; then in verse 15, *"therefore said I, that he shall take of mine, and shall shew it unto you."* The things spoken of here are **thoughts** – *"he will guide you into all truth"* – and **purposes** – *"he will shew you things to come"* – already present in the mind of the Saviour. Both the thoughts and the purposes are obtained by hearing and after that transmitted by the Holy Spirit by speaking, verse 13. This does not refer to that which Jesus spoke after His resurrection, but of that which should come to the apostles by direct inspiration.

Not only would the Holy Spirit reveal these things, but also enable them *to retain* what Jesus has already revealed to them whilst He was with them but which might escape their failing memories. The Holy Spirit would guard against this, *"he shall teach you all things, and bring all things to your remembrance, whatsoever I have said unto you"* (John 14:26). As far as the apostle Paul was concerned, there could be no remembrance brought of the ministry of the Lord in this way because he had not been with Him during His ministry on earth. Nevertheless, Paul tells us that the Lord Jesus had revealed the Gospel to him, *"For I have received of the Lord that which also I delivered unto you"* (1 Corinthians 11:23). He repeats this later in the same letter when speaking about the resurrection.

> "For I delivered unto you first of all that which I also received, how that Christ died for our sins according to the scriptures..." (1 Corinthians 15:3 ff.)

When speaking about Christian marriage in the seventh chapter of the same epistle, Paul says, *"But to the rest speak I, not the Lord"*(v.12). This statement should not be understood to mean that what he was saying carried no divine authority, but that Christ had given no directions in this particular matter when on earth. In this passage, Paul is speaking, not from memory, but by *direct inspiration* of the Holy Spirit.

> "But I certify you, brethren, that the gospel which was preached of me is not after man. For I neither received it of man, neither was I taught it, but by the revelation of Jesus Christ." (Galatians 1, 11-12)

The Lord Jesus appointed the apostles as a definite body and gave to them the task of being His witnesses in this very special and precise sense *until the end of the world.* That they might fulfil this task, He promised and granted to them the inspiration of the Holy Spirit.

## The unique role of the apostles

Apostles and prophets are spoken of together in the Bible. Both are extraordinary manifestations, both have a very specific meaning, and both are unique. Prophets are those, both in Old and New Testament times, who spoke by the direct inspiration of God to His people. Sometimes this would involve future events, but equally what they said often had reference to what was going on at the time. Sometimes what they said was recorded in writing, but often it was not. The apostles are different from prophets, but they are also quite different from ministers of God's Word today. Their office is unique.

Scripture refers to *holy apostles, holy prophets* (Revelation 18:20). This simply means that they were set apart to God for that exclusive purpose designated by Him. The apostles were set apart to a very specific task by the power of God's Spirit. In this sense they are also set apart from other men, occupying a very different level than other teachers or ministers of the Gospel throughout all dispensations. They stand with a foot in both the Old and the New dispensations and have a prophetic significance for both the Church and Israel.

> "And Jesus said unto them, Verily I say unto you, That ye which have followed me, in the regeneration when the Son of man shall sit in the throne of his glory, ye also shall sit upon twelve thrones, judging the twelve tribes of Israel."
> (Matthew 19:28)

All twelve apostles were all Jewish, also Paul, the apostle to the Gentiles.

Throughout His earthly ministry, the Lord Jesus repeatedly spoke of the very special way in which the twelve would be His witnesses, but only after they had received the Holy Spirit in a once-for-all-time extraordinary manner. Until this time, they were to keep themselves out of the public eye and to remain in Jerusalem.

> "The former treatise have I made, o Theophilus, of all that Jesus began both to do and teach, Until the day in which he was taken up, after that he through the Holy Ghost had given commandments unto the apostles whom he had chosen: to whom also he shewed himself alive after his passion by many infallible proofs, being seen of them forty days, and speaking of the things pertaining to the kingdom of God: And, being assembled together with them, commanded them that they should not depart from Jerusalem, but wait for the promise of the Father, which, saith he, ye have heard of me. For John truly baptized with water; but ye shall be baptized with the Holy Ghost not many days hence. ... But ye shall receive power, after that the Holy Ghost is come upon you: and ye shall be witnesses unto me both in Jerusalem, and in all Judaea, and in Samaria, and unto the uttermost part of the earth."
> (Acts 1:1-5; 8)

These words refer particularly to the apostles whom Christ had chosen, including verse eight.

The apostles' position with respect to the Lord was unique.

> "And the Word was made flesh, and dwelt among us, (and we beheld his glory, the glory as of the only begotten of the Father,) full of grace and truth." (John 1:14)

They were obviously not the only ones to see the Lord, but they were to be witnesses of what they had seen in a special way to bring God's revelation of His Son to His people. The life of God had thus been manifested among men in a manner apprehended by the physical senses, one that could be seen and handled. Not all, even then, had seen and handled, but the apostles most certainly had done so. This was to be declared and because of their testimony lead us to fellowship with the Father, with the Son, and with them.

It is a serious error to claim, as do Pentecostal-charismatics, that this fellowship with the apostles is perpetuated today in their churches through 'apostolic gifts', or through bishops as successors to the apostles in the case of the church of Rome. The 'signs and wonders' of today are not a sign of identification with the apostles, but reveal apostates and false Christs.

> "For false Christs and false prophets shall rise, and shall shew signs and wonders, to seduce, if it were possible, even the elect." (Mark 13:22)

The relationship we have with the apostles today will be because of their unique testimony to the Lord fixed in Scripture. This testimony of the apostles we hold in our hands is given that we may be translated from darkness into the fellowship of eternal life. There is no other testimony but theirs through which we can receive eternal life, authorised as it was by our Lord Himself.

> *As the apostles are no longer with us, as their testimony is for all time fixed in a book, there can be no continuing revelation outside the Bible.*

Those who claim new revelations, that there is more than Scripture, are deceived and deceivers.

We have fellowship with the apostles in that the preaching of the apostolic Gospel has its end in the bringing together of the one body of Christ. The Holy Spirit is given only to those incorporated into this body. Not simply individuals, but a body will be redeemed. One cannot be saved but by being incorporated into that body, there is no salvation outside it. The inflowing of the Holy Spirit came into this body at Pentecost, initially through the apostles, so that no one today can receive any spiritual gift or any experience of the Holy Spirit outside that body. Contrary to much popular teaching today, there can be no repetition of Pentecost, nor need there be. We must not interpret Pentecost in an individualistic way. We receive the Holy Spirit by virtue of being members of that one body into which the Holy Spirit was poured at a never-to-be-repeated Pentecost. Those who expect or pray for a repeat of Pentecost have thus failed to understand its true meaning and fallen into serious error.

## The apostles are the permanent leaders of the Body of Christ

Christ is the head of the Church, which is His body, and the apostles remain its designated *permanent* leaders. The apostles are not to be thought of as the foundation of the Church only in the sense of being the first pastors and teachers of the

Christian Church, to be followed by other leaders as they passed on.

> "Now therefore ye are no more strangers and foreigners, but fellowcitizens with the saints, and of the household of God; and are built upon the foundation of the apostles and prophets, Jesus Christ himself being the chief corner stone; in whom all the building fitly framed together groweth unto an holy temple in the Lord: in whom ye also are builded together for an habitation of God through the Spirit."
>
> (Ephesians 2:19-22)

The apostles remain to this day the permanent foundation of the Church of Christ. They have not been replaced nor succeeded. Such is their relationship to the Church that in Revelation, where we are given a glimpse of *"the holy city, new Jerusalem, coming down from God out of heaven, prepared as a bride adorned for her husband"* (Revelation 21:2), we find that this city has *"twelve foundations, and in them the names of the twelve apostles of the Lamb"* (v.14). The apostles have a meaning that is not passing, but permanent; so that when the New Jerusalem is built, it will rest on the same foundation as now, hence the names of the apostles on its foundations.

The apostles are unique both at the time of the Church in New Testament times and in a more extensive and permanent manner. It was given to them to found the first Christian Churches, but also to provide a written account of the revelation of the Lord Jesus valid for all time. They were given a power and authority to ordain, to command and judge in a way not seen since. The apostles are no longer with us, but their authority *remains* with us through the writings committed to them by the Holy Spirit and to which we have access in the Bible.

> *Apostolic authority is still exercised in the Church not through an office, not through charismatic gifts, but through the teaching and doctrine contained in the Bible.*

We are not at liberty to add to this seeing the apostles are no longer with us, nor are we at liberty to diminish or reinterpret it 'according to a modern idiom'. Here we have the fullest possible expression in writing of the thoughts, not simply of men, but of the Holy Spirit by whom they wrote. In many ways, this may be considered the most significant aspect of the apostles' work, but it is certainly the most enduring. The actual Churches founded by the apostles have long since disappeared, but this inheritance given to the Church of Christ remains.

The apostles were a closed circle of men and every effort made to reopen this circle is foolish and doomed to failure. Such new 'apostles' lack a call directly from Christ Himself, and the authority imparted to them by the Lord Jesus Himself. The day of 'prophets' among us too is gone. Prophets receive a revelation of knowledge directly from God that does not normally come simply through the illumination of the mind to Scripture.

There may be admitted a very general meaning to the word 'prophet' as one who today tells forth that which has been revealed in Scripture and it may be used to indicate a particular gift and insight in applying the Scriptures in the modern world, but this is the most we can say. Equally, the word 'apostle' may be applied in a very wide sense of being sent out by the Lord to preach the Gospel. Apostle simply means 'one who is sent'. It stems from Greek, whereas the more commonly used word 'missionary', with precisely the same meaning, is derived from Latin. An example of such an apostle, a missionary not among the twelve, is Barnabas (Acts 14:14). It follows that those who maintain the continuance of the apostles today either in a continuing office, as the Pope in the Roman Church or as a group of men in Pentecostal 'apostolic' sects, will also compromise the unique and sole authority of Scripture – and we must include those today who imagine the apostolic work is perpetuated in apostolic gifts. In all these cases, there will inevitably be an authority above or alongside Scripture to set it at naught. The case for a closed body of revealed knowledge is bound together with the idea of a closed circle of apostles. God gave to them what was to be known, they being gone and not continuing, there can be no further revelation.

Scriptural evidence for closed circle of apostles is clear from the fact that it was always just twelve, all appointed by the Lord Jesus and granted exceptional power and gifts in connection with their office. When Judas killed himself the number was quickly made up.

> "And they appointed two, Joseph called Barsabas, who was surnamed Justus, and Matthias. And they prayed, and said, Thou, Lord, which knowest the hearts of all men, shew whether of these two thou hast chosen, That he may take part of this ministry and apostleship, from which Judas by transgression fell, that he might go to his own place. And they gave forth their lots; and the lot fell upon Matthias; and he was numbered with the eleven apostles." (Acts 1:23-26)

It is from Paul as much as any other that we are made aware of the special nature of the apostolate:

> "By whom we have received grace and apostleship."
> (Romans 1:5)
> "For he that wrought effectually in Peter to the apostleship of the circumcision, the same was mighty in me toward the Gentiles." (Galatians 2:8)

The very fact that *Paul* was called to be an apostle is in itself evidence of the closed number of the apostles. Were the number of chosen apostles not limited, it would have made little sense to question Paul's apostleship. Many questioned his apostleship because he had not been one of the twelve. How could he have been a witness of the Lord? Forced to defend himself, Paul did so most vigorously, contending his apostleship was no different in essence from that of Peter. The Damascus experience of Paul was less a conversion, for after Pentecost this was the work of the Holy Spirit, but its primary significance lies in being a meeting with the risen Lord. He was appointed an apostle in the very Church that he was persecuting. The question as to there being twelve apostles only and Paul being added to them is not as problematic as at first appears. The twelve apostles parallel the twelve tribes. One of the tribes of Israel was replaced by *two* others. In the place of Simeon came Manasseh and Ephraim, so Judas was replaced by Matthias and Paul. We cannot say that the apostles acted precipitately in the appointment of Matthias, there was a vacancy in need of immediate filling, but the apostolate without the apostle Paul is unthinkable.

The calling of the apostles gave to the Church a power and authority not previously found among men. God's power was exercised through the instrumentality of these men. The Lord Jesus was no longer on earth to direct His Church, but He had not forsaken His Church. The Church was not to begin its life in ignorance, struggling about to find the truth, hopefully at the end to attain a clearer understanding of the truth. From the start, it would have available all the knowledge it needed. Through the apostles, the Church from the beginning stood in the light of the whole counsel of God. Nothing that would develop subsequently would surpass that committed to the apostles and through them to the Church.

There is still *a development of understanding* of that which has been revealed to us in Scripture, both as individuals and as a body of believers down through the years since. Nevertheless, we have no more knowledge in itself available to us than was available to the early Church, not a grain more than at the death of the last apostle. Nothing can be added, all is there that ever will be there. Unlike those who would modernise our Churches, bring them up-to-date, seek new knowledge in new experiences and learning, *our treasure is always behind us, we must always go back to the apostles.*

Through the apostles was given to the Church something not previously possessed by Israel, nor was it in our possession directly after the ministry of the Lord Jesus, who Himself said:

> "I have yet many things to say unto you, but ye cannot bear them now. Howbeit when he, the Spirit of truth, is come, he will guide you into all truth: for he shall not speak of himself; but whatsoever he shall hear, that shall he speak: and he will shew you things to come. He shall glorify me: for he shall receive of mine, and shall shew it unto you."
>
> (John 16:12-14)

Paul speaks of

> "...the revelation of the mystery, which was kept secret since the world began, but is now made manifest, and by the scriptures of the prophets, according to the commandment of the everlasting God, made known to all nations for the obedience of faith." (Romans 16:25-26)

Some knowledge of saving faith was available to our first parents in the garden, but also to the Patriarchs and Israel. Truth was revealed to the Patriarchs that was unknown in Paradise, and later revealed to Israel of which the Patriarchs knew nothing. Through our Lord came things unknown before in Israel. Truth was revealed to the Church through the apostles that was not given by our Saviour whilst on earth. Therefore, there can be no distinction made between the teaching of the apostles and the Lord, such as some godless theologians have suggested. All is the same doctrine of Christ;

that which the apostles received was given by Him and to us indirectly through the apostles. They were not independent persons bringing doctrine in and of themselves, but they were instruments of the Holy Spirit through whom the Lord Jesus was teaching His Church.

Had it been God's intention that the Church was to survive only during the lifetimes of the apostles and confined to the Jewish world, the spoken word of the apostles would have been sufficient.

*The purpose of God is that the Gospel should be taken to the corners of earth to every creature in all the days before the return of the Lord Jesus. A written revelation is therefore indispensable.*

As we read the writings of the apostles, we do not always seem to find any clear understanding that what they had written would reach such a wide readership. The epistles were written for particular local Churches and their needs at that time. Nevertheless, under God, they were ordained by God, with or without the writer's express knowledge, to edify the Church of all time.

We have said that these writings have two elements, that which was to be known from the apostles of the Saviour's life and teaching during His time on earth, and those things which the Lord Jesus promised would be made known to them after He had returned to heaven. Recording these things in writing was essential for the Church in its worldwide extension and its duration throughout time. As the number of Churches began to grow and the distances between them became greater, Paul was obliged to commit things to writing as the personal delivery of verbal instructions became increasingly difficult. Other apostles did the same. Alongside these epistles came the narratives of the Lord's life and teaching, His death and resurrection, the Acts of the Apostles. Finally, given direct instructions by the Lord Himself, John on Patmos wrote the book of Revelation, writing down *the things which thou hast seen, and the things which are, and the things which shall be hereafter* (1:19).

From Paul's epistles we see that he wrote much more than has been included in the New Testament, and this was doubtless true of apostolic writings in general. Under the guiding hand of God all these writings were sifted down to those we now have in Scripture. Both Old and New Testaments we have by the Holy Spirit, the veritable Word of God. To write an epistle to the Romans the Spirit of God prepared a Paul, as He also prepared a John and a Peter. This had been equally true of the Old Testament prophets and writers. All the circumstances of their lives were ordered by God to this end.

> "Then the word of the LORD came unto me, saying, Before I formed thee in the belly I knew thee; and before thou camest forth out of the womb I sanctified thee, and I ordained thee a prophet unto the nations." (Jeremiah 1:4-5)
> "But when it pleased God, who separated me from my mother's womb, and called me by his grace, to reveal his Son in me, that I might preach him among the heathen; immediately I conferred not with flesh and blood."
> (Galatians 1:15-16)

Their thoughts and reflections would arise at the behest of the Holy Spirit. By that same Spirit, they would be kept from error and be led into all truth. God foreknew in eternity what the book He would inspire was to be like, down to the last jot and tittle. God prepared in advance all those elements that were to be put together as part of His one Word.

## Inspiration essential

Not all the writers of the New Testament were apostles, nor do we have anything to hand suggesting they wrote under apostolic direction, although it is clear that both Mark and Luke had very close contact with the apostles. Nevertheless, they will have obtained much that they wrote from the apostles themselves. In the final instance, that which gives authority to *all* the writings of Scripture is not alone the apostolic connection, *but that all that was written was directly inspired by the Spirit of God.*

> *Whilst the doctrine of the apostles is authoritative as no other, the guarantee to us that the Bible we read is in all things accurate and reliable lies in the fact that it comes to us graphically inspired of the Holy Spirit.*

The apostles are the designated instruments by which the knowledge of God comes to us, but whether the New Testament Scriptures are made up solely of their writings is not the point. The important fact is that every writer was inspired of God as he wrote. Even the endorsement of the apostles would be insufficient to guarantee accuracy and authority without inspiration. The Bible derives its ultimate authority from the fact that it is the inspired Word of God and not because of anything intrinsic in the instruments through whom it comes to us.

Without inspiration, there can be no certainty that the records we have are accurate. To guarantee accuracy on a human level such accounts would have meant someone would have had to write down what was said at the time and there would have had to be countless witnesses as to precisely what happened on each occasion. Much of Martin Luther's writings have come to us second-hand. His sermons, his *Table Talk* and, although likely to be pretty close to what Luther said, we have no absolute certainty that what we are reading is an infallibly accurate account, nor would we expect it to be. This is not true of Scripture; divine inspiration is its guarantee. We cannot *prove* its truth by external evidence, nor do we need to. This would lead to a denial of it. God the Holy Spirit gave it and there can be no better surety than that. Were a thousand honest witnesses to rise from the dead and give testimony, it would still be less than sufficient. The record of the Holy Spirit is not to be surpassed nor doubted by mortal men. My eternal salvation depends upon the accuracy and reliability of the biblical account. Shall it then rest upon the testimony of men and their ability to prove anything? Shall evidence for the resurrection of our Saviour depend upon the shaky testimony of individuals? Rather, it must come to us guaranteed by the Holy Spirit, nothing less will do.

> *Let the list of witnesses for the credibility of the Scripture writers fill a book; let it stretch around the globe; let the willingness, suitability, honesty of the witnesses be impeccable, it would all prove nothing! The moment we feel the need for such proof at that same instant our faith in the Word of God has dissolved into nothing. Nothing can surpass the testimony of the Holy Spirit in giving us a divinely inspired book.*

The fact is that revelation of God came to the apostles in a manner that could not be detected by others and so there could be no external testimony to it. On the rare occasions that an audible voice was heard, it appears that it could be understood by no others.

> "Father, glorify they name. Then came there a voice from heaven, saying, I have both glorified it, and will glorify it again. The people therefore, that stood by, and heard it, said

that it thundered: others said, An angel spake to him. Jesus answered and said, This voice came not because of me, but for your sakes."

(John 12:28-30)

Both in the case of Paul on the road to Damascus and John on Patmos, the voice need to be supplemented with a spiritual operation of the God's Spirit. *The nature of Scripture is such that it cannot be verified by human evidences.* Revelation would not be revelation could other persons have had the same access to it as those to whom it came originally.

Such conviction as there can be that the Scriptures that the Bible is indeed the veritable Word of God comes to us by a conviction worked in us by the Holy Spirit as to the reliability of the Person who speaks to us in it. As we are touched by the love of our Saviour to us, even whilst yet in our sins, so our trust and faith in Him is such that we do not doubt His Word.

> *Can we then trust our Lord for our soul's salvation and at the same time doubt His Word? Impossible! We trust His Word because we trust HIM; if we doubt it, it is because we do not trust HIM.*

We have no hesitation in claiming that we have a predestined Bible, the precise content and form of which had already been given in eternity. This includes all events, means, and persons by which that preconceived form would be actualised in the created world. During the course of time, all kinds of events transpire, people appear and disappear not knowing each other. In the midst of this, a number of people are inspired to produce, without necessarily being aware of the overall higher purpose at the time, a written record of facts and thoughts given by God in a form prescribed by Him. According to a plan devised by God, a structure gradually comes about through the years where different persons have worked without consulting each other, nor having seen the whole. No one man had seen the whole plan behind Scripture. Not one writer had simply added his contribution after due premeditation, nor persuaded others to do the same. Behind that which entered the human consciousness was that which was eternally within the heart and mind of God. It was God who created each of these writers, so endowed, led and empowered them that they contributed to Scripture that which He had foreordained. The thoughts did not go forth from men, but from God. Every Scripture document by every writer down through the years both in content and form was not a matter of accident, but was predetermined by the will of God. Only in this way can we have an authoritative and infallible Word.

> *"For ever, O Lord, thy word is settled in heaven"*
> **(Psalm 119:89)**

CHAPTER 10

# The Bible and Language

*"For as the rain cometh down, and the snow from heaven, and returneth not thither, but watereth the earth, and maketh it bring forth and bud, that it may give seed to the sower, and bread to the eater: So shall my word be that goeth forth out of my mouth: it shall not return unto me void, but it shall accomplish that which I please, and it shall prosper in the thing whereto I sent it."*
(Isaiah 55:10-11)

It is a game in which nearly all of us must have participated in at one time or another. Everyone sits around the room next to each other. Someone at the start of the line whispers a sentence into the ear of his or her neighbour. The same words pass from person to person until the end of the line. The last person repeats what he has heard, everyone laughs, end of game. The fun, of course, is to compare what was said at the beginning of the line with what finally emerges at the end, the two will inevitably be quite different. The longer the line, the greater will be the discrepancy between what was said at the beginning and then at the end.

The Scriptures are fixed and pure and preserved from all the effects of sin. Human tradition, because of the fallibility of memory and the perversity of the human heart, cannot be entirely trusted. When something is fixed accurately in writing or printing there can be no dispute. That which is settled in heaven must be fixed on earth. Were the Word of God to be passed from person to person by word of mouth the danger would always be that it would be changed. Once available to us in a God-inspired written or printed form there is a guarantee that the revealed thoughts of God come to us in an authentic and fixed form. It is not by accident, but by the distinct will of God that His revelation should not come to us by oral tradition but in the permanent form of Scripture.

## The word and the letter

All things are known to God from eternity and the place of each and everything according to His purpose. Every object pre-exists its own literary life, existing first in the mind of God and then in creation. Knowledge and understanding begin in the consciousness of God. *Our understanding must be a finite replica of that which is found in God,* if it is to be according to the truth. To bring this about God has revealed to His prophets and apostles what He wants us to know. He then caused this to be infallibly recorded by them in written form in Scripture. We then take up this Word and, enlightened by the same Holy Spirit who revealed and inspired it, as we read it those sacred words will reproduce in our consciousness that which was in the heart of God from all eternity. In this whole process the utmost accuracy is essential, for without the assurance of God's preserving work down through the years with respect to the text, as well as faithfulness in the process of translation, this replication cannot take place.

A biblical understanding of language is rooted in what the Bible has to say about creation. It is to be expected that the same individuals who take on new bible translations and scorn us poor souls still wedded to the *Authorised Version* will reserve the same scorn and abuse for those still insisting upon a literal six-day creation, whilst they have themselves taken on a theologically sanitised version of evolution. The Bible tells us Adam gave names to every living creature.

> "And out of the ground the LORD God formed every beast of the field, and every fowl of the air; and brought them unto Adam to see what he would call them: and whatsoever Adam called every living creature, that was the name thereof." (Genesis 2:19)

He also gave his wife the name 'woman'.

> "And Adam said, This is now bone of my bones, and flesh of my flesh: she shall be called Woman, because she was taken out of Man." (Genesis 2:23)

These early passages of Genesis indicate that God spoke with Adam and Eve. It is evident that words as sounds were used. Right from the start, Adam was given a mind to understand God when He thus spoke along with the ability to use words and to speak, even before Eve appeared on the scene. As the experience of our first parents widened, the language they used would have become increasingly complex and their vocabulary much greater. Having had no childhood, Adam was created with an adult ability for language. We are all born with an *innate ability* for language that develops throughout our early years along with the ability to think and reason for ourselves, making use of an increasing vocabulary and ever more complex grammatical structures. Whilst most linguists today believe language is acquired rather than innate, a notable exception is the American linguist, Noam Chomsky. However, we need to be careful before drawing him onto our own side. He believes the innate 'mental representations and the operations that apply to them' are a central part of our *biologically determined nature,* which has come into being through the process of evolution.

Our mind recognises a two-fold manner of existence. It receives representations pictorially as images, but it also receives concepts as words. We see that some written languages, such as Chinese, retained the visual representation as pictorial characters or symbols. Others developed these pictorial representations into an alphabet system with each letter standing in the place of a sound. The symbols depend upon analogy and a similarity between the visible object and the mental image. All our thinking borrows from the visible. Without an analogy to the external world and the inner affinity, no unity of perception is possible. The connection between the sounds and representations of words are not arbitrary as modern linguists suppose. Words are used to express what we see and how we relate to what we see, and are drawn by way of symbolism from the world around us. These perceptions and relationships are then reflected in the way we position the words with each other, in grammar, syntax.

A child will initially view everything pictorially. As the months go by sounds and squeals express feelings and desires. These sounds and squeals eventually become words as he or she learns to speak. At first these words are used just as labels, little by little as the child grows and the ability to think develops, words are strung together in simple sentences and the world around is not only seen as pictures. Thinking and language are linked. With a constant diet of television in which visual images dominate and verbal communication is often minimal, the imagination stultifies, but more seriously the ability to think wastes.

Phonemes (from Greek *phōnēma*, meaning sound) are the smallest unit of the spoken language. A phoneme is to the spoken word what a letter is to the written word. If these are mere sounds without being words, then they are dead. If the phonemes or letters do not convey to my mind words carrying meaning, they cannot be of use to me. Paul goes into this in some detail when discussing 'tongues'.

"So likewise ye, except ye utter by the tongue words (*lógon*) easy to be understood, how shall it be known what is spoken? for ye shall speak into the air. There are, it may be, so many kinds of voices (*phonōn*) in the world, and none of them is without signification (*áphonon*). Therefore if I know not the meaning (*dúnamin*) of the voice (*phonēs*), I shall be unto him that speaketh a barbarian, and he that speaketh shall be a barbarian unto me." (1 Corinthians 14:9-11)

A 'barbarian' is someone whose language makes no sense to me. I can hear someone uttering sounds in a language I do not understand and may even be able to reproduce the sounds myself, but unless those sounds are meaningful to me, they remain just an empty noise. A word manifests itself in sound through individual phonemes, or in letters as a transcript of those sounds. Words can be manifested in the form of sound as phonemes or in writing as letters. If we only study the nature of the phonemes and letters, which is the expression of life, the meaning itself will not have been grasped. Only when we reach beyond the outward expression, which we have heard or seen, to the power, the dynamic, the life of the word, do we also reach the meaning (see v. 11 above). The word, the *lógos*, originates in the life of the consciousness. This becomes available to others when uttered or written using sounds or letters.

The 'word' (*lógos*) does not refer to the letter (*grámma*), but refers to thoughts uttered as speech. It is not thought alone, but a thought uttered as speech. The importance of this in the context of verbal inspiration becomes immediately obvious. Thoughts are not to be divorced from the words that carry them. There can be no inspiration of thought without words. The word uttered precedes the word written. The 'letter' (*grámma*) refers to anything written, to that which uses the letters of the alphabet. A 'grammar' school was where children once went to learn the art of letters. The highest academic accolade is to be made a 'doctor of letters'. The Lord

Jesus had been to no rabbinical school to learn His letters, hence the Jews remark, *"How knoweth this man letters, having never learned?"* (John 7:15). How could He thus presume to teach? The word is manifested in letters. Letters turn spoken words into writing. Words cannot be written without letters. The physical letters are of no significance, are dead, without the substance. Written language amounts to more than scribbles on a page. Letters on their own are dead, even as is the body without the spirit. When we are occupied only with the *expression,* the object itself has not been grasped. The Jews, Paul tells us, were preoccupied with the outward expression to the neglect of the substance that lies behind it.

> "But he is a Jew, which is one inwardly; and circumcision is
> that of the heart, in the spirit, and not in the letter."
> (Romans 2:29)

Paul encourages believers, *". . . that we should serve in newness of spirit, and not in the oldness of the letter"* (Romans 7:6). We must reach beyond the physical expression of that which we observe to the life behind it, in the case of a word *(lógos)* to its life in consciousness. The word we hear as sound or see on a printed page indicates what is going on within the conscious life. Without this life, the letter is dead.

Writing is a codified form of the spoken word enabling the repeated reproduction of what was originally said, and before that of what was originally thought using those same words. Although images may present themselves to our minds as pictures, we cannot have thoughts as such without words. We understand words only when we receive them together with their meaning. Therefore, if God clothes His thoughts in human words, by giving us His words He gives us His thoughts. A thought is born in our consciousness and clothed in words, which may remain in the mind or be uttered as speech. Memory and language enable what has been thought and said to travel down the years. Nothing in our mind can either be retained permanently or passed on without some means of doing this. A concept is retained by language in words. What has been uttered may then be recorded on paper using letters. Although we may still perceive pictorially, without words we cannot fully think.

Inspiration has to do with the communication of the uttered word (*lógos*) to God's chosen instruments and its accurate recording in written language (*grámma*). Writing (*grámma*) records the uttered word (*lógos*), which is vehicle or body by which consciousness is expressed externally and can be known by others. Whilst word and letter are distinct from each other, clearly without word, letter can have no meaning and expresses nothing; they become nothing more than marks on the page. *Grámma* without *lógos* is dead. Letters that do not express the living words, springing from the heart and consciousness of a living being are dead. To reduce Scriptures to arguments about scratches and marks on a bit of paper *without having regard to the living word uttered* is to kill it dead. Paul writes,

> "...our sufficiency is of God; Who also hath made us able ministers of the new testament; not of the letter (*grámmatos*), but of the spirit: for the letter (*grámma*) killeth, but the spirit giveth life." (2 Corinthians 3:5-6; see also John 7:15, Romans 2:27-29 & 7:6)

Letters as written signs cannot be divided off from the word, thought or uttered. Without them, we have no access to the Word of God. It is therefore essential that the writing is accurate down to the last jot and tittle, if we are to know in truth what God has revealed to us of His thoughts in human language. The outward physical writing alone is meaningless.

## The spoken and the written word

Writing ought to be regarded as an aid rather than an end in itself. Were our memory and ability not as limited as they are, the need for writing would hardly have arisen. Writing was also prompted by the need to preserve and guard that which had been spoken and to prevent that which had been agreed upon from being misrepresented. Material coming to us on the internet can usually quite easily be edited or changed, but once something has been committed indelibly to paper it is there forever. Writing attempts to capture the physical aspect of our language so that by seeing and interpreting these signs a second person may understand what has transpired in the unseen world of thought in another person or what has left his lips. Writing does the same as an audio recorder, but meaning is attached not to sounds but to signs made on paper or other material. Were it possible for our voice to transcribe itself immediately on paper, an absolute form of writing would exist. Writing is not produced by our voice but by our thinking mind. Our mind receives the sounds and records them by signs on paper in such a way that another who sees them is able to reproduce the sounds and impart to them the same content and meaning as the original speaker. It is impossible to tell whether without sin writing would still have taken the course it has done. Doubtless, to assist our finitude some development along the same lines would have taken place. The need to communicate across distances would have still existed as it does now. It remains to be seen whether in glory the need for such aids as writing and books will still exist. What we cannot say is that the need for writing has arisen only because of sin, although due to sin the need for writing has intensified.

As finite human beings, we are subject to the limitations of time and space. Writing enables men to speak beyond their own time and in more than one place at any one time and to a limited degree overcomes these physical human limitations. Writing brings an abiding quality and permanence to that which would otherwise be transitory. That which we produce with our voice disappears into the air and is remembered hardly by ourselves and perfectly by God alone, who hears and marks every word we speak. Our voice has no ability to preserve what it produces. The invention of writing overcomes this limitation. After many years what was spoken is able to perform the same service that it did when originally uttered. Words spoken hundreds, even thousands of years ago, come to life again in written form. As a result of being written down thought is set free from the limitations imposed upon it by time.

The whole human race does not live upon the earth at the same time, but appears in succeeding generations. Through the written Word, one Word of God can be given to the whole human race. Only through writing has it become possible to collect together human thought and hand it down from age to age. Special revelation from God was not given for the one generation in which it appeared, even as the appearance of the Lord Jesus was not simply for those who were privileged to live in Palestine at that time, but was for the *whole* world until the end of time. The necessity for this special revelation to be written down immediately becomes evident. Only in this way could it be a revelation to our whole race.

Writing also overcomes the limitations of space. It is bound neither to a single place nor people. Who can extend the sound of his voice even half a mile? The word once committed to writing knows no such bounds but travels across the world. A speaker may convey his thoughts to several thousand people at one time, perhaps aided by radio waves but even these eventually fade. He who writes will reach far more. Writing overcomes at a stroke the limitations imposed on the human voice by time and space. The written word is truly international uniting the nations of the earth. In the Bible, special revelation is freed from all restrictions of time and space. God so loved *the world*, not just individuals, not just one nation. Only through writing can the Word of God fulfil its end. Writing perpetuates and disperses thought bringing it within the reach of all. Writing gives thoughts wings. When the thoughts of God are clothed in written human language, Scripture is the form they take.

The timing of the invention of printing from moveable types was perfect in the providence of God. It rapidly accelerated the power of the written word in a manner that arguably exceeds that of the advent of the Internet in our own time. In Europe before 1500, there were possibly 35,000 printed books; they were mostly in Latin and therefore inaccessible to most people. Between the years 1500 and 1640 in England alone, 20,000 different items in English were printed; prominent among them was the Word of God. The effect of this communications revolution was the spread of books in the vernacular, particularly English and German, but also it is estimated that as a direct result of this by 1600 half the population of England could read. It can be no accident that in 1611 the *Authorised Version* appeared.

The significance of Johann Gensfleisch zum Gutenberg's invention of printing around 1450 was that he used *moveable types*, individual letters. This simplified and allowed flexibility in the printing process. The Chinese had been printing on paper from blocks for about a thousand years before this time. The fact that Chinese was written using ideographic characters severely hampered any ability to develop printing more flexibly. Good Chinese writers today are likely to use anything up to twenty thousand different characters. Ten thousand characters must be mastered to read an average book. Chinese people learn to read by committing sentences, pages, and then whole books to memory and repeating them aloud in class. It is significant that the Bible was given in alphabetic languages where letters stand in the place of sounds. This means that what God actually *said* can be recovered precisely. An alphabetic system of writing has many advantages over those using ideographic symbols. Once the alphabet has been mastered with the spelling forms and sounds, reading can begin. Thousands of different characters must be mastered in order to begin reading Chinese. In an alphabetic system decoding immediately turns writing back into speech, making learning to read a straightforward undertaking thus facilitating a rapid spread of literacy.

Divine revelation sets itself against the sinful mind and rebellious heart of men. An impaired memory, personal idiosyncrasies, and wilful modification of what was revealed according to human inclinations are all but eradicated where there is a permanent written authoritative text. If it were not to be falsified, revelation had to take the permanent form of writing. Scripture therefore came to us in God-breathed written form rather than through oral tradition, preserved and kept by God. Despite this, there have, since earliest times, been those who have tampered with the texts, and produced twisted translations in order to give their own slant on what they think God ought to have said. However, in the presence of an authentic and authoritative text in the original languages, in English, or in any other tongue, the activities of these people is more readily discernable than were we dependent on the word of mouth alone. The authentic *written* Word of God has always been the surest safeguard against falsification. Without this sure standard one begins by questioning whether what was not given was somehow different and ends up by saying that it was something different. The Word of God had to be written down and in the providence of God printed for its purity to be preserved.

> "The words of the Lord are pure words: as silver tried in a furnace of earth, purified seven times. Thou shalt keep them, O Lord, thou shalt preserve them from this generation for ever." (Psalm 12:6-7)

In the English language, God has set His seal upon the *Authorised Version*. It is a faithful translation of that which God spoke to His prophets and apostles. It is a tried and tested standard by which we may identify deceivers and falsifiers of God's Word. One of the most evil effects of the proliferation of modern bible versions, each one claiming to be more authentic than the last, is that the single standard by which we can identify deceivers has been cast aside. Which version do we follow now? Everyone is right and some more so than others! To set aside the *Authorised Version*, replacing it with something less than genuine, is like debasing the currency. Even revising or changing it in any way will have the same effect. It is robbery! Leaving the gold standard enabled banks to operate with money that does not exist. Substitute bibles open wide the door to crooks and fraudsters.

Were that which has been done to our beloved Bible visited upon the works of Shakespeare, there would be an academic uprising in almost every University English department in the land and far beyond. When it comes to changing the Word of God, it seems textual 'scholars' of every hue knock each other over in the unseemly scramble to climb on board the ghost train to oblivion. Shakespeare is far less intelligible to the modern reader than the *Authorised Version*. When writing his plays Shakespeare raided the dictionary, his vocabulary exceeds 30,000 words, whereas the average educated individual today will have a vocabulary of about 15,000. Halve this again, add 500 or so, and we have the 'iron rations' vocabulary of the *Authorised Version* – as one secular language historian expresses it. With a vocabulary half the size of the average literate English speaker, from the point of view of its language the *Authorised Version* is more than accessible to the ordinary reader. It is ignorant nonsense to suggest otherwise.

One may be tempted to think only of the giving of revelation as from God and the invention of writing and later of printing from moveable types as something human. These things are far from being accidental, but are means thought out for us by God, which in His own time He caused us to find. The divine revelation is most eminently suited to writing and printing, because God made it that way. In the giving and dissemination of the Word of God to the ends of the earth making it accessible to every individual, human writing and the art of printing can attain no higher purpose. Writing and printing liberate us from dependence upon other men as we hold the Word of God in our own hands. It thus binds us to God. For as long as the Word of God was passed on from generation to generation before the writing of Scripture began, and also during the time of its writing, the great masses of the people remained dependent on a priestly class, upon prophets, in order to have knowledge of what God had said. Through writing and printing everyone can have the authentic Word of God to read in a language they can understand. For this reason, Rome opposed the distribution of Scripture and would retain for herself the ultimate authority in its interpretation. In a similar way, there are those who claim that they alone can tell us where among the texts the authentic Word of God is to be found today, and they alone are able to tell us what it really means. No version, no translation, according to them, is the authentic, perfect Word, so the untaught, simple saint of God must turn to a priestly class of scholars.

Only in a written and printed form can the Word of God achieve its full potential of power among men. By inspiration of God, the Word of God came forth in such a manner that the thoughts of God and the product of them, the Bible, are one and the same. This is the high and majestic view we have of the Bible. That which was over and above the created world has in this way entered into it.

## Language as a battlefield

Modern linguists deny that a precise and accurate reproduction of the thoughts of another is possible using the spoken or written words. The connection between words and meaning and their expression in speech or writing is an arbitrary one. Readers are said to *create* rather than *recover* meaning. Since Saussure's *Cours de linguistique générale* was published in 1916, the study of language has moved on. Meaning according to Saussure is simply a matter of differences; 'map' is 'map' because it is not 'tap' or 'rap' (see Chapter 6). Despite his claim that language is a closed and stable system, it is blatantly obvious that every word can only be defined by an apparently unending network of differences and that it is all but impossible to nail down a word to any specific meaning at all. Opening a dictionary does not help, for here we are faced with yet another string of words, each with its own series of defining opposites.

Any translation methodology, such as that used for the *New International Version* and most modern versions, that is based on this view of language cannot give us access to the unchangeable Word of God, 'for ever settled in heaven'. Also a system of hermeneutics interpreting the biblical text according to this shifting sand of meaning can proclaim no fixed eternal truth, no eternal Gospel, but allows the Bible say anything the reader fancies at the time. We reject these views of language as contrary to what a verbally inspired Bible demands we believe about language. *Apart from textual considerations, the importance of which we do not underestimate, this is first among many reasons as to why we reject out of hand all recent translations of Scripture, which are almost all based on these godless views.* What we face is an evil and wicked deception, a deliberate attempt to deny that there can be anything such as truth.

> **We cannot use methods and ideas designed to undermine the truth in order to propagate it!**

In a delimited structure, or 'open' text, meaning runs away into chaotic senselessness. Meaning is then the by-product of a never-ending word game that prevents us binding any one word to any one meaning. Should we ever lie under a surgeon's knife, let us hope that he will not have read his textbooks 'dynamically', that he knows more than approximately where my heart is, or my lungs, liver, and kidneys. Let us hope that the words in the textbooks he studied do not mean one thing to him and another to his colleagues! In reality, reading has to do with the accurate communication of precise information following agreed conventions and codes; *it is not the elaborate guessing game many linguists would have us believe.* In this way, the Bible can be made to mean everything and nothing. A word will not yield up meaning like a mirror does an image. Verbal inspiration becomes redundant nonsense. Meaning does not correspond in any direct way to the words that carry it, nor are the distinctions fixed either.

To be fair, linguists are not entirely unaware of many of these difficulties and some have tried to circumvent or explain them, others exploit them. The Italian writer, university professor and linguist, Umberto Eco has written extensively on 'semiotics', the science of signs. This way of thinking can be applied to every part of life. He distinguishes between 'open' and 'closed' texts. Closed texts would be those such as textbooks and instruction manuals where the precise communication of information is required. Open texts are largely literary texts, novels, poems, where the author deliberately sets out to stimulate the imagination of the readers, who create images for themselves, visualising in their minds that which is suggested by the book. This cannot always be deemed negative. There are texts that swing between the two types of text. The author of a travel book may well create pictures in the mind of the places described with great skill, yet these pictures will be particular to each individual reader according to their own knowledge, experience, and circumstances. There will be a mixture of objective information, which is independent of the reader and of subjective conjecture drawn from the reader's own experience. Here we see the tremendous power of the printed page to invade the privacy of our minds and direct the way we think. Writers play games with our minds in order to change the way we think, therefore let us be careful what we read, lest unaware we fall into evil ways. We become what we read, so let the Bible dominate the time we give to reading, these are pure words.

> "Finally, brethren, whatsoever things are true, whatsoever things are honest, whatsoever things are just, whatsoever things are pure, whatsoever things are lovely, whatsoever things are of good report; if there be any virtue, and if there be any praise, think on these things." (Philippians 4:8)

Linguists often distinguish between 'open' and 'closed' texts by attributing to them what they call denotative and connotative meaning. Denotative meaning is the purely objective meaning found in a dictionary or encyclopaedia, and it means what it means whatever the experience of the reader and his ability to understand it. Strictly speaking, connotative meaning cannot really be called meaning at all because it actually describes the subjective response of individuals to an objective denotative meaning. For example, I may look up the word 'Paris' in a lexicon and find something like: 'the name of the capital city of France'. This would be the denotative, objective, unchangeable meaning. We will know what a city is by having had a city pointed out to us, so that understanding will be dependent upon memory and experience, we once more internalise that which was external. Do we not know what a city is, then it must be explained to us drawing upon other things we have seen, so that we will often be told it is 'like' this or that. The extent of our understanding will often be dependent upon our experience. *This does not determine the actual meaning of the word 'city'; it only prescribes the extent of our understanding of what a city is.* The connotative 'meaning', or better still 'response' rather than meaning, would conjure up for us pictures of the Eifel Tower, Notre Dame, the Seine, and involve my memory of these places should I have ever been there as a tourist. It is largely subjective. A daily commuter from St Denis will view Paris very differently, the crowded 'metro', the rush to the office. This subjective connotative 'meaning' is variable, unstable, dependent upon circumstances, and will necessarily be different for each person. Meaning is in essence always objective and denotative, not dependent upon the reader, and the Word of God must always be read in this way. At times, we will read things in the Bible that are outside our experience and we shall need help in order to come to a proper understanding.

Eugene Nida has drawn precisely the same distinction by describing some translations as having 'dynamic equivalence' and others 'formal equivalence'. The dynamic translation is one that deliberately exploits the connotative response of the reader to the text and calls that meaning; its meaning exists primarily in the mind of the reader. A faithful translation of the Bible communicates to us God's thoughts; they prevail over all the thoughts of men. The connotations arising as we read make up our reaction to what God has said fixedly, these will vary from reader to reader according to our circumstances, understanding, and experience, *but we must never ever confuse these with the objective meaning of what is before us on the page*. The Bible does not *mean* what it means to me, it means what God gave it to mean quite apart from me. With the gracious illumination of the Spirit of God, I can *recover* that meaning, so that God's thoughts on the page before me become mine.

The final and complete break between words and meaning, dividing 'signifier' from the 'signified', came with what is known as 'post-structuralism'. Foremost among post-structuralists is the French philosopher, Jacques Derrida. Derrida is known for a method of textual criticism called 'deconstruction'. Others who work in the same way in their own fields include: the French historian Michael Foucault, the French psychoanalyst Jacques Lacan, the feminist critic and philosopher Julia Kristeva.

In 1968 there were student riots on the streets of Paris and Berlin that swept right across Europe attacking the authoritarianism of the institutions of learning, even threatening to collapse the French state. The return of Charles de Gaulle from exile led to a crushing defeat for the 'revolutionary' student forces in France in the name of patriotism, law, and order. In Germany the resistance lingered on in the small but very active student terrorist groups, Bader-Meinhof and RAF, eventually to fizzle out altogether, disappearing into various sections of the environmentalist 'greens'. This euphoric carnival of revolutionary chaos, unable to defeat the existing structures of state institutions by physical force, turned in on itself and in post-structuralism found a way instead to subvert language and destroy institutions effectively from inside. At least, in this way it was possible to avoid having a policeman's bullet pass through your head! That which was once open now began to work secretly, hidden away from public gaze. The enemy was any coherent 'hierarchical' belief-system offering a total, or 'big picture' view of life. Anarchistic spontaneity replaced systematic thought of any kind, which was condemned as repressive. There was not even now a system as a whole to fight against, such a thing did not exist – how this was known to be so was never explained. Organised left-wing politics was abandoned for 'decentred' alternatives, local political projects. Dogma was damned, whether capitalist or Stalinized Marxism.

At this point, language itself takes centre stage displacing terror as a means of political and intellectual subversion. Derrida sought to show that all ideas of truth, reality, knowledge, and meaning depended upon a 'naïve' understanding of language in which meaning was represented directly by appropriate words, this would include a biblical view. Words, he said, are not a stand-in for reality. Meaning being the fleeting product of words and inherently unstable, it is partly present and partly absent in the word. This effectively kills off all possibility of the communication of truth, reality, and meaning. Reality is constructed immediately by language rather than language being a reflection of it. The only reality to be known is that of our own discourse. The interpretation of a text, biblical or literary, had been concerned largely with understanding the meaning of the past. It now remained to be asked whether there was any past to be known other than as part of the function of the present discourse.

Meaning is not immediately present in a word, because meaning is equally a matter of what the word is not and so is always in some sense absent from it. Words are only what they are because of what other words are and equally what they are not. Furthermore, each time a word is used, because the context of that use will be different, so too will the meaning. No two situations ever being the same – change being the constant watchword – it becomes impossible to speak of words as having an 'original' meaning. How then, we ask, can God give us His Word given this situation? He cannot. Meaning will be scattered in some nebulous and undefined way along a whole string of words. Reading becomes rather like watching one of those very jerky early movie films on a projector in which the film keeps slipping! The sense of a sentence is not mechanically found in a combination of individual words. Any meaning there may be in a text contains elements of the words gone before and those coming after them. In some way, the whole chain of meaning in any one instance is shot through with that of all other meanings. No one word is ever 'pure' or its meaning final, but together with all other words form an inexhaustible complex network meanings. We read that the *"words of the Lord are pure words"* (Psalm 12:6), they mean what they mean, words and meanings have to be identical with themselves. Furthermore, it is only possible that these words should be kept and preserved *"from this generation for ever"* (v.7), if there truly is a stability to language, something these godless philosophers and word game specialists deny. They give us language where nothing is really definable, and everything is entangled within everything else. Were all this actually the case, speaking and writing would be like untangling an endless ball of wool with which an infinite number of kittens had been playing. Words cannot mean anything definite, for nothing is ever fixedly present in them. It simply is not possible for one person to convey to another what is in his heart and mind, because the meaning will always divide up and float away. If language is so unstable, then I too am unable to communicate with myself – to think. The idea of man himself as a stable being also disappears.

A biblical view of language is 'phonocentric' in the sense that the language of the living voice precedes any written language. It is also 'logocentric' in the sense that the Word (*lógos*) of God is the foundation of all our thought, language, and human experience. As we have seen, remove this and language disintegrates. To create, it was sufficient that 'God said'. Things are what they are because God created them that way, including language. As we name these things and describe their actions and states, we convey meaning and sense only because there is an inseparable bond between signifier and signified, between words and their meaning. To drive a wedge between the two is to fall into meaningless and chaos, infinite ambiguity. The Word of God is the meaning of meanings, the fulcrum upon which the whole system of truth moves, it is *the* Sign around which all others revolve and which they reflect. For this to be so, the Word of God must have pre-existed all other words.

Jacques Derrida labels all such structured thought systems, religious, political, or philosophical, each with their own hierarchy of meaning, as 'metaphysical'. He believes it is difficult for us to rid ourselves of something that is so embedded in our history and social consciousness. Even his own work he views as thus 'contaminated' by metaphysical thought. There must be a complete break with all structured hierarchical ways of thinking – especially those including a God who defines all things. All such defining first principles are to be 'deconstructed'. Within the 'structuralist' system (Saussure), principles and meanings are defined by what they exclude. For 'man' to be defined, he must ceaselessly shut out 'woman' as his opposite. She is all that he is not, and a reminder therefore of what he is. Yet, contradictorily he needs to accept woman and give her a positive identity just as desperately as he needs to reject her for without her, *he* cannot define himself. Although parasitically dependent upon her, he feels the need to subordinate and exclude her. At the same time, she represents something within himself that he needs to repress to maintain his own identity. The negative hides within its opposite the positive. Feminists, race and gender freaks, sodomites and lesbians, all draw on this outrageous thinking.

> *Once we leave the God-revealed account of human creation and the order and meaning it provides for human existence, this sort of appalling drivel replaces it.*

Authoritarian 'ideologies' erect rigid boundaries between what is true and false, between self and 'non-self', sense and nonsense, sanity and madness. These barriers are to be deconstructed. Whilst Saussure's structuralism was content to recognise these oppositions, Derrida's deconstruction aims to show how the thesis and antithesis (Marx), truth and falsehood, light and dark, secretly exist one within the other and then to unravel the logic ruling them by exposing the inherent contradictions. Post-structuralism is an utterly hypocritical position permitting criticism of everyone else's point of view without having to suggest an alternative. Nothing is true or even serious, so no answers are postulated. Texts are squeezed until every possibility of any meaning is drained from them. The aim of deconstruction is to dismantle all systems of truth and the institutions arising from them. Ultimately, it is a reiteration of the ancient cry, *"We will not have this man to reign over us"* (Luke 19:14).

What we are determines the way we use language. Consequently, if the way in which we use language can be undermined, so can the authoritarian belief-systems which determine it and society can be changed. At least, that is the idea. The possibility of the communication of truth, as in Scripture, is intimately bound up with a particular view of language that structuralism and post-structuralism has deliberately set about to undermine. Language generally and grammar in particular reflect precisely the way we look at all things. We cannot observe or think about anything without doing so 'grammatically'. We then give external expression to the manner in which we have been thinking in speech, or in writing as the codified form of speech.

> *Those able to influence the way language is used will also direct the way in which the users of that language think. To manipulate language is to manipulate the processes by which we all think.*

Educationalists, guided by structuralist and then by post-structuralist thinking, have been training teachers in this methodology since the 1930s and have dictated the methods by which children are taught to read and use the English language. The way that children think is guided more than anything else by how they are taught the English language.

"Train up a child in the way he should go: and when he is old, he will not depart from it" (Proverbs 22:6)

Train a child in godless ways of thinking at a young age and even after a sound conversion to Christ, it can take years before this is recognised and eradicated. It is essential that our children be taught habits of thinking and reading that coincide with a biblical view of language. This will have a significant effect on the way in which they approach the reading of the Bible, and even determine to what extent they can read it properly at all. Teaching Latin in 'Grammar Schools' had more to do with teaching pupils *to think* than it did with anything else. Few would make use of it after leaving school, but all would have developed their ability to think and reason along classical lines, to a greater or lesser degree. The particular structures of different languages go a long way to explain why French people think in a somewhat different way than do their German neighbours, and English-speakers think differently again.

In his book, *The Alphabetic Effect* (1986), Dr Robert K. Logan of the University of Toronto has gone so far as to say that even the writing system itself affects the way we reason. An ideographic system of writing, such as Chinese or Japanese, he maintains, is less conducive to abstract scientific thinking than an alphabetic script. To change the way we speak, to change the way we write, will necessarily change the way we think. Fortunately, the godless purveyors of this new way of looking at language are not entirely successful, nor can they succeed as they would wish, for their views being false can never work. Despite this, the confusion they cause is horrendous.

It comes to us with little surprise that those who believe the meaning of a sentence is somehow sprinkled along its length like sugar on a pudding tell our trainee teachers that reading is for children a 'psycholinguistic guessing game'. Although these methods are not altogether successful, nevertheless, many children leave school functionally illiterate to join an increasingly uneducated and ignorant populace. Eighty-nine percent of youngsters in Britain, should they read anything, will not reach beyond the disjointed and often verbless garbage of the picture-strewn tabloid press. Even Christian classics are now being republished in 'simplified English' because they are deemed too difficult for modern readers. If this is not grossly patronising, then it is patently tragic.

> *Modern bible versions fit this mindset as a casting does its die.*

All modern bible translations, but especially those translated by 'dynamic equivalence', are largely designed for 'dynamic' reading. The reader is not recovering a communication given by God once-for-all-time in the past, but listening for the voice of God from a string of words that have no fixed meaning. They may say one thing to one person and something quite different to someone else, depending upon the circumstances. The same words may even say something different to the same person on different occasions. Truth is in the end what the reader makes it. There is no underlying fixed meaning. No single reading of this bible is right or wrong, just different. The reader is not a passive recipient but an active co-creator to whom the bible text provides reading 'cues'.

This is how our children are taught to read in state schools today. Text books used in teacher training colleges throughout the land will say that reading is not about retrieving meaning from the text, it is not *decoding*, but *creating* a variety of meanings. There can be no single given meaning for any text only *plausible* meanings – whatever that means, if it can mean anything at all! A biblical understanding of language binds it immediately to an objective revelation of the truth, something that can be known only when, with the illumination of God's Spirit, we 'decode' the authentic Scripture text accurately having regard to grammar and vocabulary. Modern translations, even those using the so-called 'formal equivalence' translation method, are not designed to be read in this way. Today's readers will often find it difficult to read the *Authorised Version,* not because it is 'old' language, but because they have not been taught to read in the way the structure of its language demands. God, not the reader, is the

**243**

Creator of the meaning of Scripture and He has something to say to us. Those who approach the Bible with any other conviction than this are condemned to remain sitting in deep darkness. Contemporary linguistic methods cast a veil over the Word of God.

# CHAPTER 11

# A God-breathed Book

*"All scripture is given by inspiration of God, and is profitable for doctrine, for reproof, for correction, for instruction in righteousness: That the man of God may be perfect, throughly furnished unto all good works."* (2 Timothy 3:16-17)

What is more refreshing or invigorating than to step out into the garden first thing on a summer's morning? Hardly a soul is about. The dew lies thickly on the blades of grass and droplets sparkle on the plants. The air is fresh and cool. At the top of a tree, a blackbird sings its tiny heart out, a dog barks in the distance. The flowers stretch upwards on their stalks, opening their petals in a display of glorious colours. The believer joins in chorus with the blackbird, if only inwardly.

> *Heaven above is softer blue,*
> *Earth around is sweeter green;*
> *Something lives in every hue*
> *Christless eyes have never seen:*
> *Birds with gladder songs o'erflow,*
> *Flowers with deeper beauties shine,*
> *Since I know, as now I know,*
> *I am His and He is mine.*

Whilst the whole of creation cries out daily in praise to God, only men remain silent. They who more than any have reason to be thankful to God fail to recognise Him. God manifests

Himself as Creator in all that He has made, around us, but also within us. The believer rejoices on recognising the revelation of God in creation. To those still in unbelief, creation indicates a breach with God before whom we are all born as guilty sinners. The godless man strives energetically to deny his Creator. Isaiah laments over Israel,

> "The ox knoweth his owner, and the ass his master's crib: but Israel doth not know, my people doth not consider."
>
> (Isaiah 1:3)

That which creation recognises, sinful men deny. This revelatory *common grace* of God, 'common' because it touches all men, condemns all, for we all without exception ought with all creation to praise our Maker but by nature do not do so.

In an act of *special grace*, God has revealed Himself in the Bible as the Inspirer. God steps into our world, as it were from outside. Special revelation is not intrinsic to creation. However, things were not like this at the beginning before sin entered. This would not have been how God entered our consciousness before the fall. The present dualistic nature of revelation and of grace, *common* and *special*, will only disappear when in glory our consciousness is fully renewed. In our sinless Saviour, there was no such distinction. That which is today supernatural knowledge will one day be natural to us. In the place of our present incomplete understanding will come a seeing 'face to face'.

> "...whether there be prophecies, they shall fail; whether there be tongues, they shall cease; whether there be knowledge, it shall vanish away. For we know in part, and we prophesy in part. But when that which is perfect is come, then that which is in part shall be done away."
>
> (1 Corinthians 13:8-10)

## All one work of God's grace towards sinners

We will be touched by Scripture effectively only when we recognise that a breach exists between God and all mankind. We reach for Scripture in earnest when we realise all other channels to God have been stopped up and that there is no other route to Him. We cannot climb over the wall and enter in by another way. Only when we see that knowledge of God does not come to us along purely natural channels, will it dawn upon our souls that something more is needed. Then, we take down our Bible. Only when we recognise that we are cut off from a knowledge of God, once natural to mankind, will we be disposed to accept the divine witness in Scripture.

The Bible is a book for sinners. Driven by the Holy Spirit, as we are touched by Scripture, a deep sense of sin and alienation from God will intensify and incline us to seek salvation in Christ Jesus. The more powerfully this inward conviction of being a sinner is upon us, the more ready we shall be to accept the Scriptures. *The very presence of the Bible tells us the world has sinners in it.* Those who refuse the testimony of Scripture will also refuse Christ and thus be lost. This work of God's Spirit as to the authenticity and veracity of Scripture can always be traced to the starting point of a conviction of sin. Equally, the degree of certainty with respect to the divine origin of Scripture runs parallel with our sense of being sinners in need of God's grace.

Knowledge of God has gone out from Him, first breathed into the minds of His chosen instruments, who then, being carried along by God's Spirit, infallibly recorded this same knowledge in writing for the rest of mankind. God then gives assurance to those reading that these words are indeed from Him.

> *The content and the eventual form as the written words of Scripture both spring from a special work of God's grace.*

When speaking of inspiration we may distinguish between the in-breathing of the content of the revelation into the mind of the individual writer and the inspiration of the actual words recorded in Scripture, we are not at liberty to look at these two elements as being separate from each other. They stand in an indissoluble union. We are looking at *one* work of God. One aspect may be viewed as the *process* of inspiration and the other as the *product* of inspiration. In this sense we can speak of having an inspired Bible, every word of which was God-breathed. Both aspects of inspiration are expressions of the one intention of God to put an authoritative revelation within reach our lost race for all time.

The action of God did not finish once His work of revelation and inspiration was over. Whilst God is near and His glory is manifested all around us, He is also afar off. He approaches us at a distance through His Word. Yet, here He reveals His presence, speaks to us as though He were at our elbow. The Bible was not simply placed in the world, at which point God simply stood back to see what men would make of it. Now follows the continuing work of God's special providence in preserving, interpreting, and applying what He has given. This too is all part of *one work* in bringing His truth to our hearts. God has brought the Bible to us and subsequently He brings us to the Bible – and all by His grace. It is not that men seek and in stumbling around somehow find the Bible and so are led to God. From beginning to end, there is *one* unbroken action of grace going out from God by which He still works upon men to bring them to a knowledge of Himself. It is all *one work* of God.

> *The work of God in giving the Scriptures is not finished until it brings forth fruit in us to His glory, His Word returning to Him.*

This is the true sense of the much-quoted verses from Isaiah.

> "For as the rain cometh down, and the snow from heaven, and returneth not thither, but watereth the earth, and maketh it bring forth and bud, that it may give seed to the sower, and bread to the eater: So shall my word be that goeth forth out of my mouth: it shall not return unto me void, but it shall accomplish that which I please, and it shall prosper in the thing whereto I sent it." (Isaiah 55:10-11)

We must remember that in Scripture, knowledge of God is invariably linked with salvation itself. The redemptive power of God has been continuously at work in the world since man first fell into sin. It is *God*, who by His power introduces a knowledge of Himself into the human consciousness. The objective product of this activity is the Holy Scripture. The action by which this comes forth we call inspiration. *Inspiration is not to be viewed in isolation from the whole redemptive purpose of God.* This would reduce it to a purely mechanical inspiration, exclusively an intellectual product remote from reality. The Bible is not given solely for the purpose of abstract intellectual contemplation but that men might be saved and *"that the man of God may be perfect, thoroughly furnished unto all good works"*(2 Timothy 3:17).

The power of God is directed to carrying through the redemptive purpose of God in the world. *The Bible has not been given just as a record of God's redemption, but is itself a redemptive act.* God gave His Son and has given us the Bible as part of this work of redemption. Sin is not just intellectual in nature. It affects the whole of our lives and so the Bible speaks to the whole of our lives. Sin has corrupted the whole of our nature and being and brought a curse upon the whole of creation. The divine power of God could not overcome the opposition of sin without directing itself at the whole of our human existence. In the face of the present disorder, God will bring about that which has been predetermined by the counsel of His will. The entire life of the cosmos will realise that purpose of glory God always intended for it. The regenerative work of the power of God that shows itself in a radical renewal of the life of man in new birth into a new humanity of which Christ is the Head will also at the end bring to pass a similar radical renewal of all creation.

Scripture is not the dictation of a law or doctrine, but is a divine in-breathing of a revelation of God Himself into the world as one element of His redemptive action towards us. Inspiration cannot be isolated from the rest of God's redemptive working in human history, but itself forms part of it. The same grace of God going out to the sinner to save him has also given us an infallible Bible.

It is God in grace, who bears witness to our hearts as to the divine origin and authenticity of His Word as one step along the road of bringing salvation to our lost souls. The Holy Spirit convinces us of the sufficiency of Scripture as He does of the sufficiency of Christ. Finite reasoning can never achieve an infinite result.

> *We can no more reason our way into a belief in Scripture than we can reason our way into heaven.*

We trust the Bible; we trust the God of the Bible. Those who doubt the Bible will doubt the Saviour too. Those who refuse the authority of the written Word will surely refuse the lordship of the living Word.

**250**

Were it ever the case that God should withdraw His grace from an individual soul, should He no longer bear witness to His Word, that person would no longer believe it. No apologetics, however brilliant they may be, would ever then be able to restore the blessing of believing the Bible. Faith in God's written Word is given by God Himself to bring us to faith in Christ, the living Word. It is invincible. Pseudo-faith worked up from 'evidences' and human reasoning is devoid of all spiritual reality and will burst like a soap bubble in the chill wind of godless human logic. The special and particular grace of God operates from the inception of revelation, through the inspiration and preservation of the written page and until that moment and beyond, when our heart has been reached and touched by it. All is of God's grace. The heart touched by God in this way can do no other than respond in faith. All faith in Scripture comes by the quickening of God's Spirit and, in turn, our faith is quickened by Scripture.

Belief in the divine authenticity of Scripture that derives its assurance from any other source than the Spirit of God will surely fail. The alternative is that each person must reason everything out for himself and not everyone has either the time or the means to do it. Such matters are then left to a privileged few upon whom everyone else will depend. This would mean having faith in human scholars and their fallible reasoning in the place of a sure and personal trust in God. Those who trust the work of 'scholars' will find one contradicting the other. One book brings one set of difficulties, another advances new objections, and so we become embroiled in an unending confusion and are torn between doubt and faith. Much that parades as 'Christian scholarship' rests on the treacherous sands of fallible human reason.

> *It is faith that gives the highest and only certain assurance.*
> *Here our heart rests upon the immediate testimony of God.*

Rather believe the revealed Word of God, eternally in the heart of God that can never pass away, than to flirt with the fading words of fallible men. *Rather believe what the Bible says about men, than what men say about the Bible.* The Bible is the highest authority on the Bible.


## Inspiration and illumination

Many confuse inspiration with illumination. Illumination is an enlightenment upon that which is already given. Illumination enables the appropriation of that which has been revealed. Illumination neither increases nor changes that which God has given by inspiration, but takes from that which is there. Inspiration is an *extra*-ordinary work of God and takes its place among accompanying miraculous works such as healings, tongues, and other wonders. For as long as the process of revelation was still on going and not yet complete, the manifestation of these extraordinary powers continued as a corollary. All these signs disappear when revelation is complete. In order for revelation to exist objectively, it must of necessity be completed. As long as it was not finished, Scripture lacked its objective and absolute character and remained attached to the persons and sphere from whence it arose.

Those who believe that God speaks to men's hearts today as He did in apostolic times in addition to Scripture will usually also believe that the day of healings, tongues and the like continues. Belief in an ever-continuing inspiration in any form and under any name amounts to a denial of the absolute authority of the Bible upon all men. Without this universal and final authority, it would be restricted only to those inspired, those alone to whom inspiration comes. To claim absolute authority for Scripture, we are bound to insist upon a completed Bible, a finished revelation with no competing voices. Inspiration is necessarily transitory in nature, so that when its immediate purpose is completed it disappears along with those miraculous workings that accompanied it. Inspiration is a temporal activity bringing about a specific result, one Word to our entire race. It has a beginning; it has an end. The benefit we derive does not come from a continuing inspiration, but from the finished product of it.

Inspiration is an activity of God in bringing about a particular end product. What we now derive from the pages of God's inspired Word is not continuous revelation, but the fruit of a finished work of inspiration. A work that is not yet completed cannot save us. An incomplete Word cannot bring to us that which we need to know in order to be saved. Inspiration is an in-working by the Spirit of God upon the mind of His chosen instruments by which He makes Himself known, communicating His will or His thoughts. By contrast, mystics falsely assume God will speak individually to each and every man, first to one then to another. Inspiration repeats itself over and over again. This is a false view of inspiration. Inspiration is not an in-shining of the Spirit of God that endlessly repeats itself in an endless number of people, but is limited to a definite period and bound to definite conditions. That which is revealed within this given time forms one whole, not by adding one revelation to another, but as one thought of God develops from one germ. This has now ended.

The process of revelation having ended, the need for inspiration has also ceased. The work of the Holy Spirit today is to illumine to our minds that meaning of that once-for-all-time revelation. The illumination to our hearts of that which God has inspired is also a work of God's special grace and without it, inspiration is of little use to us and the Bible remains then a book beyond us. One presumes the other, requires the other. The Holy Spirit explains to us the fruit of inspiration. All these operations of the Spirit of God are distinct, yet at the same time are *one* redemptive work.

That God has not spoken since apostolic days cannot be attributed to a diminishing of His power, but that it seemed good to Him not to do so. Having spoken once in Scripture, He is now silent in order that we should honour His Word. It is necessary that the one revelation should address itself to the human race as one. The Bible is the special Word of God *to the whole world*. God has nothing to say to anyone other than that which He has recorded without error in the Bible. To deny the authority of a completed, God-breathed Bible is to remove a stepping-stone along the path that leads to a saving knowledge of Christ. Those who diminish *the* Book can make no claim knowing Christ. Those with a purely human bible will have a purely human saviour, neither of which can lead to salvation.

We must distinguish between that which is completed once for all men, and that which continues and is realised within the individual. That which the Holy Spirit continues today to apply to the hearts of individuals is drawn from a work once completed for all. It is to be expected that the work of inspiration would finish, for its completed end, the Bible, is given for all. That which goes out from God to all men must appear in the completed objective form in which it is to continue down through the years and spread from nation to nation. Illumination in contrast to inspiration is directed not to all men, but to the individual. It remains subjective and mystic in the proper sense of the word. Inspiration completed revelation, now through illumination this finished work of God in the written Word performs its work in individual believers.

The process of inspiration was necessarily linked to the unfolding of time. Many years passed from the fall of man before the Lord Jesus took upon Himself flesh and made His appearance. Nevertheless, there came a moment in time when this actually happened. In the same way, however many years there were before its completion, there came a moment when the written Word too came forth and was completed. What incarnation is for the living Word, inspiration is for the written Word. The Scriptures can only be a universally objective Word when written down, even as the Lord Jesus could only be a universally objective Saviour when manifest in human flesh. As the Scriptures are the only Word of God to all men, so the Lord Jesus is the only Saviour to all men. The incarnation brought life into the centre of human *being*, inspiration brings the knowledge of God into the centre of human *thought.*

An objective finished work must become a subjective experience. That which was completed universally and objectively, must then be experienced individually and subjectively, if we are to benefit from it. We experience salvation individually as we participate personally in that which was accomplished outside ourselves on our behalf by our Saviour. We obtain a saving knowledge of God individually as we access personally that which was given outside ourselves to all men in Scripture. This does not demand the continuance of inspiration, but *excludes* it.

Included in any definition of false mysticism must be all who regard inspiration as something subjective rather than objective, individual rather than central or universal. Were the inspiration of God something individual as the mystics claim, those who do not feel this inspiration as they read the Bible can justifiably claim it has no authority over them. Where inspiration stands apart from the individual, then the authority of the Bible is the same for all men irrespectively. Many deny or relativise the inspiration of Scripture and imagine thereby to have escaped its authority over them. The Bible speaks to you but it does not speak to me, or it spoke to me yesterday but has nothing to say to me today. All this is woolly-headed mysticism. Here authority is determined subjectively by the reader and not by God. In truth, the Word of God speaks objectively to all men at all times and its authority is universal. If there is one authoritative Word for all, irrespective of the individual stance or experience, then all are under its rule whether they accept it or no.

There is no inspiration going out to individuals one by one. The content of such inspiration could never be the same in each case. There could be no universally authoritative absolute Word of God. How we read the Bible is important. Is the meaning to be recovered or created from the text? God has spoken to us once in His Word. From its depths, individual believers draw for themselves their knowledge of God. God has once given one Word for all, which neither repeats itself nor continues to expand. It is given that believers of all times and all places may draw upon the knowledge of God. Those indwelt by the Spirit of God will be driven *to the Scriptures* for what they need to know, not to visions, 'baptisms' or tongues and other individual mystical experiences that are a denial of the faith.

## The self-testimony of Scripture: the Lord Jesus and the apostles

Inspiration is something to which we ourselves are strangers, but not to those called of God to pen the words of Scripture. To understand inspiration, we must look to them, to what they wrote under inspiration, and what they taught. In them dwelt that Spirit who animates the whole of this sacred book.

In an absolute sense, only in the Lord Jesus did the self-consciousness of the Scriptures fully express themselves. When He walked this earth, the Scriptures of the Old Testament were already completed. Consequently, it is of importance for us to know exactly what the Lord Jesus Himself thought of their inspiration. In the same way, the apostles also clearly understood the idea of inspiration.

> "And they were all filled with the Holy Ghost, and began to speak with other tongues, as the Spirit gave them utterance." (Acts 2:4)

Here the apostles uttered sounds not produced of themselves but that were the result of an action going out of them from the Holy Ghost. This is inspiration in the fullest sense of the word.

First, the Lord Jesus and the apostles saw the Scriptures not simply as a varied collection of many different books, but as *one organic whole having absolute authority*. Quoting Psalm 82:6, the Lord Jesus answers the Jews,

> "Is it not written in your law, I said, Ye are gods? If he called them gods, unto whom the word of God came, and the Scripture cannot be broken." (John 10:34-35)

As Psalm 82:6 occurs in Scripture, hence it cannot be broken. In saying that the *"Scripture* (singular) *cannot be broken"*, the Lord Jesus is identifying the Old Testament specifically as one whole having an absolute character, but He is also stating a truth generally applicable to all that can be called Scripture. He speaks of the word of God, again singular, word not words, indicating a single whole – *"unto whom the word of God came"*. Jesus is saying here that whatever is Scripture cannot be broken. Today, we have also the New Testament. By implication therefore, the New Testament, because it is Scripture, cannot be broken. Otherwise, it simply cannot be Scripture – this is the nature of Scripture. We conclude that if we accept the New Testament as Scripture in like manner as the Old, then it cannot be broken. On another occasion, the Lord Jesus uses the word 'Scriptures' (plural) to indicate the same thing – an organic whole. Again referring to the Old Testament, He asks, *"Did ye never read in the Scriptures…?"* (Matthew 21:42). Although He is quoting from one passage in one book, the Psalms (118:22-23), by saying the Scriptures (plural), He is identifying the one place with the whole. The one is the same as the whole.

According to Hebrews 1:1, Scripture derives not from any human insight, but God himself spoke to the fathers by the prophets.

> "God, who at sundry times and in divers manners spake in time past unto the fathers by the prophets." (Hebrews 1:1)

Even although this took place 'in divers manners in times past', it was *all one*, God's testimony to the fathers and to us. The apostolic manner of quoting the Old Testament demonstrates this. Omitting the name of the individual author, the apostles simply say something like *"as it is written…"* (Romans 4:17), *"for the scripture saith"* (Romans 10:11), *"according as it is written"* (Romans 11:8). In this way they head off all opposition to what they are saying. They viewed the Scriptures as a *whole*, and as authoritative because it was the written Word of God. In Romans 11:2, the prayer of Elijah is quoted as *"what the scripture saith of Elias"*. In Romans 3:10-18, Paul constructs one single argument and yet it is made up of no less than six different passages from the Old Testament (Psalm 14:1-3; 5:9; 140:3; 10:7; Isaiah 59:7 & Psalm 36:1). The quotations are preceded by *"it is written"* and explained by *"whatsoever the law saith, it saith to them who are under the law"*. No importance is made of David or Isaiah, for the authority of these words does not lie with them, it is sufficient that they are found in holy writ.

Second, the Lord Jesus and the apostles recognised that in Scripture *a single word, or a fragment of it, was just as authoritative as the whole*. It could be appealed to as the final authority. Pilate said, *"What I have written I have written"* (John 19:22). In a similar way, what God has written, He has written. It is final, authoritative and irrevocable. The authority of what is written stems from the One from whom it came forth. The Lord Jesus continually uses all kind of quotations from the Old Testament in His arguments and reasoning, indicating that this was an absolute Word, a final Word not to be questioned.

Matthew 4:1-11 describes the temptation of the Lord Jesus. On each occasion, He meets every temptation with *"it is written"*. It is not simply that the Lord meets Satan with some quotation to support His argument, but He appeals to an authority that bears no contradiction. There is no other way in which the appeal to Deuteronomy 8:3 that *"man shall not live by bread alone, but by every word that proceedeth out of the mouth of God"* (Matthew 4:4) can be understood. It is significant that the Lord Jesus does not say, 'Moses said', but uses the formula, *"It is written"*. The word cited derives its divine authority from the fact *that it is written*. There is no possible mistake, but that Jesus attributed absolute and divine authority to every single word written down in Scripture.

In many cases, an argument will hang on a single word. This being so we must be sure that we still have the precise wording given by God. Only a verbally inspired Bible can provide this. Here is an example.

> "The Lord said unto my Lord, Sit thou on my right hand, till I make thine enemies thy footstool?" (Matthew 22:44)

Citing Psalm 110:1, the whole strength of the argument made by the Lord Jesus hangs on the single word *my*, or to be more precise, in the original Hebrew on a single *iod*. This is a precise example of what the Lord Jesus meant when He said, *"And it is easier for heaven and earth to pass, than one tittle of the law to fail"* (Luke 16:17). Divine authority extends even to each individual letter. The Lord Jesus does not tell us here that just meaning is inspired and preserved, but assures us that the actual written words down to the very smallest detail cannot fail. Not one 'tittle' can fail, therefore neither can it be lost. God's preserving work did not cease with the original autographs but is with us today. The 'tittle' refers to the apostrophised *iod*, the smallest letter. To say that not even one tittle shall fail means that the Scriptures are given, inspired, preserved, and are therefore authoritative down to the last detail.

---

*From the opening verse of Genesis to the last verse of Revelation, we are at liberty to change precisely nothing, not a word, not an apostrophe!*

---

> "If any man shall add unto these things, God shall add unto him the plagues that are written in this book: And if any man shall take away from the words of this prophecy, God shall take away his part out of the book of life, and out of the holy city, and from the things which are written in this book." (Revelation 22:18-19)

Bearing in mind that every single word carries with it the authority of the whole book and were one word missing the

Bible would be incomplete and imperfect, we ought not to be surprised that subtracting of even a single word put in place by God or adding a word of our own incurs a penalty of eternal loss. The book of Revelation being inseparable from the whole, this warning must apply to all Scripture. What is said about the part must be said about the whole.

Often the argument made by the apostles in their writings will rest on the importance of single words or even single letters. Unless they regarded the text as perfect because inspired, they could in no way use Scripture in this way. The entire argument of Paul in Galatians 3:16 rests on a single letter both in Greek and in English.

> "Now to Abraham and his seed were the promises made. He saith not, And to seeds, as of many; but as of one, And to thy seed, which is Christ."

Were the plural used, the argument would have been lost. This kind of accuracy must be applied to whole of Scripture, both Old and New Testaments. A similar kind of situation is found in 1 Peter 3:5-6 where the exhortation rests on the fact that Sarah called her husband 'lord'. It is impossible for the apostles to have made their argument with the same authority, if it were not that they knew inspiration extended to every word, every letter.

Third, Scripture is *grounded in every detail in the eternal counsel of God*. What men devise or think out can always be changed or corrected should things not work out quite as expected. The word of men can most certainly be broken. The only thing on this earth that 'must be fulfilled' and 'cannot be broken' is the eternal purpose of God revealed and given in definitive form in Scripture.

> "For I say unto you, that this is written must yet be accomplished in me, And he was reckoned among the

transgressors: for the things concerning me have an end."
(Luke 22:37; quotation from Isaiah 53:12)

The Lord Jesus points to a specific written text and declares that it *must* be fulfilled in Him. The Lord Jesus does not act in omnipotence, nor does He call upon a legion of angels to save Him as He faces the cross. There can be no going against the Scripture for down to the last letter it reveals the eternal purpose of God regarding His Son. Nothing God ever said, nothing God ever gave us in writing, can ever fall to the ground. Because it is written in Scripture this *prevents* anything else happening than that which is written there. Nothing else can happen than that which is written in the Bible, quite impossible. *"But how then shall the scriptures be fulfilled, that thus it must be?"* (Matthew 26:54). The prophetic programme *must* be carried through.

---

*The Bible is a carbon copy of the counsel of God concerning His Son and for this reason nothing in it can fail.*

---

Even the manner of His betrayal by Judas is unavoidable in order that the Scripture may be fulfilled.

"I know whom I have chosen: but that the scripture may be fulfilled, He that eateth bread with me hath lifted up his heel against me." (John 13:18)

Jesus did not just choose a particular text to illustrate the occasion. On the contrary, the Scripture is seen in its entirety as speaking of Him *"they are they which testify of me"* (John 5:39). As a *whole* the Scriptures point to the Lord Jesus and nothing concerning Him can fail.

The apostles too saw Scripture as the transcript of the eternal purposes of God. Peter, in his sermon on the day of Pentecost, says that the God raised up the Lord Jesus *"because it was not possible that he should be holden of it"* (Acts 2:24). Why was this? Was it because He was the Son on God? Most certainly, but this was not the reason Peter gave, rather he quotes Psalm 16 and bases his argument on the words of David,

> "For thou wilt not leave my soul in hell; neither wilt thou suffer thine Holy One to see corruption." (Psalm 16:10)

It was impossible for Christ to remain in the grave *because the Scriptures say so*, they give us details of what *must* come to pass because God has planned it that way. Peter mentions this specifically saying that the Lord Jesus was *"delivered by the determinate counsel and foreknowledge of God"* (v.23) and the Bible is a transcript of that counsel.

Something similar appears in Acts 1:16.

> "Men and brethren, this scripture must needs have been fulfilled, which the Holy Ghost by the mouth of David spake before concerning Judas, which was a guide to them that took Jesus."

Here we are told quite specifically that David was in fact the mouthpiece of the Holy Ghost in the utterance of prophetic words. What the Holy Ghost was revealing was part of the eternal counsel of God and therefore *had* to be fulfilled. It is this fact that renders the Bible an entirely trustworthy book.

## *The Bible, Old and New Testament, has only one Author*

The Old Testament cannot be considered apart from the New. Without the New Testament, we could not consider the Old as Scripture. First came the Old Testament, *then* came the living Word, God clothed in flesh. Only after our Saviour had completed His redemptive work could the New be written and *together* the Old and New Testaments make up sacred Scripture.

In the process of inspiration, God by His Holy Spirit enters into the spirit of man and introduces into his consciousness thoughts clothed in words that this man could not conceive on his own, nor derive from other men. Peter's confession was not something he produced himself nor gained from others, but it came directly from God.

> "Blessed art thou, Simon Bar-Jona: for flesh and blood hath not revealed it unto thee, but my Father which is in heaven."
> (Matthew 16:17)

Prophecy did not have a human origin within the will of the prophets themselves. As men of God, that which they spoke had entered into their consciousness as they were moved by the Holy Ghost.

> "For prophecy came not in old time by the will of man: but holy men of God spake as they were moved by the Holy Ghost." (2 Peter 1:21)

The ministry and preaching of the prophets of the Old Testament and the apostles of the New were all done in the same Spirit of Christ. Very clearly, this passage teaches the spiritual unity of the Bible, revealed and inspired by one Holy Spirit. What the Lord Jesus and the apostles testified of the Old is equally true of the New Testament.

> "Of which salvation the prophets have enquired and searched diligently, who prophesied of the grace that should come unto you: Searching what, or what manner of time the Spirit of Christ which was in them did signify, when it testified beforehand the sufferings of Christ, and the glory that should follow. Unto whom it was revealed, that not unto themselves, but unto us they did minister the things, which are now reported unto you by them that have preached the gospel unto you with the Holy Ghost sent down from heaven; which things the angels desire to look into." (1 Peter 1:10-12)

We see here that both the prophecy of the Old Testament and the reporting of those same things by the apostles, now recorded for us in the New Testament, were inspired by the same Spirit.

The New Testament contains many passages that indicate God the Holy Spirit is the speaking subject of the Old Testament. *"And God spake on this wise..."* (Acts 7:6; see also Acts 1:16; Romans 2:4; Hebrews 1:6,13; 10:15). On many occasions, the apostles string together a whole series of quotations from different parts of the Old Testament, the significance of the individual authors falling into the background. What was important was that it was clear that they understood there to be one divine Author behind the Scriptures (see Acts 1:20; Romans 11:8,26; 15:9; 1 Timothy 5:18).

This appears even more clearly in those passages where we are told that the words written contain far more than the human writers ever understood themselves. In Romans 4 there are words from Genesis 15:6 where we are told that the expression referring to Abraham, *"imputed to him for righteousness"*, did not simply refer to Abraham as intended by the writer, but also to us.

> "Now it was not written for his sake alone, that it was imputed to him; but for us also, to whom it shall be imputed, if we believe on him that raised up Jesus our Lord from the dead." (Romans 4:23-24)

Again in Romans 15, Psalm 69:9 is cited. The prophetic messianic utterances coming though David are used by Paul to make this general statement,

> "For whatsoever things were written aforetime were written for our learning, that we through patience and comfort of the scriptures might have hope." (Romans 15:4)

This could not have been part of the intention of David as he wrote. David sang when his heart was full, Jeremiah prophesied when fired burned within his bones – but both under the direction of the Holy Spirit.

As we examine the quotations of the Old Testament made by the writers of the New, we notice that they cannot be understood to be a word for word translation into Greek of the original Hebrew. This would perhaps, on a human level at least, have been understandable had they not been conversant with Hebrew, but they all invariably were. Various explanations have been offered nearly all of which are unsatisfactory to say the least. To say that they spoke Greek to Greek-speaking Churches is insufficient, to say that they always followed the Greek version of the Old Testament is inconsistent and can be objected to on many grounds. When, however, we understand that the writers of the New Testament were themselves inspired as they wrote, the question assumes an entirely different perspective. Usually, in quoting from someone else one must take care to do so precisely and literally. A writer quoting from himself is clearly allowed more liberty and is bound only to the content. It being the Holy Spirit who spoke through the prophets and at the same time inspired the apostles, it amounts to the same Author *quoting Himself.* He is therefore free to quote Himself in such a manner that applies His words to the argument in hand for which the quotation is being made, and to modify it accordingly. Only the Author Himself is competent to quote freely in this way.

The Lord Jesus accepted the verbal inspiration of Scriptures in the same way as did all believers of His day and since down to the present. Those who deny this teaching have departed from Christ. In view of how the Lord Jesus Himself viewed the Scriptures, it is not possible for anyone claiming to be His follower to take any other view than His. Our Lord shows Himself as being bound to the Word of God, the Scriptures. We cannot measure with two measures. Either what Jesus said about Scripture is true and we should kneel before Him, or it is false and He is an impostor.

# CHAPTER 12

# Inspiration and the Writing of Scripture

*"For prophecy came not in old time by the will of man: but holy men of God spake as they were moved by the Holy Ghost."* (2 Peter 1:21)

All men live, and move, and have their being in God (Acts 17:28). Human life would otherwise be quite impossible. This fact above all else enables men to act in a truly spontaneous way. That the purposes of God enclose even the evil that men do does not deny the reality that men choose wilfully to sin, nor does it absolve them of the responsibility for what they do or place the cause of their sin anywhere else but with them. Those born again of the Spirit of God having once been in bondage to sin now willingly serve the Saviour whom they love (Romans 6:16). This is a *living* relationship not a mechanical one. Doing the will of God does not suspend the human will, but the will of God and the will of man now function in harmony towards an identical end. With the Psalmist, we delight in doing the will of God (Psalm 40:8). God's thoughts become our thoughts; His words become our words. Thinking the thoughts of God does not suspend the operation of the human mind. On the contrary, without the functioning of our mind, we could neither think nor receive any thoughts at all.

There is a most amazing verse to be found in the thirty-seventh Psalm.

> "Delight thyself also in the LORD; and he shall give thee the desires of thine heart." (Psalm 37:4)

This does not teach that we can somehow bend God to our every whim, but that as we delight ourselves in Him, all our desires are found in His perfect will. Even as we are enabled through Scripture to think the thoughts of God, in a similar way our heart desires the desires of God, so that God is perfectly willing to give us what we ask of Him. Although on occasions we may be passive instruments in God's hands, more often than not our will is not put out of action so that the will of God can displace it, but rather it is active within the will of God. The options are not that either my will prevails and I please myself and sin or else God's will operates *in its place* and I please Him. Instead, the one is superimposed upon the other so that both act together. Our wills work in harness with God. We are submissive in love to God, but not necessarily inactive. This coincidence of wills is best exemplified in the life of our Saviour.

> "Then answered Jesus and said unto them, Verily, verily, I say unto you, The Son can do nothing of himself, but what he seeth the Father do: for what things soever he doeth, these also doeth the Son likewise. ...I can of mine own self do nothing: as I hear, I judge: and my judgment is just; because I seek not mine own will, but the will of the Father which hath sent me." (John 5:19 & 30)

What was perfectly enacted in the life of the Lord Jesus is only imperfectly realised in us.

## The will of God and the will of man

First, inspiration is possible because God is both omnipresent and immanent. We live only of Him, through Him, and in Him. Second, inspiration is only possible because we are made in His image. Inspiration is based upon a special affinity between God's Spirit and ours, an affinity true of no other creature. Human consciousness is the distinguishing mark of a spiritual being. Thus is opened up the possibility of communion between our spirit and the Spirit of God, by which the thoughts of God can become our thoughts.

God uses man's spirit as His organ, consciously or unconsciously, actively or passively. Sometimes, for example in the New Testament epistles, the human activity appears to be the only factor and inspiration is hardly observed. At other times, the human spirit appears almost only as a vessel to catch the action of God's Spirit, as for example in the visions of Ezekiel. Despite the superficial appearances, in neither case is the one portion of Scripture less inspired than the other. Nor can we construe an explanation suggesting that the human element is greater in one and the divine greater in another.

In the process of inspiration the mind and consciousness of the writers of Scripture were so elevated that the thoughts arising there came solely from the Spirit of God, unhindered by the intervention of anything originating from within the individual concerned. Moved, or borne along by God's Spirit, the thoughts of God become the thoughts of these men. Nevertheless, the functioning of the human personality was not set aside, but its faculties operated coincidentally and utterly in tune with the Spirit of God. We cannot think without words, the writer of Scripture would have been conscious of God's thoughts as words. He then, still under the perfect guidance of the Spirit of God, commits these same words to writing without error. This is inspired Scripture.

The prophet is an instrument whilst God speaks the word. From the descriptions of many prophetic visions and from the words of the prophet himself, it is clear that he often regarded himself as being taken hold of by God and being compelled to speak not his own thoughts but those of God. This is indicated by the constant phrase *'thus saith the Lord'*. It is shown too by Jeremiah's great struggle (Jeremiah 20:7-9). At first the prophet Nathan speaks from himself, encouraging David to build the Temple, *"Go, do all that is in thine heart; for the Lord is with thee"* (2 Samuel 7:3). Later this is contradicted when it is reversed by a word from the Lord, recorded in the verses following and announcing that David's son would build a house for the Lord. The distinctive element in prophecy is that the prophet is always an instrument for the words of the Lord.

The Bible does not teach that men can only act spontaneously when, to a greater or lesser degree, they do so outside God's determinative will and counsel. God's plan enables and guarantees human spontaneity and freedom. God wills it. This makes us something more than captives to chance or immoveable natural law. It makes us responsible beings, answerable to our Maker for all that we do. A freedom conceived outside God's will can only amount to an assumed and sinful human autonomy, an impossible desire to break with God completely. Were a true spontaneity upheld by His sovereign will not possible, *God would be reduced to dictating Scripture word by word in a lifeless way to ensure its accuracy.* The writer is then nothing more than an inanimate writing tool. There can be no adequate defence of the inerrant inspiration of Scripture that sets aside the biblical teaching of the sovereignty of God and the free agency of the human will within it. This enables the coincidence of the will of God and the will of the believer without disabling either.

Speaking presumes a person who thinks and intends that what is said should pass into the consciousness of another person. When God speaks, it is His intention that what He says is received by men. The result of this is that there arises in the human consciousness a thought that previously existed only in the mind of God. For human beings to communicate with each other, the content of what we have to say must pass through the physical world. In the case of speech as sound waves, they must pass through the air to be picked up by the ear and passed through the nervous system to our mind. Anyone whose ears do not function properly, or at all, is unable to receive speech. God is not limited by our imperfections. He can access the human heart and consciousness directly from within, even reaching to the stone deaf. In order for us to receive the thoughts of God, they must be clothed in words we can understand. If there are any obstructions, they exist with us and not with God.

Revelation is the name we give to the miraculous operation by which God communicates His thoughts to men. Inspiration is the work of the Holy Spirit by which God's thoughts infallibly fill and direct the minds of His servants *as they speak or write*. Revelation will have come to both prophets and apostles not everything of which was recorded as Scripture. They will have spoken under the inspiration of God. Again, not all of this will have found its way into Scripture. Whether the writers were always conscious of their inspiration is not the point, the Holy Spirit sharpened their mind in the choice of expression and vocabulary so that their choice would always have been that directed by God's Spirit – they *always* chose the right word. Sometimes God spoke audibly to men, sometimes He spoke directly to their souls, but always in words. Whether He dictated what was to be written as is the case with the book of Revelation, or whether He governed the writing in a more indirect way, as in historical parts such as the Gospels, the result will always be the same. The Bible is a book in form and content down to the last jot and tittle designed by the Spirit of God, inerrant and infallible. Inspiration does not exclude the normal collation of documents, literary style, structure, choice of vocabulary, but what we must insist upon is that the resultant writing is in every detail given of God and carries divine and absolute authority for all men at all times.

In inspiration there is the Spirit who inspires, the spirit of man that is inspired, and the content of what is inspired. The nature of all consciousness is determined by consciousness in God. His thought goes before any other. Our consciousness is not an unknown sphere to God. He made it. Inspiration assumes a God who has the *will* to inspire with one or the other thought. Unlike us, who do so much without even realising what we are doing, everything that God does is because He has willed it so. Through inspiration God wills that from His divine consciousness He will introduce into the consciousness of man this or that thought in a form within our capacity to receive. In this way, He introduces His thoughts among men.

Scripture will show as many different dispositions towards inspiration as there are authors. In the Temple, Simeon showed a strong inclination towards that which was given him. Jeremiah, on the other hand, showed a severe disinclination towards inspiration (cf. Jeremiah 20). In the case of the Lord Jesus, the Holy Spirit did not simply descend upon Him but remained upon Him. He is a model of the way in which the human spirit ought to respond towards inspiration. His was an ever-continuing inspiration within His human consciousness.

> "I can of mine own self do nothing: as I hear, I judge: and my judgment is just; because I seek not mine own will, but the will of the Father which hath sent me." (John 5:30)

Although the Bible is word-for-word given by God, we must not automatically assume that the character and personality of the Scripture writers are set aside and become matters of indifference. It is not as though God just looked around for someone who would be suitable for what He had in mind. Instead, God caused these men to be born with the idea of using them for a purpose He already had in mind. He caused them to spend their early years in those circumstances and surroundings best suited as a preparation, so that in due time they would be entirely suitable instruments. Personality sets the tone for what is written. Isaiah will not speak as Jeremiah or Luke as Paul. The instrument was designed to accomplish the task God had in mind for each one. God made a Jeremiah to exercise the ministry of Jeremiah and write his prophecy.

> "Then the word of the Lord came unto me saying, Before I formed thee in the belly I knew thee; and before thou camest forth out of the womb I sanctified thee, and I ordained thee a prophet unto the nations." (Jeremiah 1:4-5)

He made a Paul to be an apostle; he too was preordained of God to his apostolic task and to the writing of Scripture.

> "But when it pleased God, who separated me from my mother's womb, and called me by his grace, To reveal his Son in me, that I might preach him among the heathen..."
> (Galatians 1:15-16)

This predestination is not to be limited to these people as individuals, but is to be extended to the whole circumstances of the life from which they sprang. If there is any predisposition to inspiration, it is in the fact that they were created and chosen by God to that end. This disposition was moulded and tuned and gifts of God's grace endowed to suit each one to their particular task. There is an election to service as much as there is to salvation. Many are the leadings of God's providence in the education and background of God's chosen instruments: Moses in Pharaoh's court, David the shepherd boy, Peter and John to become 'fishers of men', Paul sitting at the feet of Gamaliel. It was God who created and chose an Isaiah or a John, He it was who animated and inspired them.

There are considerable differences between all the writers of Scripture. What one cannot do the other is able to accomplish. The personal stamp of the human author remains upon his writing. At the same time, the thoughts must not be viewed as *originating* with the man – not even the words in which those thoughts are clothed – but as coming from the consciousness of God. In the providence of God, the background, education or lack of it, the development of the writer and his general lot in life are all available to God to bring the Word He wants to and in the way He wants to do it.

## How God inspired His servants

When thinking of how God inspires, we must distinguish between that which is already present in man and in the world about him, and that which God purposely brings about to effect inspiration. In order to speak to men, God sometimes uses what is already to hand, but at other times He brings things about that would not otherwise occur.

God spoke to men audibly using the ears He gave us, but also He spoke internally, bypassing the physical organs of hearing reaching directly into the world of thought. This would be much in the same way as when we hold a dialogue with ourselves – thinking. Here God intervenes directly into the thought processes. This is a speaking within by which God has direct contact with the human consciousness and causes such thoughts to arise within us as he wills. Of course, we cannot do this with each other. Communication among men goes out through our nervous system and organs of speech, from there the sound travels through the air and affects the auditory nerve of the other person. Only in this way can our thought reach the consciousness of someone else.

In thinking, or speaking within ourselves, our organs of speech and hearing are not involved. Nevertheless, moment-by-moment successive changes of thought take place in us. We note once more, that God does not think in this time-bound moment-by-moment manner. Yet, God has direct access to human consciousness, outside and inside and He cannot be limited to organs of speech and hearing. In this kind of inspiration, God brings thoughts into the human mind directly. Jesus experienced a constant internal dialogue with His Father.

We can probably assume that God spoke to Adam in this way *before* the fall. Only *after* the fall do we read that he heard God as though His voice walked in the garden in the cool of the day. God's voice is no longer within but outside. Evidently, because of sin, the susceptibility for internal address by God may have been blunted, but it was not removed. After the entrance of sin, but exclusively within His redemptive purpose, God still revealed His thoughts directly to man in the prophets and the apostles.

There is a kind of speaking that does not arise from within the normal human consciousness. Examples of this would be *glossolalia* or tongue speaking, speaking done by parrots and the like, the speech of Balaam's ass, also in demon possession. There is the inspired speech promised by Christ to the apostles.

> "For it is not ye that speak, but the Spirit of your Father which speaketh in you." (Matthew 10:20)

At times, God also spoke audibly as one man does to another.

> "And the Lord spake unto Moses face to face, as a man speaketh unto his friend." (Exodus 33:11)
> "With him will I speak mouth to mouth, even apparently, and not in dark speeches…" (Numbers 12:8)

The emphasis here is more upon what a man hears, rather than upon what he speaks after the suggestion of God.

> "And the Lord said unto Moses, Lo, I come unto thee in a thick cloud, that the people may hear when I speak with thee, and believe thee for ever. ..." (Exodus 19:9)

> "And ye said, Behold, the Lord our God hath shewed us his glory and his greatness, and we have heard his voice out of the midst of the fire: we have seen this day that God doth talk with man, and he liveth." (Deuteronomy 5:24)

> "And when Moses was gone into the tabernacle of the congregation to speak with him, then he heard the voice of one speaking unto him from off the mercy seat that was upon the ark of testimony, from between the two cherubims: and he spake unto him." (Numbers 7:89)

Perhaps the most obvious example of this manner of speaking is the call of Samuel, when the boy Samuel heard what he first took to be Eli's voice. Only after speaking with Eli did he recognise it as the voice of the Lord.

> "And the Lord called Samuel again the third time. And he arose and went to Eli, and said, Here am I; for thou didst call me. And Eli perceived that the Lord had called the child. Therefore Eli said unto Samuel, Go, lie down: and it shall be, if he call thee, that thou shalt say, Speak, Lord; for thy servant heareth. So Samuel went and lay down in his place. And the Lord came, and stood, and called as at other times, Samuel, Samuel. Then Samuel answered, Speak; for thy servant heareth." (1 Samuel 3:8-10)

Sometimes when God spoke audibly, what He said could be heard by others standing by. Jesus prays to His Father,

> "Father, glorify thy name. Then came there a voice from heaven, saying, I have both glorified it, and will glorify it again. The people therefore, that stood by, and heard it, said that it thundered: others said, An angel spake to him. Jesus answered and said, This voice came not because of me, but for your sakes." (John 12:28-30)

In Acts 8:29, we read that *"the Spirit said unto Philip"*. We are not told that a thought occurred within him, but that there was an actual speaking.

At Sinai, God's voice came down from above. Moses heard a definite voice from between the cherubim. Samuel too heard a voice. At the baptism of the Lord, there was a voice from heaven. Peter testifies of what he saw and heard,

> "For we have not followed cunningly devised fables, when we made known unto you the power and coming of our Lord Jesus Christ, but were eyewitnesses of his majesty. For he received from God the Father honour and glory, when there came such a voice to him from the excellent glory, This is my beloved Son, in whom I am well pleased. And this voice which came from heaven we heard, when we were with him in the holy mount." (2 Peter 1:16-18)

We have the testimony of Paul on the road to Damascus, of John on Patmos. We set aside the question as to whether in each case the sound was produced by a vibration of the air waves or whether it was a sensation on the eardrum. In either case, it would have been a physical hearing. God who made the voice, vocal cords, waves of air, the eardrum, auditory nerves, can He not make all of them perform a task appointed by Him seeing that He maintains them moment by moment?

> "He that planted the ear, shall he not hear? He that formed the eye, shall he not see?" (Psalm 94:9)

What is clear is that each of these people heard a voice speaking *in a language they could understand* as though a friend or neighbour were speaking to them.

Another form of inspiration where God makes use of that already to hand is that which we can call impulse. We read of Samson, *"And the Spirit of the Lord began to move him at times..."* (Judges 13:25). Peter writes,

"For the prophecy came not in old time by the will of man: but holy men of God spake as they were moved by the Holy Ghost." (2 Peter 1:21)

Someone who is moved is given a push, an impulse is a mental push urging the mind to move. Jeremiah could not contain himself however hard he tried.

"Then I said, I will not make mention of him, nor speak any more in his name. But his word was in mine heart as a burning fire shut up in my bones, and I was weary with forbearing, and I could not stay." (Jeremiah 20:9)

Inspiration here is a push, an impulse of the Holy Spirit.

At other times, God purposely brings something about in order to bring His Word to the human mind. One of these is sleep.

"In a dream, in a vision of the night, when deep sleep falleth upon men, in slumberings upon the bed; Then he openeth the ears of men, and sealeth their instruction." (Job 33:15-16)

We are not thinking here about something that comes about in a purely natural way, but a sleep that is brought on by God for a specific purpose. Such a sleep came upon Adam (Genesis 2:21), upon Abraham (Genesis 15:12), upon Saul and his men (1 Samuel 26:12). In each of these cases, it is specifically stated it was a *deep* sleep. Men dream, we are told, during periods of light sleep, but here the body of those affected was cut off from all contact with the surrounding world. It was a form of revelation, totally isolating the person from the things of this life.

That revelatory dreams in Scripture are something more than common dreams is clear from 1 Samuel 28:6,

"And when Saul enquired of the Lord, the Lord answered him not, neither by dreams, nor by Urim, nor by prophets."

Godly and demonic influences can be at work in dreams, there are false prophets and pseudo-dreams. Dreams were a common means of revelation used by God to speak to those outside Israel. Anyone dreaming such a dream would have understood it to be symbolic and immediately sought the reality behind it. Abimelech, Pharaoh, and Nebuchadnezzar are cases in point. These dreams all needed interpretation, Joseph for Pharaoh and Daniel for Nebuchadnezzar. Both the dream itself and the interpretation of it were supernatural and given directly by God.

The difference between a dream and vision – also something brought about deliberately by God – is that a dream occurs in sleep whilst a vision takes place at the periphery of the inner consciousness when wide-awake. Visions were often experienced by false prophets. In the prophetical books of the Old Testament and in the Apocalypse in the New we find symbolic prophetic visions followed by an interpretation.

We cannot assume that the words recorded in Scripture are the only ones ever spoken under inspiration of the Holy Spirit by a particular person. A man like Amos, a prophet inspired by God, would not only have spoken under inspiration whilst writing the short book bearing his name. He doubtless preached many sermons under direct inspiration, yet not all are recorded. The Lord Jesus, to whom the Holy Spirit was given without measure, always spoke under inspiration and most of what He said was never written down.

> "This is the disciple which testifieth of these things, and wrote these things: and we know that his testimony is true. And there are also many other things which Jesus did, the which, if they should be written every one, I suppose that even the world itself could not contain the books that should be written." (John 21:24-25)

Those words of the Lord Jesus not recorded cannot be thought to be less inspired that those that are.

> "For I have not spoken of myself; but the Father which sent me, he gave me a commandment, what I should say, and what I should speak. And I know that his commandment is

> life everlasting: whatsoever I speak therefore, even as the
> Father said unto me, so I speak." (John 12:49-50)

What is lost of the inspired words of our Saviour does not detract in any way from the inspiration of Scripture. These different elements in inspiration need to be distinguished from each other. Inspiration is to be thought of as the means employed by which God caused those instruments of His revelation to speak, sing, or write what He desired and purposed.

For the greater part in Scripture, that recorded by the writers, whilst being directly inspired by God, gives us the distinct impression of being the result of their own subjective consciousness. Scripture is not, however, as some have portrayed it, part the work of God and part the work of men. Scripture is not God plus men. At the back of *everything* written lies a higher motive from another consciousness above that of the writers. Again, the will of God does not strike out the will of man, nor does the will of man preclude the work of God behind what is done. Instead, it is the will of God, and the action of God, that sustains and enables the will of man to act as it does. This happens not mechanically like a robotic machine but willingly and freely so that what is done is truly the work of the writer, yet at the same time is something totally determined by God.

## The inspiration of the Lord Jesus and of the apostles

To say that the man Christ Jesus knew everything without inspiration is to deny the incarnation. The consciousness of God and the consciousness of the mediatorial Saviour are not one, but two. The transfer of divine thoughts from the consciousness of God to His Son is not common inspiration but inspiration of the highest degree. It occurs because of the union of the divine and the human nature. This is what Christ Himself said.

> "I can of mine own self do nothing: as I hear, I judge: and my judgment is just; because I seek not mine own will, but the will of the Father which hath sent me." (John 5:30)
>
> "Jesus answered them, and said, My doctrine is not mine, but his that sent me." (John 7:16)
>
> "I have many things to say and to judge of you: but he that sent me is true; and I speak to the world those things which I have heard of him." (John 8:26)
>
> "For I have not spoken of myself; but the Father which sent me, he gave me a commandment, what I should say, and what I should speak." (John 12:49)
>
> "Believest thou not that I am in the Father, and the Father in me? the words that I speak unto you I speak not of myself: but the Father that dwelleth in me, he doeth the works."
> (John 14:10)
>
> "He that loveth me not keepeth not my sayings: and the word which ye hear is not mine, but the Father's which sent me." (John 14:24)

This was to be expected when the divine Son of God took upon Himself human nature. It was the more necessary because He assumed that nature in all its weakness, with the single exception of sin.

> "For we have not an high priest which cannot be touched with the feeling of our infirmities; but was in all points tempted like as we are, yet without sin." (Hebrews 4:15)

This means that in Jesus there was no lie, no falsehood to set itself against the truth and be overcome, as would have been the case with the prophets. The Lord Jesus *increased* in wisdom. He became gradually more enriched as He went through the world in the consciousness of God. This came about as He read the Scriptures, saw the created world and by His life in Israel, as well as through direct inspiration. The Holy Spirit was also *given* to Him. The precise process of this inspiration is described for us.

"For he whom God hath sent speaketh the words of God: for God giveth not the Spirit by measure unto him." (John 3:34)

It was not possible for the Lord Jesus to be passive towards inspiration without being active at the same time. It is interesting that the Lord Jesus never received a vision, all inspiration came to Him directly as a clear concept. Before coming to earth, Jesus had seen the heavenly reality which in prophecy had come in visions.

"Verily, verily, I say unto thee, We speak that we do know, and testify that we have seen; and ye receive not our witness." (John 3:11)

"And no man hath ascended up to heaven, but he that came down from heaven, even the Son of man which is in heaven." (John 3:13)

"I speak that which I have seen with my Father: and ye do that which ye have seen with your father." (John 8:38)

The instrumental means necessary to the prophets because of sin was unnecessary for the Lord Jesus for whom there could be no individual limitation. This is why the Lord Jesus spoke 'as one having authority'. What He spoke was the fruit of direct inspiration because of the divine union. All inspiration, in fact, has Christ as its centre. He is *the* Prophet who in the Old Testament spoke by the prophets and after His ascension bears witness by His apostles. It is He who is still today our prophet through His Word.

"I will raise them up a Prophet from among their brethren, like unto thee, and will put my words in his mouth; and he shall speak unto them all that I shall command him."

(Deuteronomy 18:18)

"Howbeit when he, the Spirit of truth, is come, he will guide you into all truth: for he shall not speak of himself; but whatsoever he shall hear, that shall he speak: and he will shew you things to come." (John 16:13)

"Of which salvation the prophets have enquired and searched diligently, who prophesied of the grace that should come unto you: Searching what, or what manner of time the

Spirit of Christ which was in them did signify, when it testified beforehand the sufferings of Christ, and the glory that should follow." (1 Peter 1:10-11)

If we make the inspiration of the prophets the measure of all inspiration, not only will we find it difficult to understand the inspiration of the Lord Jesus, but also we will be bound to conclude that the apostles could have not have been inspired. The nature of the apostles' inspiration is quite different from that of the prophets. First, the *Holy Spirit had not yet been poured out* and had taken up His abode in believers. Before Pentecost, the Holy Spirit came upon men in the Old Testament and then departed. The *indwelling* of the New Testament is quite different from the *inshining* of the Old. Second, the inspiration of the apostles came in conjunction with their *official role* in the Church and adapted itself appropriately. Third, the apostles *came after the incarnation*, which was anticipated by the prophets of the Old Testament.

The book of Revelation is somewhat different than the rest of the New Testament in that it does not deal with that which appeared in Christ, but it moves on to that which is yet to come, it is prophetical. The vision that came to Peter in Acts 10 with respect to Cornelius is also unusual. Paul was not one of the immediate circle of the Lord's disciples, but had received a separate calling from Him. Everything he needed in order to fulfil the office of apostle was given to him directly. Apart from these examples, most of what appears with the preaching of the apostles as recorded in Acts and the epistles comes across as though they are speaking and writing in quite a normal manner and of themselves. There is little to suppose it was any different from the preaching and writing that has not come down to us in Scripture. Paul's reference to the "cloke, books and parchments left at Troas" (2 Timothy 4:13) gives the letter very much of an everyday feel. With the prophets the phrase *"thus saith the Lord"* shows at least a claim to inspiration. Such a suggestion of inspiration rarely occurs in the New Testament. Indeed, there seems to be some kind of opposition between inspiration and words like *"I command"* and *"speak I, not the Lord"* (1 Corinthians 7:10 & 12). This, however, is explained by the difference between what Paul knew from the special revelation given to him (see 1 Corinthians 11:23) and that which came as normal apostolic inspiration, to which he refers in the words *"and I think also that I have the Spirit of God"* (7:40).

Clearly, the apostles were inspired

> "But the Comforter, which is the Holy Ghost, whom the Father will send in my name, he shall teach you all things, and bring all things to your remembrance, whatsoever I have said unto you." (John 14:26)

> "I have yet many things to say unto you, but ye cannot bear them now. Howbeit when he, the Spirit of truth, is come, he will guide you into all truth: for he shall not speak of himself; but whatsoever he shall hear, that shall he speak: and he will shew you things to come. He shall glorify me: for he shall receive of mine, and shall shew it unto you."
>
> (John 16:12-14)

> "But God hath revealed them unto us by his Spirit: for the Spirit searcheth all things, yea, the deep things of God. For what man knoweth the things of a man, save the spirit of man which is in him? even so the things of God knoweth no man, but the Spirit of God. Now we have received, not the spirit of the world, but the spirit which is of God; that we might know the things that are freely given to us of God."
>
> (1 Corinthians 2:10-12)

Only the Holy Spirit could reveal to the apostles the 'deep things of God'. Paul, along with the other apostles, had not received the spirit of the world but the Spirit which is of God, and the direct effect of this was that he knew the things that were freely given by God.

Paul states that the mystery that had been hidden from former generations *"is now revealed unto his holy apostles and prophets by the Spirit"* (Ephesians 3:5). He also does not hesitate to say that what they had heard from him was *"not as the word of men, but as it is in truth, the word of God"* (1 Thessalonians 2:13). John writes in Revelation (1:10), *"I was in the Spirit on the Lord's day"*.

With the apostles, inspiration came about because of the Holy Spirit *dwelling in them* not coming upon them, possible only after Pentecost and therefore different than the Old Testament prophets. This deserves emphasis. First, they had received in-workings of the Holy Spirit before the day of Pentecost. In breathing upon them, the Lord Jesus had officially communicated to them the *gift* of the Holy Spirit. Despite this, the Lord Jesus repeatedly declares that only when the Holy Spirit shall have been sent to them from the Father can real apostolic inspiration begin, as it did at Pentecost in the sermons of Peter. *After* Pentecost there was the indwelling of the Holy Spirit, *before* that day there were in-workings from without. This gave inspiration a modified form. From within the Holy Spirit was able to use, guide, and enlighten the consciousness of the apostles in a more immediate way, and without any break, even without them knowing.

Second, the impulse for the working of this inspiration lay in their official function as apostles. There are instances where there was a break, inspiration coming from without, as for example the vision of Peter at the house of Simon the tanner (Acts 10:19), or the vision of Paul of the man of Macedonia (Acts 16:9). Nevertheless, as a general rule inspiration came to them on a continuous basis as they discharged their duties as apostles. This went on until they died. Inspiration was given to them so that they could discharge their duties as apostles. They do not write simply because the Holy Spirit impels them irresistibly to write but because this was part of their office of being apostles. Inspiration flowed into their everyday activities.

Third, the apostles stand in a different position to the centre of all revelation, Christ Himself. What was vague with the prophets was concrete with the apostles, they testified of what they had seen and heard, the prophets could not do this. The inspiration of the apostles was an inspiration first of remembrance.

> "But the Comforter, which is the Holy Ghost, whom the Father will send in my name, he shall teach you all things, and bring all things to your remembrance, whatsoever I have said unto you." (John 14:26)

They had not to stop there but to proclaim the message of the Gospel and for such they were given remembrance by the Holy Spirit. Then, they were to announce the things to come and for this they receive apocalyptic vision. Finally, they had to give apostolic reflection concerning the 'Word of life' and for this the Holy Spirit led them into the deep things of God (1 Corinthians 2:10-12).

## The inspiration of Scripture

The inspiration of the writers by the Holy Spirit and the inspiration of Scripture ought to be kept distinct in our minds. That which originated within the consciousness of God through the working of the Holy Spirit's inspiration entered the consciousness of the Scripture writers. We now need to consider how what is in Scripture has come from this sphere of inspiration to be written down in a totally authentic and reliable form and free from error.

We have taken great care to distinguish between the inspiration of that which was written and all other forms. In writing, Scripture inspiration took place by the direct influence of the Holy Spirit upon the minds of the writers of Scripture through which their writings took on that form, even down to the words and syntax used, which was in the eternal counsel of God and was predestined by Him to be the means of grace to us that it is. In most of the epistles, apostolic inspiration will completely overlap with the inspiration of that which was written. The two aspects of inspiration thus coincide. Nevertheless, the two do not always overlap in this way. There may have been a choice between several epistles or even different copies of the same epistle whereby another factor is introduced. The fact that an epistle to the Colossians is preserved but one to the Laodiceans is lost can only be that the choice lay not in the hands of men but in the providence of God by which He permitted one to be lost and the other preserved. This does not mean that the one lost was not inspired, but that it was not intended by God as part of Scripture. The psalms of David would have been inspired to him as he sang them, but this alone did not give them a place in Scripture. Even as the notion of revelation and inspiration overlap at times, so too does that of the preservation of that which was inspired. God is directly at work in inspiration in the compiling of and, where applicable, the editing of the books of Scripture.

Inspiration is least obvious in forms such as the epistles, since their form is that of writing anyway. In those sections of Scripture taking the form of poetry, it is unlikely anything would have been changed, certainly were this the case those changes must have taken place under the inspiration of the Holy Spirit as they were written down. The working of inspiration is more obvious in the recording of apocalyptic visions, especially one of such proportions as the Revelation of John. To obey the command to *"write the things which thou hast seen"* (1:19) when the visions were finished required a special sharpening of the memory. It was also necessary that the descriptive language in particular be appropriate to what John was writing.

It would have been different again in the writing of the historical books where the author may well have begun to compile what he wrote from data already available to him, perhaps gleaned from the testimony of others. Luke's preface to his Gospel and the Acts provide an interesting insight.

> "Forasmuch as many have taken in hand to set forth in order a declaration of those things which are most surely believed among us, Even as they delivered them unto us, which from the beginning were eyewitnesses, and ministers of the word; It seemed good to me also, having had perfect understanding of all things from the very first, to write unto thee in order, most excellent Theophilus, That thou mightest know the certainty of those things, wherein thou hast been instructed." (Luke 1:1-4)
>
> "The former treatise have I made, O Theophilus, of all that Jesus began both to do and to teach." (Acts 1:1)

We learn that Luke was not the only one to have made a record of the things that Jesus said and did. As is implied by John at the end of his Gospel some of these may not have been entirely reliable and the need for something fixed and trustworthy was now becoming increasingly essential. Not being present himself, nevertheless, Luke had established for himself a perfect understanding of all things from the very first. In this, he had been guided by the testimony of those who had heard and seen the Lord. Having done this he then deemed himself competent to write down a narrative of all these things in good order. This procedure was doubtless followed by all writers of historical events of the Bible of which they were not themselves witnesses. The inspiration here lies in the preserving of the account from all error and its phrasing in precisely those words and structures determined by God, the Author behind the author.

No human being was present at creation, therefore no one but God Himself can be the author of information about what actually happened. Those things that happen to men are matters of human experience, so that the compiler of history would have probably followed a method similar to that followed by Luke. Their task then consisted in committing to writing a representation of the past that had thus formed itself in their minds. We must see at this point that that which was thus formed in their minds was itself in every detail facilitated by the inspiration of the Holy Spirit. That whilst what they were doing had the outward appearance of a work of purely human origin, in reality it was a work done entirely under the direct inspiration of the Spirit of God.

Often in Scripture there will appear more than one account of the same incident. This is particularly true in the Gospels. These are not repetitions but independent representations formed in the consciousness of the different writers under inspiration of the Holy Spirit giving different perspectives on the same incident and event. Inspiration does not override intellect, but subjects it to itself and uses it as an instrument. The words *"all scripture is given by inspiration of God"*(2 Timothy 3:16) clearly refers not to the writer, but to the products of the inspired writers. They remained writers, even compilers and poets, but in all their functions, the Holy Spirit worked upon their hearts and minds so that what they produced was error-free and carried divine authenticity and authority.

All those born again of the Spirit of God testify to the divine authority of the Bible by their submission and obedience to it as the written Word of God. The Lord Jesus, whose Spirit witnessed beforehand in the prophets, attributes absolute divine authority to the Scriptures and through His apostles He gives us the ground for that authority in divine inspiration.

We can do no other than accept the same to be from God. Not to recognise it is to admit that the Lord Jesus Himself was mistaken about these things.

## Loss of an inspired Bible means loss of an infinite Saviour

Were the Bible not inspired, the reading of it would never bring a single soul from death to life. Those not born of God will invariably see the inspired Scriptures as a dead book. All within them tends to disown the authority of Scripture and resists it with every human effort.

Inspiration at its heart amounts to this, that God in His sovereignty employs all the faculties He created in man that He might communicate to men what He has purposed to reveal with respect to the maintenance of His glory, the execution of His plan for the world, and the salvation of sinners.

# CHAPTER 13

# Whatever happened to the Originals?

*"The words of the LORD are pure words: as silver tried in a furnace of earth, purified seven times. Thou shalt keep them, O Lord, thou shalt preserve them from this generation for ever."* (Psalm 12:6-7)

Take up a copy of any of Shakespeare's plays, what certainty is there that the words we are reading were penned by the bard himself? We have no certainty at all. Textual critics will have examined first and second quartos, folios and reprints, printings 'newly corrected, augmented, and amended'. They will have seen pirated, reported, and cut versions of the play. There will be versions perhaps printed from a prompt copy containing corrections and additions in the margin. Arguments abound among critics as to correct and incorrect quarto readings, mistakes, which then may have been repeated in folios – all critics are fearful of attributing frightful rubbish to this prince of pen pushers! Daggers are inserted for swords, spitchcock for pilcher, shog for shake, stage directions are added that at times make havoc of a scene. Few would claim more than probability for an authentic and authoritative Shakespearean text. It may be intensely irritating to Shakespeare aficionados not to have a certifiably authentic text, but in the end what does it matter? The plays have bored the senses out of generations of schoolchildren and still provide amusement for those with time to go to the theatre, and so they have served their useful purpose.

No one's life is going to be radically changed by reading a corrupted version of Shakespeare, but relying on a corrupted version of God's Word has eternal consequences. When the meaning of a verse hangs on a single word or even a single letter, we cannot afford to have an unsure and approximate text.

> *The probability ascribed to a Shakespearean text is simply not good enough when it comes to the Bible.*

The Bible is not a text penned in the heat of literary and human inspiration, but it was given in words carried into the minds of its human authors on the breath of God, and then written by that same breathing onto holy pages. Why should we think that God would take such great care by a divine act of inspiration to secure the perfect recording of His every word, if at the last all is lost? The Word that God gave, He also keeps. Those who treat the text of God's Word like a Shakespeare folio will end up with a text like Shakespeare, a probable text with no certainty at all. It must be obvious that all those, professed friend or patent foe, who treat the Bible as though it were a human text will be unable to give us any more certainty for the Bible than they can for any human book. This is completely inadequate.

> *The textual integrity of the Word of God can only be guaranteed by a work of God in its preservation equal to that displayed in its original inspiration.*

Nothing less will do. The choice is clear, do we follow the pathway of textual criticism that can only give us a probable text, or do we take the texts preserved among God's people and still with us as the fulfilment of His promise? The first choice completely sets aside divine intervention and relies upon the rationalist methodology of critics. That which God has done is discounted, only that which is measurable by physical human senses is allowable. Once again, faith is set against autonomous human reason. *The reason of faith is settled on the plain statements of Word of God.* There is no point in defending a book we cannot take as being wholly trustworthy. Even a rationalist *defence* of textual integrity, however well intentioned, is just as inadequate. If we need to *prove* it true before we *believe* it to be true, we have already declared beforehand our lack of faith in it. If we begin, even if only by implication, with the assumption that the Bible is not true, that God has not preserved His Word intact, this is what we shall 'prove'. There can be no other outcome. What we say about Scripture must be based upon statements it makes about itself, believing these same statements to be wholly reliable because they have been made by God Himself. Believe it or bin it!

There are two ways and two ways only of approaching the whole issue of the preservation of Scripture. Those who seek a middle road delude themselves, there is none. God does not preserve Scripture using men and methods rooted in a denial of what He has said. As the actual autographs written by the prophets and apostles are long since gone, what guarantee can we have then apart from a divine promise that the words once given have been preserved and can be perfectly *recovered* in the copies, or 'apographs'? The best we can hope for otherwise is to *reconstruct* something as near as possible to what we imagine the originals to have been like employing methods textual critics would use on Shakespearean manuscripts and the early printed copies of his works. This approach is a total waste of time since all it can give us is a thoroughly human book. It flies in the face of all the Bible itself tells us about its own preservation. A book that tells lies about itself cannot be a book from the God who cannot lie!

> *Those who tell us that the only inspired Bible that ever existed is now gone for good are deceived. They would fob us off with false bibles they have cobbled together themselves – and we will not have them!*

There is no point in proving a book to be from God, if we start out by denying clear statements in its pages about its own preservation. The critical and rationalist route can never lead us to a Bible with word for word accuracy and thus makes the defence of verbal inspiration a pretty pointless undertaking. To profess verbal inspiration and at the same time to subject the Scripture texts to rationalistic critical methodology is to live in a crazed schizoid world, denying on the one hand what is confessed on the other. An inspired Bible that only lasted a couple of centuries or so is of little use to us today and makes a mockery of any claim that the written Word of God is given to all generations of men. We need certainty and not guesswork, this only God can give us. God's work with Scripture continues beyond inspiration, it is alive today in keeping that Word, applying it to human hearts and saving us. No human book can do that! All is one work of God's infinite grace.

## God has kept His promise

Those who begin the New Year with a resolution ought to know that if true to form they are hardly likely to carry it beyond a few weeks. Since none *"by taking thought can add one cubit unto his stature"* (Matthew 6:27), when resolving or promising anything our words ought to be tempered by an awareness of our own finite weakness. We ought to guard our words before making a commitment to God or man. The truth is that we fail so abysmally in these areas largely because we do not have complete control over all the circumstances of life. The reason God can be relied upon is that He is omnipotent, sovereign, and true, and so He will neither deceive nor fail us. We must be ever mindful that in looking into the question of manuscripts and translations, what we are really asking is whether God has made a promise and is able to keep it! The preservation of the Scriptures can only be maintained on the basis that God *"works all things after the counsel of his own will"* (Ephesians 1:11).

---

*If God cannot keep a promise to preserve His Word, how can we be sure He can keep His promises concerning salvation through repentance and faith in His Son?*

---

Throughout the twentieth century, a view of inspiration gained ascendancy among evangelicals and many fundamentalists that marked a departure from that which was previously confessed by believers since New Testament days. (This does not include many, if not most neo-evangelicals, who now frequently hold a neo-orthodox view of inspiration based on the philosophical musings of Barth and Brunner.) Recent scholarship has shown that men like Princeton professor, Benjamin Warfield (1851-1921), were not as committed to the biblical doctrine of verbal inspiration as we are sometimes led to believe. Thinking to answer rationalist theologians on their own ground and legitimise textual studies, these men began to suggest that only the autographs (originals) were inspired, apographs (copies) were not. For this reason many of the Statements of Faith issued by various bodies now speak of the Scriptures being inspired 'as *originally* given' whereas before this time the conviction was that inspired Scripture was preserved in the copies. All this took place almost unnoticed, but we are being asked to swallow a real whopper! What this means is that as the originals have long since turned to dust, *no inspired text exists today.* All we have available to us are non-inspired copies. Those who speak of reading an inspired Bible must therefore be mistaken.

Now the door stands open for all those of a mind to do so to engage in critical studies. This discipline will generally proceed on the assumption that God has not preserved His Word, but that it is now left to men to put together something as best they can. This cannot be thought of as inspired because God has not preserved an inspired Word beyond the original writings of the prophets and apostles. Having only non-inspired copies with which to work, it would seem, were this in fact so, that all we *can* do is apply human means to a reconstruction of what we think the originals may have said. The conclusion from this must be that however accurate such a reconstruction may or may not be is not really the point, what matters is that this man-made literary patchwork will lack the absolute certainty and therefore the authority of an inspired text. A non-inspired text cannot suddenly turn into an inspired one the moment our back is turned! To lose inspiration *at any point* is to lose an authentic and wholly reliable Bible altogether. We can then never be sure whether the Bible is full of errors or has none. Warfield's book on biblical inspiration is still hailed as a 'classic', but his viewpoint has done more to undermine confidence in Scripture than almost any other in the last 150 years or so.

Without a work of God, there is no way we can be sure whether the manuscripts we possess today are precisely as the originals. Alternatively, the Bible will be exposed to the ravages of the years as any human book. We are being asked to believe that God has allowed His authentic Word to disappear into the mists of time, in direct contradiction of what the Bible itself says. This view provides an excuse for rationalistically orientated 'scholars' to set their grubby little fingers to work on the sacred page. It gives opportunity for strangers 'to grace and to God' to rewrite the Word of God in their own image.

If we are to read *a word for word reliable Bible*, any view of the preservation of Scripture must extend the life of the inspired text beyond that of the autographs. Only an inspired text can give us an inerrant Bible. Without the precise words, we do not possess the precise thoughts of God. The promise of God is to preserve **His words** *"from this generation for ever"* – this presumes the perpetuation of an inspired text. Are we to believe that the Lord Jesus Himself was mistaken or that He was ready to mislead us? Never!

> "For verily I say unto you, Till heaven and earth pass, one jot or one tittle shall in no wise pass from the law, till all be fulfilled." (Matthew 5:18)
>
> "Heaven and earth shall pass away, but my words shall not pass away." (Matthew 24:35, cf. Luke 21:33 & Mark 13:31)
>
> "And it is easier for heaven and earth to pass, than one tittle of the law to fail. "(Luke 16:17)

We include *ALL* Scripture in this promise, for the Word of God is to be thought of only as an organic whole.

> "My spirit that is upon thee, and my words which I have put in thy mouth, shall not depart out of thy mouth, nor out of the mouth of thy seed, nor out of the mouth of thy seed's seed, saith the Lord, from henceforth and for ever."
>
> (Isaiah 59:21)
>
> "But the word of the Lord endureth for ever."
>
> (1 Peter 1:25)

After the exile, the law was once more taught in Jerusalem.

> "This Ezra went up from Babylon; and he was a ready scribe in the law of Moses, which the LORD God of Israel had

> given: and the king granted him all his request, according to
> the hand of the LORD his God upon him. ... For Ezra had
> prepared his heart to seek the law of the LORD, and to do it,
> and to teach in Israel statutes and judgments."
>
> (Ezra 7:6 & 10)

It was Ezra, doubtless assisted by others, who gathered all the books of the Old Testament together. They were preserved like this through to when the Lord Himself appeared. It is interesting to note that although the Jews were accused of many things, the *corruption* of the Old Testament was never once suggested by either the Lord or the apostles. After this time, the traditional Old Testament text was faithfully transcribed by Jewish scribes. They took exceptional care about accuracy, ensuring all copies were made without error, developing a complicated system of checks and counterchecks involving the counting of every letter. Each letter had its correct place in the overall text. Any copy under the slightest suspicion was discarded despite all the hours of work that may have gone into its preparation. In 1488, the whole Hebrew Old Testament in the Masoretic text was printed complete, a second edition appeared in 1491, a third in 1494. It was this last edition that was used by Luther and also later by the translators of our own *Authorised Version.*

Paul's writings are referred to by Peter as being Scripture; this was the *nature* of these writings.

> "And account that the longsuffering of our Lord is salvation;
> even as our beloved brother Paul also according to the
> wisdom given unto him hath written unto you; As also in all
> his epistles, speaking in them of these things; in which are
> some things hard to be understood, which they that are
> unlearned and unstable wrest, as they do also the other
> scriptures, unto their own destruction." (2 Peter 3:15-16)

Gradually, all that was recognised as Scripture was gathered together by the believers of the time into what we now recognise as the New Testament. By the fourth century, there was no dispute among believers as to what belonged in the New Testament. All were agreed that it was to be placed alongside the Old Testament to make up the whole Word of God. There were many false writings, false Gospels and epistles. There were other writings too, although perhaps helpful, they were not inspired Scripture. All these were excluded. Not only false writings but also *false readings* of the authentic Scriptures were recognised and rejected in the same way. To summarise: trustworthy copies of the original writings were produced by conscientious scribes; their copies were re-copied down the centuries by believers; unreliable copies, which would have been easily recognised by those who knew their Bible, were laid aside.

The traditional text of the New Testament was handed down through generations of genuine believers who rejected the false and kept the true. This traditional text is known to have been in use in the Greek Church during what is called the Byzantine period (452-1453) so that it is often referred to as the Byzantine text. It was seen into print by Erasmus of Rotterdam (1466-1536) in 1516. The printed text is referred to today as the *textus receptus*. The first edition of Erasmus was printed in some haste so that it is known that some minor oversights crept in. Although such blemishes persisted in some later printings, they were gradually spotted and removed. When speaking of blemishes, we need to remember that they were wholly inconsequential and relatively obvious. They would generally approximate in English the spelling of 'judgement' with or without an 'e', or 'honour' with or without a 'u'. Apart from this, it would have been in all respects as the traditional text. Theodore Beza produced five editions between 1559 and 1598, such was the desire to get things right. It was printed later by Stephanus in 1550, and by Elzevir in 1633. This Greek text, along with the Masoretic Hebrew text, that was used by the translators of the *Authorised Version* of 1611. We use this Bible because it is a faithful translation of the originals as preserved by God for us in the traditional texts. Reliable authors have written extensively and helpfully on the history and preservation of the Scripture texts and they should be consulted for a more exhaustive account.

*It continues to be the task of all who love the Word of God to reject all that is false and preserve that which is true.*

> **Would so-called believing scholars confine their energies to the task of sifting the wheat from the chaff, the true from the false, rather than co-operating with godless men in the destruction of the Word of God as preserved by Him in the traditional text, we could have more confidence in them. Until they do so, we shall continue to reject their inane ramblings out of hand!**

Such men as this have nothing to say to us and we nothing to them other than that they should change their ways and submit to God's Word. Sorting the true from the false is doubtless perceived by them as a far more limited role, and is one that satisfies their academic aspirations less than the one they have assigned to themselves. For now then, we cannot assume they are our friends.

Either we will accept without reservation and in faith what the Bible says about itself, or we will subject what the Bible says about itself to some other authority. Many *say* that they accept the Bible's own statements about itself, but then question it. A Bible worth receiving is a Bible worth believing. Do we or do we not have God's *inspired* Word in our hands today? This is the question. Many say we do not. We have His Word because God said He would preserve it and it needs no endorsement from us. Against all others, we say with Luther, "*Arguments* based upon reason determine nothing, but because the Holy Ghost says it, it is true". To move off the ground of faith, is to move off redemption ground, it is to be found "walking in the counsel of the ungodly, standing in the way of sinners, sitting in the seat of the scornful" (Psalm 1:1). As His children, we are by faith bound to believe the Word of God, in similar manner as rationalists are by reason bound to believe the judgements of men. Scripture says that Word carries within it the assurance of its own authenticity. Of the Scriptures John Owen says: "we are obliged, upon the penalty of eternal damnation... to receive them, with that subjection of soul which is due to the word of God." (Works XVI, p. 307, 1968 reprint). The Word of God itself must be sufficient authority for us.

### There can only be one Word

We acknowledge the final authority of the Word of God, a revelation of the mind of God, of His unbreakable purpose. If we refuse the authority of sola scriptura, we must replace it with another, whether this be the ultimacy of 'make up your own mind' rationalism, of Pope, church, human tradition or visionary hallucination. The rationalist, Romanist, and religious mystic have always sought to undermine the absolute authority of Scripture by introducing another word in its place or alongside it. They have all recognised too that if the Scripture can be shown to speak with more than one voice, clearly an adjudicator is required to bring clarity in the place of uncertainty. We shall find many volunteering to fill this place.

> "For if the trumpet give an uncertain sound, who shall prepare himself to the battle?" (1 Corinthians 14:8)

Sola scriptura is rightly perceived as a threat both to the claims of Rome and to rationalism. In a book of 1689 called Critical

301

*History of the Text of the New Testament,* and sounding for all the world like a modern textual critic, a Roman priest by the name of Richard Simon wrote,

> "A true Christian who professes to follow the Catholic faith must no more call himself a disciple of St. Augustine than of St. Jerome or of any other Church Father, for his faith is founded on the word of Jesus Christ, contained in the writings of the apostles as well *as in the firm tradition of the Catholic Church.* ...The great changes that have taken place in the manuscripts of the Bible—as we have shown in the first book of this work—*since the first originals were lost,* completely destroy the principle of the Protestants and the Socinians, who only consult these *same manuscripts of the Bible in the form they are today.* If the truth of religion had not lived on in the church, it would not be safe to look for it now in books that have been *subjected to so many changes* and that in so many matters were dependent on the will of the copyists. It is certain that the Jews who copied these books took the liberty of *adding certain letters here, and cutting out certain letters there,* according as they judged it suitable; and yet the meaning of the text is often dependent on these letters. *If traditior is not joined to scripture,* there is hardly anything in religion that one can confidently affirm." (ed. italics ours)

Simon uses tradition, another 'word', to undermine the *one Word* of Scripture. He continues his attack on the authority of the Bible by pointing to the loss of the originals and whilst acknowledging the authority accorded to the traditional or received text by 'Protestants', he denied its acceptability. He then speaks of a variation in readings, the intentional corruption of manuscripts, and an alleged unreliability of copyists, just as do his modern counterparts. Rationalist theologians must show the same thing, for any absolute biblical authority snatches all self-assumed autonomous reason from its throne.

If they would do away with the authority of Scripture, the critics must first demonstrate that there is no single Word of God but many. What they must then show us is that as the original writings have turned to dust many centuries ago and although they alone were written under inspiration, we now have no inspired Bible but only one in which the words are uncertain. They will then proceed to tell us that most manuscripts are unreliable and that many were corrupted by the Jews with respect to the Hebrew or by the early Christians with respect to the Greek. Copyists are not to be relied upon as most wanted to show their case in the best light and so made embellishments as they went along.

The Bible is then not the only voice. Another voice needed, a 'priestly class' of scholars to unscramble the jumble of manuscripts for the layman, to *reconstruct* for us what the original Scriptures must have been like. The Holy Spirit illuminating one inspired and divinely preserved sacred text to the heart of the individual believer as it is read or proclaimed is not enough. Strange, just when we think God will speak to us in Scripture, someone else always seems to appear on the horizon. We can never be trusted to be alone with our God and His one Word!

An easy way to show that no two texts or versions are the same is to quote or print them side-by-side. The modern preacher quotes from this version or that at a whim, just where his fancy leads him. In the end, it is completely unclear as to where the authentic Word is to be found. The very fact that many different translations are deemed equally worthy of our attention deflects the authority of the Word of God. It allows the sinner and the trifler to unhook himself from the barbs. He can always turn to another version that seems to support him, the apostate to one, the worldling and the sodomite to another.

> *Where there is no one Word, there is no one authority.*

Rome tried to discredit the authentic Scriptures by publishing *polyglot bibles*. Most well known of these is the *Complutensian Polyglot* (1513-17). Its purpose was to establish the defective Romish Latin Vulgate of Jerome as the standard of correctness rather than to allow the traditional text. The Vulgate was printed with the Greek Septuagint Old Testament on the one side and the Hebrew on the other. Christ at the centre, two thieves on either side, so they boasted! The other two versions were deemed corrupt where they differed from the Vulgate at the centre. This was intended to demonstrate how 'unbelieving Jews' had corrupted the Hebrew and 'schismatic Greeks' the Greek of the Old Testament.

There were other polyglot bibles, even one published by an Anglican, Brian Walton, in 1657. The Puritan and non-conformist turned to the authentic Word of God in matters of church practice. This undermined the Anglican stance and threw into doubt the 'apostolic succession' of the bishop and thus the authority of the clergy. Walton was suggesting the Puritan recourse to Scripture alone was untenable because of the great variety of readings. By gaining the assistance of leading Orientalists at the universities of Oxford and Cambridge, anyone raising a voice in opposition to his work could be labelled ignorant and foolish. Nothing changes, does it? The enemies of God's Word still attempt to belittle the learning of any opposing their viewpoint. A rat will run when it is chased – clobber it with a shovel, if you can – but when cornered, it will strike back. Such abuse only suggests to us a weak argument.

Since Bible days and through the Reformation to the present day, godly students of the Word believed that they were in possession of an inspired text, preserved, and kept pure by God. Even the enemies of God were prepared on occasions to concede that believers treated Scriptures as though they were perfect. Canon I of the *Formula Consensus Helvetica* (1675) holds that the *textus receptus* and the Hebrew Massoretic text along with the vowel points are the Word from which not a jot or tittle shall fail.

> "God, the supreme judge, not only took care to have His Word … committed to writing … but has also watched and cherished it with paternal care ever since it was written up to the present time, so that it could not be corrupted by craft of Satan or fraud of man. Therefore the church justly ascribes it to His singular grace and goodness that she has, and will have to the end of the world, a 'sure word of prophecy' and 'holy scriptures' (2 Tim. 3:15), from which, though heaven and earth perish, 'one jot or one tittle shall in no wise pass' (Matt. 5:18)."

The miraculous preservation of the original manuscripts themselves – Old or New Testament – is unnecessary as God has preserved faithful copies, as much the Word of God as the originals, because He *"has also watched and cherished it with paternal care ever since it was written up to the present time"*. The meaning is abundantly clear. No one at the time thought to draw the distinction made later by Warfield that sets the copies at odds with the originals.

Whilst we do not share all his theological insights, John Owen (1616-1683), ranks among the finest and most spiritually minded of theologians that God ever gave to the British people. Certainly, his defence of the Scripture texts has stood the test of time and is a position we find to be in almost all respects in conformity to what the Bible teaches about itself. He began where we all must begin. He believed most firmly that God has kept His promise to preserve the Word He inspired entire and without corruption.

"But yet we affirm, that the whole Word of God, in every letter and tittle, as given from him by inspiration, is preserved without corruption." (*Works,* XVI, p.301)

"Surely the promise of God for the preservation of his word, with his love and care of his church, of whose faith and obedience that word of his is the only rule, requires other thoughts at our hands. ... We add, that *the whole Scripture,* entire as given out from God, without any loss, is preserved in the *copies of the originals* yet remaining; what varieties there are among the copies themselves shall be afterward declared. In them all, we say, is every letter and tittle of the word. These copies, we say, are the rule, standard, and touchstone of all translations, ancient or modern, by which they are in all things to be examined, tried, corrected, amended; and themselves only by themselves." (*Works* XVI, p.357, ed. italics ours)

We have the Word of God because God *has* preserved it in its entirety.

"...the purity of the present original copies of the Scripture, or rather copies in the original languages, which the church of God doth now and hath for many ages enjoyed as her chiefest treasure" (*Works* XVI, p.353)

The Genevan theologian, Francis Turretin (1623-87) makes this same point.

"By the original texts, we do not mean the autographs written by the hand of Moses, of the prophets and of the apostles, which certainly do not now exist. We mean their apographs which are so called because they set forth to us the word of God in the very words of those who wrote under the immediate inspiration of the Holy Spirit." (*Institute of Elenctic Theology,* I, 2, p.106)

He attributes authenticity to the copies and to the original writings.

"However, a writing can be authentic in two ways: either primarily and originally or secondarily and derivatively. That writing is primarily authentic which is *autopiston* ('of self-inspiring confidence') and to which credit is and ought to be given on its own account. In this manner, the originals of royal edicts, magistrates' decrees, wills, contracts and the autographs of authors are authentic. The secondarily authentic writings are all the copies accurately and faithfully taken from the originals by suitable men; such as the scriveners appointed for that purpose by public authority (for the edicts of kings and other public documents) and any honest and careful scribes and copiers (for books and other writings). The autographs of Moses, the prophets and apostles are alone authentic in the first sense. In the latter sense, the faithful and accurate copies of them are also authentic. ... But the latter consists in this, that the autographs and also the accurate and faithful copies may be the standard of all other copies of the same writing and of its translations. If anything is found in them different from the authentic writings, either autographs or apographs, it is unworthy of the name authentic and should be discarded as spurious and adulterated, the discordance itself being a sufficient reason for its rejection. ... The various readings which occur do not destroy the authenticity of the Scriptures because they may be easily distinguished and determined, partly by the connection of the passage and partly by a collation with better manuscripts." (*op cit* p.113-114)

A number of points deserve our attention here. Underlying what Turretin writes is the assumption that accurate and faithful copies exist and are to be taken as the standard for all other copies and translations. Furthermore, if copies appear that do not match the authentic standard copies they are to be discarded as spurious and adulterated. It must not be overlooked that copyists are to be *"suitable men ... honest and careful"*. All too often, those have set themselves to work with Scripture, who knew no call of God to such a work and for this reason alone, if no other, exclude themselves as unsuitable. Finally, various readings are not a denial of the authenticity of the Scriptures as such deviations are easily identified.

> *What godly men such as Turretin and Owen tried to do, rather than cobble together a noxious pot-pouri (French for 'rotten pot') using every manuscript to hand, was to separate out the bogus and forged to reveal the genuine!*

The suggestion of some that Erasmus had access only to a few rather inferior manuscripts and that Stephanus and Beza largely followed him will not stand the test of honest historical scrutiny. Rome had a long history of forging all kinds of documents right, left and centre. There were the 'Pseudo-Isodorian Decretals' and the forged 'Donation of Constantine'. Men like Erasmus and Luther would have watched like hawks for the slightest indication of corruption in any texts. Furthermore, present research has shown that these men and their successors were invariably correct, as for example in the eventual rejection of *Codex Cantabrigiensis* (D). In imitation of the Reformers' resort to ancient Greek documents, Rome had used this manuscript to support their infamous doctrine of celibacy at the Council of Trent.

The greater number of manuscripts available today can only support the work of Erasmus and Stephanus, because they measured everything they looked at against the traditional text. They would work today as they did then, were they still with us. They had some alternative readings from which to choose, but after comparison with the traditional text, they either kept them as such in textual notes or laid them completely aside, but nothing was added or removed from the traditional text. The question here is not one of manuscript availability, but of methodology.

> *All new manuscripts were measured by these men against that which was already recognised by believers as being the Word of God.*

That there are variant readings in the Greek text is not in dispute and Owen offers a number of suggestions as to how they got there. What he vehemently objects to is the practice continued to this day of imposing them upon us as an alternative and thereby equally authoritative readings.

> "Hence it is come to pass ... that whatever varying word, syllable, or tittle, could be by any observed, wherein any book, though of yesterday, varieth from the common received copy, though manifestly a mistake, superfluous or deficient, inconsistent with the sense of the place, yea, barbarous, is presently imposed on us as a various lection." (*Works* XVI, p.363)

Owen, like Turretin, insists that there is a God-preserved original to hand by which all else is to be measured.

Variants, whatever their source, are to be treated *as deviations from the true text*. Owen is someone who recognizes the true purpose behind the appearance of the 'spurious brood' of manuscripts.

> "...I presume I may take liberty without offence to say, I should more esteem of theirs who would endeavour to search and trace out these pretenders to their several originals, and, rejecting the spurious brood that hath now spawned itself over the face of so much paper, that ought by no means to be brought into competition with the common reading, would reduce them to such a necessary number, whose consideration might be of some other use than merely to *create a temptation* to the reader that nothing is left sound and entire in the word of God."
> (*Works* XVI, p.364)

The effect of granting authenticity to these various readings will always be to undermine the conviction that God has preserved His Word.

Owen laments that as knowledge of the original languages of Scripture increased, the ground of legitimate textual study having already been occupied by eminent scholars, others wanting to make a name for themselves abused their position so that boldness in criticising the Scriptures increased. At first variant readings were simply compared one with the other, but this soon degenerated into a pernicious principle that *"sundry corruptions crept into the originals, which, by their critical faculty, with the use of sundry engines, those especially of the old translations, are to be discovered and removed"* (Works, XVI, p.290). The suggestion was that the copies of Scripture in the original languages then to hand had been corrupted – this has a peculiarly modern ring to it – they were to be corrected by textual criticism. In particular, comparisons were made with early translations as it was claimed they would have been made from texts that were more reliable. If there were indeed corruptions in the immediate copies of the original, it would be impossible to correct them having no standard by which to judge them. Incidental errors by scribes do not call for a revision of the text, but only for a recognition of what they are. There could be no place for mistakes in the Word of God. They were according to Owen little more than the *"conjectures of men conceited of their own abilities to correct the Word of God"* and we agree with him still. God is as much concerned in the preservation of the book itself as the teachings contained in it. Only because of the reliability of the text can the doctrines be established and so attacks of Satan will be directed as much against the book itself as against the teaching it contains.

## The rise of rationalist criticism within conservative theology

The orthodox Presbyterian school, Westminster Theological Seminary, was heavily involved in the original *New International Version*. Despite this, the project has an interesting pedigree, the roots of its family tree reaching deep into seventeenth century German rationalism. Princeton Seminary founded in 1812 was for many years a bastion of orthodoxy. The rise of liberals within northern Presbyterianism, exemplified by the tirades against 'fundamentalism' by Harry Emerson Fosdick, began to make its mark. In 1903, the standard of the *Westminster Confession* had been watered down somewhat to the advantage of liberal theology. By 1914, Princeton Seminary began to make adjustments to reflect the growing influence of liberals within Presbyterian ranks. Princeton soon disappeared into a cesspit of godless theology where it still wallows to this day. At the frontline in opposing these changes stood Drs. Gresham Machen, Oswald T. Allis, and Dick Wilson. Whilst we cannot share all their perspectives, we stand in awe at their courage. By 1929 conditions within Princeton had become too much for many, this led to the departure of Machen, Wilson and others to found Westminster Seminary in Philadelphia. The great problem at Westminster was that although they left behind every vestige of modern theology, and whilst they abhorred 'higher criticism', little was done to divest themselves of the rationalist methodology of Warfield in the field of textual studies, 'lower criticism'. Had they taken the biblical course, maybe, just maybe, we would not have seen the involvement of Westminster Theological Seminary in the birth of the *New International Version*. For a mother to give birth to a stillborn child is tragedy enough, but to wrap it in swaddling clothes, feed and nurture it, is sad beyond words. Here we observe an *alma mater* whose milk appears to have turned distinctly sour!

As there is a direct godly line, so there is an ungodly line of unbelief and rebellion. Richard Simon's book, *Critical History* (1689), greatly influenced the father of German rationalist theology, J. S. Semler (1684-1766). This was the cradle of godless higher criticism. The very sad fact about Semler is that before taking up his professor's chair at Halle University, he was educated at the pietist Orphan Schools of August Hermann Francke, which so inspired the godly George Müller in his work in Bristol. Semler had a markedly negative stance towards the Bible, rebuilding nothing he tore down; his was a lifelong revolt against the Word of God. He thought to defend 'the faith' against deism, pantheism, and atheism by laying bare the foundations upon which it was built, the Scriptures themselves. He moved onto his opponents' ground in order to defend that which they were attacking, he fought unbelief with yet further unbelief. He ended the conflict by capitulating to the enemy. Student of Semler and arch-sceptic towards the New Testament text, J. J. Griesbach (1745-1812), was professor at Jena. He continued the crusade begun by the Roman priest, Richard Simon, to discredit the text by trying to show a single *sola scriptura*, one authentic text, could not exist. If it cannot be banned or burned, butcher it! Griesbach wrote, in 1771 that the New Testament *"abounds in more glosses, additions, and interpolations purposely introduced than any other book"*. Apparent differences in the four Gospels have long been used to discredit verbal inspiration. Around 170 A.D., Tatian composed his *Diatessaron*, meaning 'through the four', a harmony to demonstrate their agreement. Griesbach constructed a synopsis to highlight the *differences* in the Gospel accounts of the life of the Lord Jesus with the express purpose of showing them to be not entirely reliable.

Perhaps, this is where the story becomes all rather sad. Between 1826 and 1828, Charles Hodge of Princeton Seminary was in Germany studying theology, despite the misgivings of the seminary's founder, Archibald Alexander. Here he made the acquaintance of the church historian, Neander. He also became friendly with the theologian, Tholuck, responsible for disseminating the myth that Luther had a loose view of Scripture. He would also have heard apostate Schleiermacher, (English, 'veil-maker'!). Hodge was tutored in the German language by a young and recently converted George Müller. Müller had, according to his *Autobiography*, fallen into a period of backsliding at the time. Whilst Hodge retained his orthodoxy, his subsequent writings on biblical criticism betray the influence of Griesbach, despite hanging on to the received text as standard at Princeton. Hodge would have been very much aware that Griesbach denied the deity of the Lord Jesus and was otherwise far from orthodox in theology. What father Hodge had begun, his son, C. W. Hodge, continued. As is often the case, the son took matters further than had his father, even refusing to acknowledge the most obvious link between 'lower' and the 'higher' criticism of Semler. He believed matters of the biblical text belonged to an essentially neutral realm.

The word 'criticism' when applied in any sense to the Bible ought to arouse more than caution in the mind of any Bible believer. In this context, it is used to mean the exercise of judgement based on human reason. Criticism is never neutral. To make autonomous human reason the final court of appeal when considering the Bible is entirely misplaced. Quite the opposite, we take what the Bible says on any issue as being a statement that is true and beyond question because it comes from God. From such statements, we then interpret the world about us, which will involve the use of reason subject to Scripture. Our reason must always be subservient to Scripture and not stand above it as judge or critic. 'Lower' criticism concerns itself with a literary text, be it Shakespeare, Goethe,

Dickens or the Bible. Its task is to recover the best possible original text. As we have seen, the Bible cannot be approached in this way without first setting aside God's promise to preserve His Word. Textual criticism can only give us an approximate text of the Bible and this is inadequate and unthinkable. Who then can trust a Bible upheld only by fallible human reason?

'Higher' criticism concerns itself with such matters as authorship, dates, and structure. Critics will compare what evidence is found within the Bible itself with the findings of secular historians, archaeologists, and others. Again, the final judge is human reason. Early critical studies by Astruc (1753), Eichhorn (1783), De Wette (1805), and Ewald (1823) gave rise to the now notorious 'documentary hypothesis' of the Pentateuch, postponing its written form until four or five centuries after Moses death. It was said that writing was not invented until after Moses. Although archaeological discoveries have since shown this to be untrue, the theory has not been thrown out! The first five books of Scripture were said to be a compilation from sources beginning before Moses rather than the work of one man. Critics then began crawling all over the sacred text, even splitting single verses into two, deciding who wrote what. This hypothesis was developed into a more stable form by two Hebrew scholars, Graf and Wellhausen. Criticism did not stop there. Isaiah was supposed to be the product of multiple authorship and Daniel could not possibly have written the book that bears his name. In this way, the entire prophetic and supernatural element in the Old Testament could be attributed to myth and legend and Bible history made to conform to its rationalist counterpart. Does one believe the plain statements of Scripture or those of godless men intent on pulling the Bible apart?

In Britain, the Graf Wellhausen hypothesis was expounded by men like Professor Driver, who published his *Literature of the Old Testament* in 1891, and by Robertson Smith in Scotland. Robertson Smith was tried for heresy by the Scottish Church, who took a dim view of these things and deprived him of his professorship. Some prominent voices thought he was suffering persecution caused by ignorant prejudice and so the decision was reversed. Many found some reassurance in Driver's claim that his views 'did not affect the authority or inspiration of the Scriptures'. Unless he had something else in mind than that which others would have understood by the words 'inspiration' and 'authority', his comments were blatantly untrue.

The New Testament fared no better than the Old at the hands of critics. A theological professor at Heidelberg University, H. E. G. Paulus (1761-1851), tried to provide natural explanations for all the miracles of the Lord. When the disciples saw Jesus walking on the water, they were hallucinating. Jesus fainted on the cross and it took the coolness of the tomb to revive Him. Let us be clear, crucifixion is not an experience anyone survives and lives to tell the tale. The disciples then wrote down these events as miracles. In 1835, David Strauss' book *Leben Jesu* appeared, in which he does not see the miracles just as the supernatural embroidery of everyday events, but as total myths – they never happened. Eventually, an Englishman, J. A. Robinson (1902), came up with a clever explanation for the miracles. He reckoned that when John wrote his Gospel, he was getting on a bit and his memory was failing, a touch of dementia perhaps, and he got a little confused about what was real and what was mythical. Other scholars tell us that John's Gospel was not written by the apostle John at all, but by someone else of the same name!

Both higher and lower criticism are the seriously deformed children of rationalist theology. They are Siamese twins, and the separation of either one from the other would spell instant death for both. The connection between higher and lower criticism is plain enough. The American literary critic, Northrop Frye, makes the point in his book, *Anatomy of Criticism* (1957), that 'higher criticism' is in fact but another kind of 'lower criticism'. *Semler* made no secret of the fact that he believed that manuscripts had been edited and not just copied by scribes, who altered them in their favour. Graf-Wellhausen and those who have followed them rest on a rationalist approach to handling the Old Testament text – 'cut and paste' theology! The New Testament critics would assume that the writers would have either added bits and pieces themselves or introduced the mythology that had grown up around the life of the Lord Jesus, providing 'supernatural' explanations of events. Griesbach believed orthodox Christians had corrupted their own texts. As copyists had tended to favour their own teaching, this was to be edited out, especially any references to the trinity or of the Lord Jesus as God. He wrote,

> "When there are many variant reading in one place, that reading which more than the others manifestly favours the dogmas of the orthodox is deservedly regarded as suspicious."

To help in the dismantling of the text, he classified manuscripts into three ancestral groups called 'rescensions'. What is a man like Warfield doing even contemplating co-operation with the successors of such men?

> ***Working with God's enemies can never deliver us victory over them, but is always a sell-out to evil!***

Like many since, Warfield made the mistake of thinking he could answer rationalism by moving across to its own ground without becoming infected with it himself. The scandal is that today most conservative evangelical and fundamentalist institutions of learning still repeat Benjamin Warfield's mantra that textual criticism is neutral. Warfield regarded textual criticism as dealing with 'facts' rather than with the speculation of higher criticism. Yet, facts are what the Bible says they are.

In defending the doctrine of 'verbal inspiration', Warfield was convinced that after careful revision, the Scripture could be placed beyond the machinations of rationalist critics. In this he went so far as being prepared to say the account of the Lord's resurrection and ascension in Mark 16:9-12 was not part of the Word of God. In 1876, Warfield also undertook the now customary pilgrimage for a year's study to Germany at the University of Leipzig. In 1887, he became professor at Princeton. By this time, the New Testament text was being worked over with such rigour that someone mockingly suggested that the critics must be questioned each morning as to what was now the Word of God lest it had changed over night! It did not take C. W. Hodge and Warfield long to embrace the work of Westcott and Hort, followers of Griesbach's methods. Westcott and Hort's text, they claimed, was neutral and arrived at scientifically, it represented that from which all others had diverged and would become the standard. The Westcott and Hort text was carried uncritically across to Westminster. Only one small piece of leaven was all it took for the whole lump to be contaminated.

By now, Warfield is caught in something of a cleft stick. On the one hand, he wants to preserve his growing reputation in textual criticism and on the other, defend his position of a verbally inspired Bible. Some balancing act would now be required. What he emerged with was quite simple: *only the original autographs were inspired!* Error in Scripture could then only be proved, if it had been in the original texts. Clever that, since he has already said we do not have them. Off the hook! Warfield's view states that God has not preserved the *inspired text* of Scripture beyond the original autographs. The conclusion must be that we therefore cannot know with certainty the precise wording of Scripture. He wrote in the *Presbyterian Review* in 1881,

> "We do not assert that the common text, but only that the original autographic text was inspired. No 'error' can be asserted, therefore, which cannot be proved to have been aboriginal in the text."

This was an innovation. Owen made clear that God had preserved that which

> "As the Scripture of the Old and New Testament were immediately and entirely given out by God himself, his mind being in them represented unto us without the least interveniency of such mediums and ways as were capable of giving change or alteration to the least iota or syllable; so, by his good and merciful providential dispensation, in his love to his word and church, his whole word, as first given out by him, is preserved unto us entire in the original languages; where, shining in its own beauty and lustre (as also in all translations, so far as they faithfully represent the originals), it manifests and evidences unto the consciences of men, without other foreign help or assistance, its divine original and authority." (*Works*, XVI, p.349-50)

No real criticism could now be levelled at the Bible and he was free to join every higher and lower critic in the task of reconstructing what might be the inerrant original. This remains the position of virtually all evangelical and many fundamentalist seminaries to this day.

This marks a significant change from the conviction that was formerly held with respect to *both the originals and copies*. The test of Presbyterian and 'reformed' orthodoxy since 1643 has always been the original unaltered *Westminster Confession*.

Those who claim to be the heirs of the Puritans must be held to their own confession!

> ... The Old Testament in Hebrew, (which was the native language of the people of God of old,) and the New Testament in Greek, (which at the time of the writing of it was most generally known to the nations,) being immediately inspired by God, and by his singular care and providence kept pure in all ages, are therefore authentical so as in all controversies of religion, the Church is finally to appeal unto them. But because these original tongues are not known to all the people of God, who have right unto and interest in the scriptures, and are commanded, in the fear of God, to read and search them, therefore they are to be translated into the vulgar language of every nation unto which they come..."

(Chapter 1; Sections IV & VIII, ed. italic ours.)

The originals were immediately inspired and "...*by his singular care and providence kept pure in all ages, are therefore authentical so as in all controversies of religion*". The originals being no longer available, these words can only properly apply to the copies. If the copies are already pure and they are still in our hands because kept by God's singular care and providence, why is there then all this talk of a reconstruction of the text?

In 1855, C. H. Spurgeon republished the 1689 *Baptist Confession of Faith*. It is in effect the *Westminster Confession* given a Baptist slant. It repeats these words almost word for word. In 1966, the Strict Baptist denomination in the UK, many of whose members would consider themselves the heirs of men like Spurgeon – mistakenly, we believe – adopted a new *Affirmation of Faith*. Two things are strikingly different, although it takes a sharp eye to spot them. Evidently they have swallowed the Warfield line "we accept the whole Bible, in the very words of the *original* Scriptures, as given by inspiration of God, to be our rule of faith and life" (italics ours). What they are telling us is that their 'rule of faith and life' is a book that is no longer available to us – not much use that! Just as worrying is the statement "the divine authority of the Bible is *not contrary to reason, but is demonstrated by convincing evidence* " (italics ours). This is the credo of rationalists. These people have to squeeze themselves somewhere into the picture with their tuppence worth of wisdom. Note the words of the 1689 Confession (identical to the *Westminster Confession*), which are very different:

> "The authority of the Holy Scripture, for which it ought to be believed and obeyed, dependeth not upon the testimony of any man or church, but wholly upon God, (who is truth itself,) the author thereof; and therefore it is to be received, because it is the word of God." (I, 4)

Scripture is to be received, not because it can be upheld by human reason and demonstrated as though it were part of some laboratory experiment, *but 'because it is the word of God'*. God says it, so it is true! *That* is believing the Bible! All we need to do now is look at the world and all things in the light it sheds and *that* is biblical reasoning! Missing in this later confession too is all reference to the Scriptures being 'sufficient, certain, and infallible'.

> *These changes have been introduced by leaders intent on taking their people in a different direction whilst at the same time pretending it is the old.*

This is quite scandalous and sooner or later they will reap what has been sown. Certainly, these people are not treading in the footsteps of their great men of the past, whom they say they honour.

The suggestion made is that only scholars can tell us approximately what the inspired text was like, but as this has now gone, the possibility of having an inspired Bible has also gone. This is an unbelievable travesty of the truth. Who are these men who would take from us an inspired Bible? Sure, the originals were God-breathed and that which God breathed was written by the authors on a piece of paper. So what? It was written down, captured for posterity. What they wrote was the product of the inspiration of the authors by the Holy Spirit; this ensured total written accuracy. A copy of what these men wrote is not less the authentic Word of God for that. It is totally illogical to conclude that copies of the words of that which was God-breathed, inspired, become less the product of inspiration for being copied. This is utter nonsense. These people are either saying there was something magical or mystical in the original documents that disappeared when they were gone, or they concentrate so much on the process of inspiration that the product of it and God's purpose for it are ignored. Must God then inspire every copyist for us to have an inspired Bible; must He inspire every printer? If I copy John 3:16 word for word as God breathed it out, does it become any less the inspired word of God? Original or copy, what is the difference? The words that God gave are identical, and they *remain* words God gave; they carry the thoughts of God; they still exist, whether we have the actual paper on which the authors wrote or no. Has God taken His hands off His Word? Never! No one seems to have thought to ask these people how they would know without doubt when their task would be complete, since they have no originals to signal their arrival at journey's end.

*Only a Bible upon which we can depend is a book we can defend!*

We have a clear choice between one of two diverging pathways, the road of faith or the road of human reason and unbelief. Do we begin with the Word of God or do we begin with the word of men? *This* is the question and it has in the first instance little to do with texts, but with the faithfulness of our God. To decide these things we need only a believing heart and the ability to read. Of course, textual scholars will deem all non-academics meddling in what they regard as their exclusive area of work unworthy to tie their bootlaces, still less to steal their clothes! Only after giving a positive answer to this question, do we turn to the manuscripts and texts, and scoop away the dross and scum from the gold, to uncover the authentic Word of God. For it to be of any use, textual study must be grounded upon what the Bible already says about itself.

> *If we do not begin with the Word of God, we shall never end with it!*

## A replacement for the received text

Around 1860, more Greek manuscripts became known and New Testament criticism received further impetus. The oldest and most complete of these manuscripts were Vaticanus (B) and Sinaiticus (Aleph). As its name suggests, Codex B was uncovered in the Vatican library and is thought to have been written around the middle of the fourth century. The discovery of Codex Aleph in a wastepaper basket in St Catherine's Monastery at the foot of Mount Sinai in 1859 by Tischendorf is well known. This was perhaps written in the late fourth century. Alexandrinus (A), thought to date from the first half of the fifth century, was considered for many years to be the oldest New Testament manuscript. Given to the English king in 1627 by the Patriarch of Constantinople, it still sits today in the British Museum.

Professors B. F. Westcott (1825-1901) and F. J. A. Hort (1828-1892), two Anglican theologians – by no stretch of the imagination to be regarded as anything approaching Bible believers – found themselves appointed to correct alleged 'errors' in the Authorised Version and work on a Revised Version. They seized the moment to falsify the Greek text. Avowed followers of Griesbach, they made no secret of an aversion to all orthodox readings and texts or of their intense dislike of the *textus receptus*. Their contention was that the traditional text was corrupt having been put together from selected readings from various texts already to hand to create a completely new text. As Griesbach, Westcott and Hort believed orthodox scribes had altered text in favour of such doctrines as divinity of Christ and the trinity, which is why they struck them out. This is hardly surprising given that the revising committee also included a Unitarian.

This all flies in the face of Bible teaching on two grounds. The first is doctrinal in that the deity of our Saviour and the trinity are integral to the faith once delivered and not to be denied. Even today, these two doctrines are the first to be attacked by our enemies. Denial of the deity of the man Christ Jesus, according to 1 John 4:3, is the spirit of antichrist! Second, we reject Westcott and Hort because the traditional text, which they sought to destroy, has been carried to us directly on the breath of God! That which was found in the hands of true believers is the true Word of God for *God has preserved what the prophets and apostles wrote even as the Bible says He would*. All textual evidence coming our way must be interpreted in the light of *this fact,* which is founded on the rock of Scripture. What Westcott and Hort did was to call false that which had always been recognised among genuine believers as the text preserved by God and to substitute it with a *false text* of their own making. Their reconstructed text was to replace the *textus receptus* as that which was nearest to the originals. This latter claim appealed to Warfield at Princeton. Westcott and Hort refused to accept that *heretics* had tampered with text Aleph and B, they implied rather that *believers* had tampered with the traditional text. When textual questions arose, error was invariably left in and that which reflected the truth was taken out.

These two men were not even consistent with their own rationalist principles for much was done without 'evidence', relying purely on conjecture. Much was obscured behind ingenious theories and technical terms that would bamboozle the uninformed. They spoke of 'intrinsic probability', 'transcriptional probability', 'internal evidence of readings', and 'internal evidence of documents'. This is all, as literary criticism in other fields can sometimes be, 'expert' opinion plus a little subjective guesswork. They are little better than saloon bar cardsharps trying to win their game by sleight of hand. Those who begin by denying what the Bible says about itself will build up a dossier of 'evidence' and argument that demonstrates their point of view. Sure, we too are prejudiced and do nothing to conceal this. We are prejudiced in *favour* of the unadulterated Word of God preserved among His people and of the teachings contained within it.

Their underlying principle was that these early texts, being in almost perfect condition, were the nearest we could have to an authentic New Testament. The text they most favoured was B along with Aleph and other texts such as D. D, we recall, had already been rejected in the 17th century. Their rationalistic methodology was much the same as that used by any literary critic on the works Shakespeare or other writer, and perhaps with even less honesty because they were dealing with matters of personal belief. The fact that they were handling the Word of God was in this respect entirely ignored. Their approach was,

> "We dare not introduce considerations which could not reasonably be applied to other ancient texts, supposing them

> to have documentary attestation of equal amount, variety, and antiquity."

What we see evolving here is not only a godly and ungodly line of scholars, but also of texts and readings. Believers working on the principle of faith accept that God has preserved His own sacred Word as a deposit of the truth and reject that which is false. Scholars relying on rationalist methodology thereby already have a predisposition to refuse the true and accept the false, which is precisely what Westcott and Hort did.

The preference for earlier texts is often supported on the grounds that being older they would have been closer to the originals. Against this, it can also be said that early manuscripts, which differ from the traditional text, survived only because they had been laid aside as unreliable and had therefore fallen into disuse. Genuine texts would have been worn out with constant use and so few are likely to have remained. We are thrown back repeatedly on God fulfilling His promise to preserve Scripture as the final guarantee of a reliable text. Let us be clear as to what these men are doing. They are taking the words God has given and changing them so that they mean something else.

Our methodology in approaching the sacred text must begin and end in faith. There are those who, whilst abhorring Westcott and Hort's work, have sought to substantiate the authentic texts using what are in essence rationalistic methods. The last thing we would want to do is diminish the most valuable insights emerging from the writings of men like Dean Burgon. Despite this, the evidence for the authenticity of Scripture must lie in the first instance within Scripture because it is the only authoritative Word of God and we accept it for that reason alone. Our faith cannot be built on anything less than this, however well intentioned. Burgon's premise is insufficient, when he says that,

> "We imitate the procedure of the courts of justice in decisions resulting from the converging product of all evidence, when it has been cross-examined and sifted."

We cannot drag God's Word before the bar of human judgement, no way! 'Facts' are always what God's Word reveals them to be. The only safe judge of Scripture is Scripture and we begin with its own statements to determine what is true and what is false. We must also reject revisions of the *textus receptus* such as Hodges-Farstad, *"The Greek NT according to the Majority Text"* (1982). It is a rationalist reconstruction. Based as it is on statistical probability, it cannot give us the Word of God, but can only lead in the end to yet more uncertainty.

Conservative textual critics still live in hope of restoring word for word that which God gave by inspiration. To be fair to Warfield, this is doubtless what motivated him. His mistake was to think that he could do so by leaving the ground of faith; this is where he went astray and many there are who have followed his in his steps with the inevitable tragic consequences. Liberal critics have long since recognised that restoring the texts is impossible and in this respect they are right, for this is where a rationalist route must inevitably lead. An authentic text can only be assured us by *supernatural* means, through inspiration and preservation. To unbelievers this is not possible, they do not believe in an inspired Bible, let alone one preserved miraculously by God in our own age. Indeed, they see their work as a means of combating what the Bible presents as the truth.

J. L. Hug (1765-1846) and Carl Lachmann (1793-1851) shared the scepticism of Griesbach. They believed the New Testament text was corrupted beyond the recovery of the original.

Lachmann claimed we could only go back to around the fourth century using extant manuscripts. To bridge the gap between these and the original we must use 'conjectural emendation'. In plain English, this amounts to little more than guesswork based on theological prejudices! Eventually, liberal scholars gave up all pretence of recovering original texts. In *History of New Testament Criticism* (London 1910), W. J. Coneybeare said, *"the ultimate text, if there ever was one that deserves to be so called, is for ever irrecoverable."* The New Testament critic, Kirsopp Lake, wrote in 1941 *"we do not know the original form of the Gospels, and it is quite likely that we never shall"*. Whilst still respected among their own, the consensus that had surrounded Westcott and Hort has eroded. The hope of ever recovering the originals has been abandoned. The task was now to uncover the 'process' by which the New Testament acquired its form. Now many 'Matthews' and several 'Lukes' appeared on the scene. What confusion! As long as there was the goal of recovering an original, the discipline at least had some sense of direction even if it was heading straight for the rocks. Without the divine preservation of the originals, we have no way of knowing whether any single word in it is from God or no. It is precisely to this point that the enemies of God would lead us. The rival to the *textus receptus* today is the Nestle-Aland Greek New Testament.

The infallible Spirit of God continues His work after the completion of inspiration in preserving that which was given in an extraordinary manner. All those who have transcribed Scripture since have done so under the special providence of God. Not that any of them were inspired as were the writers, for they brought nothing new. To say that scribes may have slipped here and there for one reason or another is one thing, but to claim that the original text has been deliberately corrupted is quite another. They would have been diligent to see that every jot and tittle was as it should be, believing as they did that these were matters of eternal import. Assuming there were any error in any document, there would have been innumerable other copies by which to identify the mishap and overall this in no way distracts from the fact that God has kept His promise despite the weakness of men. In the case of the Old Testament, men like Ben Asher spent years making perfect copies of it. What we must say is that the whole Bible as it came from God has been preserved by Him without error, to use Owen's words, *"in the copies of the originals yet remaining"* (XVI, p.357). Every letter, every word that God ever gave is to be found there and is the standard by which all else is measured or corrected. The text has been preserved by the special providential care of God not in the least through the care of believers who have since watched over God's Word, preserving authentic copies. If our generation does not do the same, we shall be found wanting, for this task is now committed to us.

So many today *claim* to believe in Scripture and yet demand proof of us based on unbelief. These are they of whom John Owen said, *"they render themselves obnoxious unto every testimony that we produce from it that so it is, and that it is to be received on its own testimony"* (XVI, p.314). We have no need of any other testimony to Scripture than Scripture itself. It is the Word of God and not to be refused. If we will not accept its own testimony, then we deny it and there is little point to trying to prove it to be true, for then we do not accept it from the start. The test of all the words of men must always be:

> "To the law and to the testimony: if they speak not according to this word, it is because there is no light in them."
> (Isaiah 8:20)

# CHAPTER 14

# The Authentic Word of God

*"For ever, O Lord, thy word is settled in heaven"* (Psalm 119:89)

It is vital when considering matters of text and translation to take into account that which has had the seal of God upon it over the years and has had the acceptance of God's people. A faithful translation is as much part of the divine preserving work of God as is the preservation of the original texts. The 1611 Bible we use is not reliable because of some argument to do with manuscripts and texts, but because it has been given and kept by God to perfectly reveal that eternal purpose which cannot fail. The Bible *we already have in our hands*, the *Authorised Version*, is a reliable and faithful translation because it is itself an integral part of God's eternal purpose to bring salvation to the world through His Son and it is therefore unthinkable that He should give us anything other than a totally reliable Word. This is the ground of our defence of the *Authorised Version* of 1611. We *reject* the newer modern versions, not because they are new or modern, but because when they are not misguided attempts to improve on what God has in His providence already given us in the English language, they are a deliberate attempt on the part of known apostates to change and pervert the Word of God.

> *The* Authorised Version *of the Bible comes to us as foreordained of God down to the very smallest detail in order to bring us His Word as He has beforehand determined it should, and for this reason alone it cannot be anything other than an error-free, a holy Bible, perfectly prepared and given by God for its task.*

A rather misleading leaflet was recently circulated by two fundamentalist pastors of whom one would have expected better things. They sought to bring into disrepute arguments favourable to the *Authorised Version* by in many cases misusing quotations from well-known figures in the Christian world past and present. The suggestion seems to be that all these giants of the faith would have been quite happy to use modern translations. It is possible to show that almost anyone said almost anything by wrenching the quotation out of the context in which it was first written. Arguing for a plurality of translations, a quotation from John Owen is used to suggest that he believed a translation must necessarily be less than the originals. They quote, *"To advance any, all translations concurring, into an equality with the originals, – so to set them by it as to set them up with it on even terms, … – is to set up an altar of our own by the altar of God"*. Perhaps, we can be generous and grant the writers of this leaflet the luxury of being ignorant rather than to accuse them of deliberate dishonesty. The answer is to return the quotation to where it came from and look at it in its proper context.

> "Translations contain the word of God, and are the word of God, perfectly or imperfectly, according as they express the words, sense, and meaning of those originals. To advance any, all translations concurring, into an equality with the originals, – so to set them by it as to set them up with it on even terms, – much more to propose and use them as means of castigating, amending, altering any thing in them, gathering various lections by them, is to set up an

altar of our own by the altar of God, and to make equal the wisdom, care, skill, and diligence of men, with the wisdom, carp, and providence of God himself."

(*Works* XVI, p.357)

What we must remember is the circumstances in which Owen wrote these words. Rome was suggesting that the Hebrew text had been perverted by the Jews and the Greek by others so that the original text was to be corrected from the Jerome's Latin *Vulgate*, the official Roman bible of the day. Polyglot bibles were compiled expressly to demonstrate this superiority. Jerome was said to have had access to more accurate texts than were to hand later. Indeed, *the originals were to be corrected from the translation!*

"That translations were of any other use formerly was not apprehended. They are of late presented unto us under another notion – namely, as a means and helps of correcting the original, and finding out the corruptions that are in our present copies, showing that the copies which their authors used did really differ from those which we now enjoy and use!" (*Works* XVI, pp.406-7)

All this Owen was at pains to dispute. Far from saying a perfect translation is not possible, he says that translations *"are the word of God, perfectly or imperfectly, according as they express the words, sense, and meaning of those originals"*, but they could never be used as a standard by which to correct the original Hebrew and Greek texts from which they derive. Translations may reflect the originals *perfectly* or imperfectly, and to that extent they must be acknowledged as the inerrant Word of God. The order must always be to check the faithfulness of a translation against the originals preserved by God among His people and against other translations, in whatever language, known to be faithful. This does not make translations less the inspired Word of God for that. A perfect translation of Scripture made at the behest and under the providential guidance of its Author is without doubt possible. With this conclusion Owen concurs in the above passage. Owen's words have been grossly misused to support something with which he would not have agreed.

## Bibles before 1611

Even before the days of the Reformation, John Wyclif (1320?-84) had already translated the Bible into English from a reconstructed Latin Vulgate text. Wyclif was critical of both the then reigning popes at Avignon and at Rome. After 1378, he became increasingly critical of Romish doctrine. Despite the evident shortcomings of this translation, its dependence on Jerome's Vulgate and being a rather stilted and mechanical rendering in Midlands English, it nevertheless grew from this brave man's conviction that the surest way to defeat Rome was to place the Bible within the reach of ordinary people. Men ought, he claimed, to have the Scriptures in the 'vulgar tongue'. He devoted the last years of his life to this task. As with many Bible translators, Wyclif did not work alone. Whilst the New Testament, which he completed in 1380, was largely his own work, the Old Testament was in great part that of Nicholas of Hereford. A revision by a follower of Wyclif, John Purvey, was completed in 1408. Nicholas was excommunicated; Purvey imprisoned; and on the orders of the Council of Constance in 1415, Wyclif's bones were disinterred from their resting place at Lutterworth Church were burned, and thrown into the local river. 1414 saw a law introduced in England that forbade the reading of the Bible in English on the pain of death. At least one hundred and seventy handwritten copies still survive, more than the copies of Chaucer. An historical reprint was made in 1850. The first complete English Bible, it was used right through to the Reformation. Our 1611 Bible owes to it expressions such as 'the mote and the beam', 'to make whole', and 'enter thou into the joy of the Lord'.

The influence of Martin Luther's (1483-1546) translation of the Bible upon our own English translations is much underestimated. At the time of Luther, many different German dialects were in use. By the late fifteenth century, the Saxon chancery language, providentially that of Martin Luther, was widely used outside Saxony itself. Consequently, his writings and translations were extensively read and understood throughout the German-speaking world of the day. Whilst hidden away by his friends in the Wartburg, Luther set to work on his translation of Scripture. He began his actual work of translation in 1521. There had been numerous translations of the Bible into German made before this time. Between 1467 and the first appearance of Luther's New Testament in 1522 there were already fourteen in 'high' German and four in 'low' German dialects. The main weakness of these earlier Bibles was a heavy reliance on the Latin text. Luther had a good knowledge of Greek and used the text published by Erasmus in 1519, completing the New Testament in just eleven weeks. With the help of friends, he translated the Old Testament directly from Hebrew. In 1534, Luther's complete Bible appeared with original illustrations by Lucas Cranach. It was revised judiciously several times by Luther himself until his death in 1546. The influence of Luther's Bible upon the German language was profound. The German poet, Klopstock (1724-1803), said of Luther, "Among no people has one man done so much to create their language". As readers of the English *Authorised Version*, we owe Luther a debt for coining words such as 'mercy seat' (*Gnadenstuhl*) and 'shewbread' (*Schaubrot*). William Tyndale and also the translators of the *Authorised Version* were well acquainted with Luther's Bible and consulted it. England lagged behind Europe in producing vernacular Bibles and no complete Bible translated from the original languages had yet appeared in English, but between 1526 and 1611, nine English translations of Scripture of significance were made.

The Cambridge of 1520 was an overcrowded market town. Historians tells us that geese and pigs ran through its main streets and the inhabitants lived under the constant threat of catching the plague. It was here that the Christian humanist, Erasmus, taught Greek. Here too, in a quiet room behind the White Horse Tavern, a small band of students gathered to read Luther's works in secret. Among them were William Tyndale (1494-1535) and Miles Coverdale (1488-1568). William Tyndale emerges as a man of singular gift and significance in the eventual making of the *Authorised Version* of the Bible. He possessed an excellent knowledge of New Testament Greek. Apart from knowing Spanish, French, German and a number of other languages, he had a sound knowledge of biblical Hebrew, something most unusual in the England of that time.

Around 1522, Tyndale resolved that he would translate the Bible into English so that, as he boasted to a cleric, "the boy that driveth the plough shall know more of the Scriptures than you do." He sought the help of Cuthbert Tunstall, Bishop of London, who was also a Greek scholar. He had hoped that the bishop would act as patron and assist him to translate the New Testament. Turned away, Tyndale concluded "there was no room in England" for his project, and so he left for Germany in 1524 never to return to his homeland. The following year, in just ten months, Tyndale completed his translation of the New Testament. He used Erasmus' second edition of the Greek text of 1519 in which the reference to the Trinity in John 5:7 was rightly restored. His debt to Luther's recently completed translation is evident, even following the unusual order of the books adopted by Luther. Tyndale's work was, in fact, an improvement on Luther. After being chased out of Cologne, his translation was eventually printed in Worms in 1526. Although incomplete, his were the first printed Bibles in English; Wyclif's Bibles of course had each been meticulously copied out by hand. Printed copies of

Tyndale's Bible were smuggled into England inside bales of cloth by sympathetic merchants. Once in England, they were bought by booksellers and eager readers alike. Equally, they were sought by the church authorities. At the instigation of Cardinal Wolsey his Bibles were collected and burned. Bishop Tunstall, from whom Tyndale had originally sought help, now piled up his Bibles outside St Paul's Cathedral and set fire to them. Ironically, the spot can only have been yards from where one of the remaining copies lies today in the cathedral library. Out of the 15,000 copies printed only two have survived in England until today, quite recently a third copy was discovered in Germany.

As though divinely appointed before the time as a member of the translators' committees of the *Authorised Version*, Tyndale's influence for the good on their work is unmistakeable. It is too infrequently acknowledged that about eighty percent of his translation of the New Testament and the books of Moses has been taken directly into the pages of the *Authorised Version*. Readers of the 1611 Bible taking up Tyndale's Bible will find themselves on comfortingly familiar ground. Many phrases later found in the *Authorised Version* appear first in Tyndale: 'A city that is set on a hill', 'No man can serve two masters', 'Ask and it shall be given unto you'. It is almost as though he completed a 'first draft' in preparation for 1611. This is fully in line with the stated aim of the translators of the *Authorised Versions*, who say in their preface, now omitted from modern printings,

> "Truely (good Christian Reader) we never thought from the beginning, that we should need to make a new Translation, nor yet to make of a bad one a good one, … but to make a good one better, or out of many good ones, one principall good one, not justly to be excepted against; that hath been our indeavour, that our mark."

Drawing on that which had gone before, these men sought to produce one translation that could stand as the measure of all, one that could not with good reason be set aside. Their aim was to procure *one indisputably authentic Word* and indeed, under the guidance of God's Spirit, in this they were more than successful. This worthy purpose stands in stark contrast to translators of today, who seem to be obsessively occupied with producing as many different versions as possible, not one remotely like the other. This is a backward step, moving away from securing a faithful and authentic translation. What remains is not clarity and unanimity as to what constitutes the Word of God, but a complete confusion of voices. This work of the enemy is nothing new, the 1611 translators write in defence of their work,

> "...doth not *Sixtus Quintus* confesse, that certain Catholikes (he meaneth certain of his own side) were in such a humour of translating the Scriptures into *Latine*, that Satan taking occasion by them, though they thought of no such matter, did strive what he could, out of so uncertain and manifold a varietie of Translations, so as to mingle all things, that nothing might seem to be left certain and firm in them, &c?"

They argue that those who have themselves caused confusion through a multiplicity of Latin translations were really in no position to criticise them for a yet further translation in English that would draw together all others and be final and authoritative. So today, we expect the Word of God in English to be *one Word* speaking to us clearly, without equivocation or confusion.

The last ten years of his life, Tyndale spent as a refugee in Holland and Germany. He had revised his New Testament and was engaged in making new translations of the Old Testament. 1530 saw the appearance of the Pentateuch in English and the following year he worked on the book of Jonah. He was a man of fervent faith and exceptional scholarship – he had no helpers with the Old Testament as did Wyclif or Luther. He possessed amazing courage. Shipwrecked on the way to Hamburg, he lost his complete translation of Deuteronomy. In 1525, he went to live in what we would now call a 'safe house' in Antwerp. There he lived with his good friend, Thomas Poyntz, whilst still working on the Old Testament. Sadly, his presence was discovered and he was betrayed to his enemies. Henry VIII, whose divorce Tyndale had condemned, did not stir a muscle to intervene on his behalf. After being confined in prison for more than a year, he was finally convicted as a heretic, cruelly strangled, and burned on 6th October 1536. From his lips fell his well known dying prayer, "Lord, open the King of England's eyes".

After his death, the demand for a vernacular Bible grew apace so that four others appeared between 1535 and 1539. Portions of Tyndale's Bible also appeared in pirated editions. Having finally broken with Rome in 1534 and wishing to appear in a favourable light with German protestant prices in order perhaps to join the Smalkald League, Henry's stance towards the English Bible was slowly changing. In Tyndale's place, Miles Coverdale (1488-1568) rose to the challenge. Coverdale's Bible appeared in 1535; a product of exile, it is thought to have been printed either in Cologne or Zürich. It was the first complete Bible to be printed in English, but had the weakness of being a patchwork of other Bibles more than a pure translation. It drew on a new version of the Latin Vulgate by Pagninius, the German Zürich Bible and Luther, and as was to be expected, it relied heavily on Tyndale. Coverdale's rendering of the Psalms was carried over into the Great Bible and are those found in the *Book of Common Prayer*. These Psalms demonstrate unmistakeable traits of the Lutheran chorale that Coverdale had encountered in Germany.

Whilst in prison, Tyndale had continued his work on the Old Testament. Although these papers were never published, somehow they fell into the hands of John Rogers, a chaplain living in Antwerp. Rogers was to become the first martyr under 'Bloody' Mary, burned to death as his wife and children were forced to stand and watch. Whilst serving as a pastor in Wittenberg, Rogers compiled and saw printed there in 1537 what became known as the 'Matthew's Bible', possibly being given this name after its financial backer. Significant is the fact that it was licensed by Henry VIII. The New Testament was Tyndale's last edition, the one burned in London. The Old Testament was also his, right through to 2 Chronicles, some of it newly printed. The rest was Coverdale's work. Tyndale's dying prayer was strangely answered in that although doubtless Henry did not known it, he was licensing what was largely Tyndale's work, the man whom he had done nothing to save.

Both Coverdale's Bible and Matthew's were recognised as being somewhat unsatisfactory compilations. To Coverdale was now committed the task of producing the first truly *authorised* Bible in English. It was known as the 'Great Bible' because of its large physical size. It appeared in 1539 and enjoyed the benefit of massive promotion through a decree requiring that every parish was to set up the whole Bible in English for the common people to read, which they did avidly and with great joy. So many wished to read the Bible that reading aloud had to be forbidden whilst Church Services were taking place in the same building. Although it was left in the shadows because of the Great Bible, an improved revision of the Matthew's/Tyndale Bible was produced in 1539 by another from Cambridge with a good knowledge of Greek, John Taverner. This was the very first English Bible to be printed entirely in England. Just seventeen years had now elapsed since Tyndale first travelled to London to meet with a rebuff from Tunstall. So much had now changed decidedly in favour of translating and reading the Bible in English. There was still no single translation acknowledged by all as definitive.

In 1547 Henry VIII died. The godly boy-king Edward VI reigned in his stead, tragically dying of consumption at only sixteen years-of-age. His successor, 'Bloody' Mary Tudor, set a cruel torch to the damp faggots of the martyrs' pyres. Thousands died an agonising death for refusing to renounce their faith in Christ. Many fled as refugees to John Calvin's Geneva. William Wittingham, later to become bishop of Durham, married the sister of Calvin's wife. He, together with others in the city, set themselves to produce yet another translation. The contributors were excellent scholars. Whilst Tyndale contributed his own unique literary turn of phrase to the stream of Bible translation, the Geneva Bible brought even greater precision and accuracy. It was to have a strong influence upon the translators of 1611. Published in 1560, it became the 'authorised' Bible for Calvinists everywhere; so much so, that they were most reluctant to relinquish it when the *Authorised Version* appeared. It was well received in England, where during Elizabeth's reign alone it went through over ninety editions. Two innovations were later carried over to the *Authorised Version*. Theodor Beza, Genevan theologian and successor to Calvin, used italics to indicate words not found in the original but which were essential to the sense in translation. Following Robert Estienne (also known as Stephanus), who was both a scholar and a printer, the English Bible was for the first time divided into verses. This Bible was also printed for the first time in Roman type, which made it much easier to read than the old English Black Letter, which had tried to imitate handwriting.

As a direct result of the popularity of the Calvinistic Geneva Bible, the officials of the Church of England then felt they must produce a version to counter it. It was left to Archbishop Matthew Parker to draw up plans for this Bible. It came off the press in 1568. As most of those working on it were bishops, it became known as the 'Bishops Bible'. The Old Testament bore a striking resemblance to the Great Bible. Due to their use in the *Book of Common Prayer*, the Psalms of Coverdale eventually replaced the original rendering. The New Testament was better than the Old, largely because of borrowings from the Geneva Bible. In 1571, it was decreed by the Church that every bishop, cathedral, and Church should have a copy and although it became the official Bible of the Church, it never replaced the Geneva Bible for private use.

All the English translations of Scripture to this point had their strengths and their weaknesses, but no single version had yet gained universal acclaim. As tributaries of some great river, they were now about to pour of their best into a translation that was to stand almost uncontested as the authentic Word of God in English in the coming three-and-a-half centuries. Strongest of these streams were, without doubt, the translation of Tyndale and to a lesser degree, the Geneva Bible through the Bishops' Bible. It will be recalled that Tyndale accomplished his translation of the New Testament whilst in Wittenberg, so that towering behind all, if now somewhat in the shadows, is the unmistakeable figure of Martin Luther.

The opening years of the seventeenth century saw Elizabeth I die childless in 1603. There being no one to carry forward the Tudor line, she was succeeded by James VI of Scotland. He was a son of Mary Queen of Scots, whom Elizabeth had imprisoned and then executed. James became James I of England. He is an interesting, if somewhat controversial, figure. Some have made him out to be a profligate wastrel;

others honour him almost as a saint. What must be acknowledged by all is that he was certainly no one's fool. Although many dismiss him as an amateur pedant, this was far from so. Under the guiding hand of his tutor, Scotland's greatest scholar at the time, George Buchanan, as a youth James read Plato, Plutarch, and Aesop, and was taught mathematics, logic, geography, grammar, and rhetoric. He studied the Old and New Testaments, and Church history. He was made aware of the differences between views of the Reformers in Zürich, Geneva and Wittenberg. It was the upbringing of a Scottish Calvinist. He learned Latin, Greek, besides the modern languages of French, Spanish, and Italian. He absorbed much before he was of an age to go to university. This man now sat upon the throne of England. We do not make the reliability of the Bible that so often carries the name of King James dependent upon our ability to demonstrate historical facts about his character. This would be to rest upon the wisdom of men rather than to have faith in God who preserves His Word. What we will not accept are the scurrilous ramblings of those who attempt to besmirch James' character using the flimsiest historical 'evidence', thinking thereby to discredit the *Authorised Version*.

Led by Dr John Reynolds president of Corpus Christi, Oxford, the puritans suggested to the king that a new translation of the Bible should be made. Their proposal presupposes their recognition that a definitive translation in English had yet to be made. The idea of 'one uniforme translation' found ready favour with James, despite protest from some bishops. It took only six months to draw up a plan to determine how the work was to be executed. Originally, there were to be 54 scholars involved, but for various reasons, in the end it was reduced to 47. They were divided into six groups. Two groups worked in Westminster, two in Oxford, and two in Cambridge. Particular pains were taken over the work, and a series of fifteen procedural rules were strictly adhered to. Each group was charged with checking the work of the others. Finally, a review by a committee of six looked through the completed Bible and it was prepared for printing. The new translation was to be based upon previous *English* Bibles, but undeniably, the greatest external influence came from Tyndale.

When translating, the divine originals always took precedence. Once more the testimony of the words of the Preface of the Translators, written by Dr. Miles Smith,

> "If you ask me what they had before them, truly it was the *Hebrew* text of the Old Testament, the *Greek* of the New. These are the two golden pipes, or rather conduits, wherethrough the olive branches emptie themselves into the gold."

From the start, the translators were conscious of the gravity of the task allotted them. They were conscious throughout of the providential guiding hand of God and their trust was in Him. The *Preface* again,

> "And what sort did these assemble? In the trust of their own knowledge, or of their sharpnesse of wit, or deepnesse of judgement, as if in an arm of flesh? At no hand. They trusted in him that hath the key of *David*, opening and no man shutting; they prayed to the Lord the Father of our Lord, to the effect that Saint *Augustine* did; *O let thy Scriptures be my pure delight, let me not be deceived in them, neither let me deceive by them.* In this confidence, and with this devotion did they assemble together; not too many, lest one should trouble another; and yet many lest many things might haply escape them."

John Bois has been described as 'the sort of scholar people like to gossip about.' He was born in 1560, just four years before William Shakespeare. Many modern scholars consider themselves to be somewhat superior in knowledge to their predecessors in earlier times, suggesting that our 'understanding has moved on' since those days. It must be asked how many of them with John Bois at the tender age of six, could read the whole Bible through and who among them at that same age would have had little difficulty reading Hebrew. At fourteen, Bois became a classics scholar at St John's College, Cambridge and soon became a Fellow. He would rise at four to conduct classes in Greek, reading whilst standing he would work until eight at night. Few today are of the measure of this man! After the expiry of his fellowship, Bois became rector of a Church at Boxworth, travelling into Cambridge on horseback to teach. John Bois was recruited to the Cambridge committee. It took six years of sustained effort for the committees to complete their task. Finally, what they had accomplished was taken to London. Each translation centre then provided two scholars to work on the review. John Bois and old his tutor, Dr. Anthony Downes, were sent from Cambridge. Much of the work of this review committee was recorded by Bois in a diary that has survived to this day. It took nine months work of refining and revising the text throughout 1610 to produce the final draft ready for printing.

There are those who facetiously demand of us an answer, either through ignorance or malice, which 'Authorised Version' we hold to be the definitive Word of God because there have been several revisions since 1611. As the changes were without exception non-substantial ones, such as orthographical improvements, inconsequential alterations to punctuation, all of which were designed to give the original text more clarity when rendered in English, the objection fails before getting up steam!

## The translation of the Authorised Version

An oft-repeated but ill-informed criticism of the *Authorised Version* is that its language is 'archaic'. In truth, such a comment is generally made in ignorance by those who thereby show how little understanding they have of what they are actually reading. If the language of the *Authorised Version* is 'archaic', it was already 'archaic' in 1611. The English of the *Authorised Version* is like no other and was certainly never spoken or written by anyone. A. T. Robertson, no friend of verbal inspiration, in his *Grammar of the Greek New Testament*:

> "No one today speaks the English of the King James Version, *or ever did for that matter,* for though, like Shakespeare, it is the pure Anglo-Saxon, yet unlike Shakespeare it reproduces to a remarkable extent the spirit and language of the Bible." (Ed. italics ours)

The language of the translators' preface is very different in style from the text of the Bible itself. The distinctive sentence structure, the vocabulary, and the turn of phrase found in the *Authorised Version* are all unique. What gives this translation its so-called archaic feel?

Too many assume without reason that the aim of the 1611 translation committees was identical to that of their modern counterparts. Whilst the style of language used must be readily accessible to readers, it was not the intention of the translators to produce a contemporary Jacobean version, but rather to mirror the linguistic framework and preserve literary integrity *of the original Hebrew and Greek text.*

> *The so-called archaic feel to* **Authorised Version** *is generated in large part by its unusual syntax, something that has been brought about by following the Hebrew and Greek as closely as possible.*

Critics of the *Authorised Version* quickly point to the use of 'thee, thou and ye' as outdated and unnecessary and having now been replaced by 'you' and 'thy and thine' by 'your and yours'. Deliberate misinformation surrounds much that is said and written on this matter. The use of these pronouns had already been in decline for around three hundred years by 1611. Using them in everyday speech would have been seen as outmoded even then. Whilst they have disappeared in English, these pronouns have survived in a number of European languages. The translators retained the older pronouns in order to reflect the grammar and therefore the full meaning of the originals accurately. By using 'thou' (singular) and 'ye' (plural), it can be shown whether one person or more than one is being addressed. The same is true of 'thee' (singular) and 'you' (plural). Luke 22:31 reads,

> "And the Lord said, Simon, Simon, behold, Satan hath desired to have you, that he may sift you as wheat: But I have prayed for thee, that thy faith fail not: and when thou art converted, strengthen thy brethren."

In verse 31, the plural 'you' is used. Here the Lord speaks of all the disciples. In verse 32, the singular 'thee' is used. Here the Lord is speaking just of Simon Peter. This significance of this distinction, lost were the translation to read 'you', becomes clearer in verse 34 where our Lord tells Peter that he will deny Him thrice before the cock crows. An accurate translation is indispensable to a proper understanding of Scripture. Unlike the *Authorised Version*, Shakespeare uses the plural 'you' in much the same way as we do today. This had already begun to be customary towards the end of the 13th century and by the 16th century had established itself as the polite form. 'Thee, thou and ye' are used by the bard only in particular circumstances: when addressing close friends and family, children, those of a lower social class, and in abuse. In all other circumstances, the polite form 'you' is used. This is very similar to their usage in modern German. The use of these pronouns in the *Authorised Version* does not follow that of Shakespeare, *but strictly replicates their use in the original texts.*

Language with its words and structures is the essential medium through which the original writers under the inspiration of the Spirit of God give expression to their meaning. The 'message' or content of Scripture cannot be separated from the literary and linguistic form in which it comes to us. The translators of the *Authorised Version* translated not only words, but they took with them the linguistic structure of the text. Wherever possible they retained the punctuation, clauses, and subordinate clauses, figures of speech, and more besides. They have given us a virtual *transcription* of the Hebrew and Greek texts in a style of English that has never been surpassed. Modern versions violate the integrity of the text, they break up the syntax, regularly ignore figures of speech, and frequently reconstruct the text in such a way that the meaning is changed, obscured, or even lost altogether. Modern versions are consequently rarely a genuine translation but an equivalent, a rewriting of the Bible. We do not need an 'equivalent', either formal or dynamic, but a faithful and sympathetic rendering of the Scriptures in a language we can readily understand.

In the *Authorised Version,* we are reading in English something as close as it is possible to get to the original. The translators do not play fast and loose with the original text; they strive in a sensitive way to find some English form even for its literary play and rhythm. One Hebrew scholar has drawn attention to this very good example of the way in which the carefully constructed Hebrew is replicated in English is found in the Song of Solomon.

> "Thy teeth are like a flock of sheep that are even shorn, which came up from the washing; whereof every one bear

twins, and none is barren among them.

Thy lips are like a thread of scarlet, and thy speech is comely: thy temples are like a piece of a pomegranate within thy locks.

Thy neck is like the tower of David builded for an armoury, whereon there hang a thousand bucklers, all shields of mighty men.

Thy two breasts are like two young roes that are twins, which feed among the lilies." (4:2-5)

Many modern renderings completely break up these sentences or shorten them thus destroying the whole rhythm of the passage. Still less is any attempt is made to reproduce any of the Hebrew poetic alliteration. By contrast, the alliteration in the *Authorised Version* is obvious, as for example in verse 2, *like a flock, sheep* that are even *shorn, bear* and *barren*, this latter being strikingly similar to *shekulam* and *shakulah* in the same place in the Hebrew.

According to modern 'analytical' linguistic theorists, such as those behind the *New International Version* and the *Good News Bible*, for a modern reader to appreciate and understand an ancient text in his or her own language the old must be 'resituated' in the new because languages are said to be also historical and cultural as well as grammatical. They speak in this context of 'radical translation' and attempt to achieve something more than a simple transfer of meaning from one language to another. Modern translations will thus be more than just 'free', and will try to relocate the text in a new and alien 'conceptual framework'. The translators of 1611 had a very different understanding of their task.

These days, translators will try to use equivalent contemporary idioms or expressions rather than making a slavish word-by-word rendering. Certainly, when learning to speak a modern foreign language there is much to be said for an idiomatic approach in which one learns to express oneself in ways that would not necessarily occur to a non-native speaker, both in terms of syntax and vocabulary. An equivalent for 'hello' in other languages may be 'ça va' or 'hallo' in French; whilst Germans say 'wie geht's' or 'hallo'; Italians say 'olà', 'pronto' just on the telephone, and 'ciao' on arrival or departure. A modern translator will first identify 'hello' as a form of greeting, and will then look for a suitable phrase carrying the same idea in the second language. Some modern linguists call this 'interlingual transposition'.

The question now arises as to whether a translator should try hard to reproduce the original text or produce something idiomatically akin to the original in contemporary English regardless of the nature of the text. What we are really asking is whether a travel guide demands the same measure of exactitude as an instruction manual. Many texts, quite apart from Scripture, do not lend themselves to an idiomatic approach. Let us hope that modern idiomatic bible translators do not try their hands at translating cookbooks or worse still – medical textbooks!

Not only the content of the original text but also the grammatical structure of the language in which it was written must have a bearing on the way it will eventually be rendered. Each language, whilst having an essentially similar structure to every other, will also have its own idiosyncrasies. Some languages have more adjectives, adverbs, or nouns than others and account must then be taken of this when translating. The translators of the *Authorised Version* have tried to preserve many of these peculiarities of language in Greek and Hebrew and have done so in a way that has enriched the English language. Whilst trying to produce a bible in modern idiomatic English, translators tend to suppress idioms found in the original text. In 1 Chronicles 12:8, we read of 'men of might' (*AV*). Whereas in English we might use the adjective 'mighty' in front of the noun 'men', the *Authorised Version* retains the Hebrew idiom using the two nouns. The *New International Version* seeking to avoid this substitutes an English equivalent, something quite different, 'brave warriors'. This is a perfect example of translation by equivalent idiom.

It is to be expected that the apostle Paul being a Hebrew would use these Semitic idioms when writing in Greek. In Ephesians, we find similar constructions, 'children of disobedience' (2:2 & 5:6), 'children of wrath' (2:3), and 'children of light' (5:8). In the *New International Version* these verses become 'those who are disobedient', 'by nature objects of wrath', yet 'children of light' is retained. The metaphor of children runs right through the epistle, the 'adoption of children' (1:5), 'be no more children' (4:14). In translating idiomatically, the *New International Version* translators make it impossible for English readers to track this thread of thought through the book because the metaphor is lost. Three words, each different but with closely related meanings, are used in Greek: *nepios*, a baby without the full power of speech; *teknon*, a child, one born; and *huios*, son. The metaphor in the original is carried over into the *Authorised Version*, whereas in the *New International Version* it is completely demolished by the idiomatic English. The doctrinal implications of such changes are huge. 'Children of wrath' has the idea of those *born*. An 'object' does not convey the notion of something that can either be *dead* in trespasses and sins (v.1) nor *quickened* together with Christ (v.5). By using the word *tekna*, children, the idea emerges of those who are *born* in this condition, that we are all born under condemnation and, until by God's grace we are saved, the wrath of God abides upon us. All this disappears with the loss of the metaphor.

Translating idiom for idiom, equating what the native speaker would say in the same circumstance in each language, cannot be carried over to Bible translation. When applied to the Bible, the integrity of the verbally inspired biblical text is thereby violated. Not only each word *but also the linguistic structure in which it is found* was fixed by the inspiration of God's Spirit. Words are assembled into an appropriate order or structure and when taken together they convey a particular meaning. It is essential that this structure as well as the individual words used be replicated as closely as possible if the identical thoughts are to be awakened in the consciousness of the reader of the translation. Where a key structure in the original is translated in different ways each time it occurs, as is common in idiomatic translations, the understanding and interpretation of the passage is severely hampered. No connections of meaning can then be made between similar passages by a monolingual reader who would have no way of recognising the existence of such links. For the same reason, there should also be some consistency in the translation of individual words.

Idiomatic speech expresses a manner of thought belonging to a particular culture and time. In translating the Bible almost supra-cultural linguistic conventions and codes must prevail, determined by the biblical text itself, producing a form of language peculiar to the Bible, but at the same time understandable across the barriers of both time and culture. An idiomatic bible must by definition deviate from the originals as it is bound by its own limited temporal and cultural norms. The ways of giving expression to our thoughts are deeply rooted in the culture from which they emerge. This fact alone really rules out all idea of a so-called 'modern version'.

> **An idiomatic bible translation is a trade-off in equivalents rather than the recovery of the divinely inspired originals.**

It must be the aim of the Bible translator to produce a good translation, but one through which both the words and the structure of original are transparent. Those having a good knowledge of both languages ought then to be able at the very least to discern something of the structure and vocabulary of the original without necessarily having to refer back physically to the original text. Anyone fluent in more than one language will recognise this phenomenon – it is almost like reading two languages simultaneously. The real skill of the translator is to create this phenomenon and at the same time to produce a perspicuous and readable translation. The translation must reveal not veil the original text. It is rarely possible to accurately perceive the original text in this way in a modern translation. The *Authorised Version* makes the originals clear, retaining its repetitions, structures, inversions of word order, it varies the tone and register of vocabulary appropriately. *It preserves the original texts; it does not obscure them.* The vivid imagery of the Hebrew and Greek is all too often lost in modern versions. The poetic language of the Lord Jesus in the Sermon on the Mount is reduced to the worst doggerel. *"Blessed are they which do hunger and thirst after righteousness..."* is debased to *"Happy are those whose greatest desire is to do what God requires"* (Matthew 5:6) in the *Good News Bible*.

Modern idiomatic versions more often than not say something quite different than the original. Although the change at times may seem so inconsequential as to be overlooked by the ordinary reader, it is nevertheless still a change. The accumulation of such changes means that in the end, we are reading a quite different book. Such changes would hardly be tolerated in a secular text, so why should tolerate them in the inspired Word of God where we have the authority to change not one jot or tittle? Changes may at times appear to be trivial, but such trivialities do invariably have a quite substantial effect upon the meaning. The changed nature of the translated text dramatically affects the way in which the Word of God is interpreted and consequently also taught and preached.

What is overlooked is that the translators of the *Authorised Version* often reproduce the original text in English in almost the word for word order. Tyndale was of the opinion that the English language in particular lent itself to such translation methodology. His view was that often such word-by-word translations from Hebrew or Greek do work in English whereas in other languages they are more difficult to achieve. Let us look for a moment at Genesis 1:4. The Hebrew reads word for word 'And-he-saw God the-light that-good'. The translators of the *Authorised Version* retained Tyndale's, "And God saw the light, that it was good." Whilst some may view the rather odd syntax as archaic, it reproduces the original, whereas the *New International Version,* for example, does not. It reads: "God saw that the light was good". Modern version enthusiasts would doubtless argue that this is how it would be said today, perhaps so, but this is not the point. The *Good News Bible* comes nowhere near accuracy with "God was pleased with what he saw". Go to the bottom of the class for that translation!

The *Authorised Version* translators sought at all times to let the original shine through the translation in order to retain the identical meaning. Grammatically, 'light' is retained as the direct object of the transitive verb 'saw' with 'that it was good' as a subordinate clause. The *New International Version* uses the verb 'saw' intransitively – God saw, which then demands no direct object. There is a change in the grammar. To change the grammar is to change the meaning. We may then ask what is the difference in meaning. To answer, let us put this into a different context. The difference is precisely the same between 'I see the child that is mine' and 'I see that the child is mine'. In the first instance, the subject *must* actually be looking at the child – *I see the child*; in the second, the subject may have simply understood an explanation without the child being present – *I see*, in the sense of 'I understand'. The important point in the translation of both Tyndale and the *Authorised Version* is that *God saw the light*, He actually looked at it, from which direct action He concluded that the light was good. Somewhat anthropomorphic perhaps, but it shows God to have been intimately involved with creation and at the same time it draws a sharp line of distinction between God and that which He has created and the resultant conclusions He draws from looking at what He had made. The seeing of God in the *New International Version* is weakened to a *realisation*, an *understanding*, or *recognition* of the goodness of the light. The meanings and theological implications of these two sentences are quite different from each other. The change from a God who actually sees to a God who merely recognises goodness in creation in some abstract way is a theological change. The reading in the *Authorised Version* is consistent with the immediate creation of the heaven and the earth by God and equates with the way other verbs are used in the same passage: "*God created...*(v.1), *the Spirit of God moved...*(v.2), *God said...*(v.3), *God saw...*(v.4), *God divided...*(v.4), *God called...*(v.5). The immediacy of the language of the *AV*, with God directly involved with creation, leaves *no place whatever for impersonal evolution*. The *New International Version* alternative – 'God saw that...' – is deviant in that it removes this immediacy and provides an accommodation for evolution, which doubtless many of its supporters welcome.

Important to the accurate interpretation of any biblical text is the recognition that key words are deliberately repeated throughout to enable the reader to make those links essential to a proper understanding of the passage or book. In the name of supposed greater accuracy and textual fluency, modern versions deliberately and constantly translate the same word with many different English words. This means that links essential to a proper understanding of the passage are lost. Neither the Calvinist translators of the Geneva Bible, nor for that matter Tyndale, were so careful. The *Authorised Version* is more faithful to the original text as such key words tend to be given their proper prominence.

The translators of the *Authorised Version* not only carry over the grammatical structures, but they try also to follow through with words, translating them with rigorous consistency. We give yet another example from the Hebrew scholar previously mentioned. In Genesis and the account of the Fall, the Hebrew word *yada* appears repeatedly. It is consistently translated each time as 'know' or 'knowing', including in 4:1 where we read, "And Adam knew Eve his wife". The same word is used in these early chapters in three ways: 'to know', 'to understand', and 'to have carnal knowledge of'. The *Good News Bible* translates the word variously as: 'know', 'realised', and 'had intercourse'. There is no indication here that these are all the same word in the original text. In the name of removing 'archaic' usage, the linkage of meaning disappears.

We should not imagine that the translators of the *Authorised Version* slavishly followed the originals never introducing variety to the English syntax or words in order to achieve an artificial accuracy. Again the translators' *Preface*,

> "Another thing we think good to admonish thee of (gentle Reader) that we have not tyed our selves to an uniformitie of phrasing, identitie of words, as some peradventure would

wish that we had done, because they observe, that some learned men somewhere, have been as exact as they could that way. Truly, that we might not varie from the sense of that which we had translated before, if the word signified the same thing in both places (for, there be some words that be not of the same sense everywhere) we were especially carefull, and made a conscience, according to our dutie. But, that we should expresse the same notion in the same particular word; as for example, if we translate the *Hebrew* or *Greek* word once by *Purpose,* never to call is *Intent*; if one where *Journeying,* never *Travelling;* if one where *Think,* never *Suppose;* if one where *Pain,* never *Ache*; if one where *Joy,* never *Gladnesse,* &c. ...For is the kingdome of God become words or syllables? why should we be in bondage to them if we may be free, use one precisely when we may use another no less fit, as commodiously?"

Completely correct! However, they acknowledge, in a manner that seems to have escaped their modern counterparts, that very often the repetition of certain 'key words' is a literary device essential to a real understanding of the passage.

The translation of the Bible into 'modern English', whatever this may mean, masks both the diversity and unity of Scripture, reducing it to one level. The *Authorised Version* translators will consistently translate a Hebrew and a Greek word having the same meaning and similar connotation using the same one English word. An example of this is their translation of both the Hebrew word 'leb' and the Greek word 'kardia' in English as 'heart'. By varying the words used modern translators pull apart the original text and this unity of meaning throughout the whole of Scripture is lost with serious implications for the doctrine of verbal inspiration. God spake *'at sundry times and in divers manners'* but one Word. The diversity of Scripture can be addressed only in terms of a single divine Author behind the many human writers. Equally, the use of a one word persistently in the same book marks it out as being different from the others. If the same English word is not used each time as in the originals, the whole effect of this is lost. One scholar has rightly drawn attention to the constant use of the *leb* in the book of Ecclesiastes, translated 'heart' in the *Authorised Version* – a word full of meaning that cannot be substituted by 'mind' or 'thought' without being considerably diminished. The word is found sprinkled on every page! It is used in very many different and imaginative ways. This is lost in most modern versions where instead of 'heart' as in the *AV* many other substitutes are used.

> "And I gave my heart to seek and search out by wisdom..." *AV* (1:13)
> "I devoted myself to study and explore by wisdom..." *NIV* (see also v.17)
> "I said in mine heart..." *AV* (2:1; 3:17, 18) *NIV* uses 'heart' in 2:1 & 3:17
> "I withheld not my heart from any joy..." *AV* (2:10) *NIV* uses 'heart'
> "...his heart taketh not rest in the night..." *AV* (2:23)
> "...at night his mind does not rest..." *NIV*
> "God answereth him in the joy of his heart." *AV* (5:20) *NIV* uses 'heart'
> "...by the sadness of the countenance the heart is made better." *AV* (7:3)
> "...a sad face is good for the heart." *NIV*
> "I applied my heart to know..." *AV* (7:25)
> "So I turned my mind to understand..." *NIV*

The *New International Version* misses fewer than the *Good News Bible*, which does not use the word 'heart' even once in any of the above instances. These omissions will be justified by modern translators on stylistic grounds, avoiding the 'archaic' again along with constant repetition, but far more is thereby lost of the spiritual meaning than is gained by a 'modern' tone. Modern versions deny us access to the original inspired texts rather than opening a door to them. Where the Old and New

Testaments appear in one language a unity will emerge where the same word occurs throughout, saying the same thing, carrying the same idea, each time.

Reducing the unity of vocabulary and syntax, in one place or throughout the whole Bible, fragments and ultimately tears the Word of God apart. The *Good News Bible* is bad news as one of the chief offenders in this area. The enduring enmity between the seed of Adam and the serpent in Genesis 3:15 is identified by using the same Hebrew verb *shup* – bruise. The *Authorised Version* reads,

> "And I will put
> enmity between
>     thee and the woman,
>  and between
>     thy seed and her seed;
> it shall bruise
>     thy head,
> and thou shalt bruise
>     his heel."

The continuing enmity between the serpent and the woman is reflected in the structure of the verse, which in the *AV* follows the Hebrew. The repetition of 'seed' and 'bruise' is an integral part of this structure. Tyndale preserves this, but uses the English verb 'tread' – perhaps drawing out the meaning of *shup* to its limits somewhat – in both places where 'bruise' appears in the *Authorised Version*. The *New International Version* breaks up the rhythm of the verse and then uses two different verbs in the place of the one in Hebrew – 'crush' and 'strike'. The *Good News Bible* offers its usual banal rendering.

Hebrew scholars tell us that in 1 Samuel 15 *a single word* links an apparent contradiction. That word is *nikham*, 'repent'. By using another word, modern translators change and weaken the passage in an attempt to provide a solution. Verse 11 tells us that God said, "It repenteth me that I have set up Saul to be king." In verse 29, Samuel tells Saul that God "is not a man, that he should repent". Finally, in verse 35, the same word appears again, "the Lord repented that that he had made Saul king over Israel." The *New International Version* uses 'grieved', 'change his mind', and 'grieved'. The *New King James Version* uses 'regret', 'relent', and then 'regret'. The idea in these modern renderings is that as God cannot repent, change his mind, relent as do men, He can only grieve or regret. They make a distinction between these verses that the Hebrew does not make. In all three verses, the word is the same 'repent', *nikham*. According to the Bible God does repent. We do not need to think that God has inspired a mistake in His Word that needs correction! How can the unchanging God repent? Repentance in man is due to a change *within himself*, within his heart. Repentance in God is due, not to any change within Himself for He cannot change, but to a change *outside Himself* and His unchanging response to it. In this passage, God repented because of what Saul had done. No change had taken place in God, His unchanging person simply responded as it should to Saul's sin. Significantly, the word 'repent' is missing in most modern versions. This is hardly surprising in a day when sins are deemed mere 'mistakes' or 'errors'.

Apart from a doctrinal slide away from the truth, a widespread Philistinism and aesthetic illiteracy now dominates much of the professing Christian world. As sophisticated prose is indicative of an advanced culture so decadent language is indicative of one that is disintegrating. Following Hebrew and Greek vocabulary and syntax enables the English reader to enter into the atmosphere and the meaning of the passage as though he were reading the original. Modern versions deprive the reader of this privilege.

## The more the merrier and the greater the confusion!

The church of Rome, unable to forbid the reading of Scripture, took the next best course available to see as many *different* bible versions circulate as possible. Humanist theologians will work until their fingertips are calloused to the same end. As long as there are many different bibles, the authority of one can be denied by pointing to another that seems to say something else. The possibility of *one* authoritative Word has then gone. No sooner is one version off the press than another comes along. With so many different bibles, godless religion or reason remains the final arbiter of the truth. This is why those whose cry is – *there is only one Book!* – will always be reviled. The argument has little to do with scholarship and everything to do with faith in the one Word God has given us.

---

*This is what is* **really** *at the heart of the* **King James Bible** *only debate – how spiritual renegades can escape the absolute authority of the one authentic Word of God!*

---

It is astounding to what lengths many are going to be rid of the *Authorised Version*. Let us remember that this hatred or even distaste for the *Authorised Version* is directed towards what remains the Word of God. Those who despise God's Word despise Him who gave it. Those who in this way mock God's Word, judged even by their own standards, mock God and from such we turn away even as our Lord has bid us.

# CHAPTER 15

# Where is the Word of God Today?

*"Ye shall know them by their fruits. Do men gather grapes of thorns, or figs of thistles? Even so every good tree bringeth forth good fruit; but a corrupt tree bringeth forth evil fruit. A good tree cannot bring forth evil fruit, neither can a corrupt tree bring forth good fruit."*
(Matthew 7:16-18)

Johann Wolfgang Goethe (1749-1832) was, by common consent, Germany's greatest secular writer. Considerably less well known is the fact that Goethe's mother and sister moved in Lutheran 'pietist' circles. So committed were they that a group of believers met regularly in the Goethe home. The curious but sceptical Goethe attended their meetings from time to time and joined in the prayers and sang the magnificent hymns. He found in the warmth apparent in these gatherings a refreshing contrast to the coldness and meaninglessness of what went on in the average Lutheran Church of the day. Although well acquainted with Christian teaching, he quite deliberately turned his back on it all. He hardened his heart against the truth of God and he became an implacable foe of all pietist belief. At times, he would give vent to his anger by dancing manically around the room and speaking venomously of Christian friends. Such was his deep hatred of all things truly Christian.

Against the protestations of some scholars, it can be argued that much of Goethe the man is but thinly veiled in his

'Werther', in 'Faust', and in other of his characters too. In *Faust*, Dr. Faust surveys all his learning, in philosophy, jurisprudence, and in medicine – all subjects in which Goethe was knowledgeable – and concludes that despite all his knowledge, he is but a poor fool, no wiser than he was before he began his studies. Furthermore, he finds himself guilty of leading his students around by the nose. He has learned nothing and therefore has nothing to pass on. His world of books and papers has become his prison. A 'Master', a 'Doctor' even, and all that he has learned is that we can know nothing! He ought therefore, he concludes, to stop his empty talking. The solution to his dilemma is a particularly modern one: he turns to the world of the occult, a decision that ends in his own destruction. The magician does not communicate meaning in words. His words bypass the mind; they do not take thoughts captive. The mere *act* of reciting the words is sufficient. Uttering unintelligible formulae is an *action* that is expected will of itself mysteriously bring to pass things otherwise impossible.

Sometime later in the play, Faust becomes an aspiring bible translator! Sitting at his desk, finding satisfaction no longer rising up within him, he turns to the New Testament. This emptiness, he muses, may be filled by revelation. To what better place can he turn than the opening verses of John's Gospel? With Mephistopheles ever at his elbow, taking the passage in the original language, he begins to turn it into his beloved German. He stumbles from the start at the words, 'in the beginning was the Word'. His business was with words, but truth could not be incarcerated in this way and so he must render this verse in some other way. Words stand for thought, but the truth, he concludes, does not originate in the mind. He rejects 'senses' as a substitute for 'Word' – a swipe at the ideas of the 'sensualist' writers, who believed truth is received passively through the physical human senses. Then, even as he is setting pen to paper, he rejects 'power' too as a replacement and with it the ideas of his friend, Johann Gottfried Herder. Helped by the 'spirit' and relieved at finding a solution, he commits to paper 'in the beginning was the *deed*'. In this phrase, the emphasis no longer falls upon the Word of God revealed in the flesh or in the written word. Truth originates not in the mind, be it of God or man, *but in the deed, in what is done, in what takes place*. Actions speak more truth than words! Only what is *done* is true.

Faustian truth is dynamic. It can never be some static thought revealed and held captive in the mind by words. Christianity, according to the first draft of Goethe's doctoral thesis, is not the work of Christ as recorded in Scripture, but the present work of each of His followers living out their faith within the limitations of time. It consists not of revealed truth, but of a multiplicity of human actions. Man is a creative spirit. God does not come down to man, but Prometheus-like, he must climb the heights to steal the sacred fire. There is consequently no one objective Word of truth given once to all men for all time. Truth is not 'out there' to be discovered, still less revealed, – taken down off a shelf as it were, already encased in words. Truth is entirely subjective; it is what each individual makes it to be *by what he does*.

This change from 'word' to 'deed' accurately describes the difference in emphasis between the work of men such as Luther, Tyndale, the translators of the *Authorised Version* and that of modern 'dynamic' bible translators. Modern versions exhibit frighteningly Faustian overtones.

---

*The underlying premise of modern translation methodology denies all possibility of the precise reproduction or anything approaching a recovery of the thought of the writer by the reader.*

---

Instead, what takes place *in the act of reading* is alone of any real significance. The text provides only the occasion.

## Modern translation methodology and the rejection of verbal inspiration

A Mephistophelian move from 'word' to 'deed' is discernable when comparing verbal inspiration with the 'dynamic' understanding of inspiration among the neo-orthodox. In his heterodox scribblings, the Anglican 'priest' and self-appointed bible translator of the 1950s, J. B. Phillips, shows sufficient insight to put his finger on the central issue with respect to what he abusively refers to as the 'extreme fundamentalist' position of verbal inspiration and translation. His assertion that the 'theory' of verbal inspiration is bound to break eventually in the world of translation is correct, given his assumptions.

The possibility of God reproducing His eternal thoughts within human minds through the medium of Scripture can fall at several hurdles. It would fall first, were God's Word not inspired word for word. It would fall second, had God not perfectly preserved what He has given by inspiration in Hebrew and Greek manuscripts now in our possession. It would fall third, could those inspired words not be replicated in languages other than the original Hebrew and Greek using vocabulary and grammatical structures that give rise to identical thoughts in us that were originally found only in the mind of God.

Individuals and churches using modern bible versions have effectively forsaken the pathway of sound doctrine. Given time, other doctrines will be set aside too, if this has not already happened. Six-day creation is often the next to go.

> *Abandonment of the Authorised Version for a modern version is an implicit rejection of the biblical doctrine verbal inspiration.*

Modern version translation methodology does not demand a careful reading of an inspired given text. It is concerned with the subjective *response* of the reader rather than the infallible transmission of the objective truth of God to the minds of men through the written Word. Those who use translations such as the *New International Version* are identifying themselves with a neo-orthodox understanding of inspiration. Many 'new' evangelicals would not flinch at this suggestion as it is becoming increasingly common to find that those once sound in theology have abandoned all thought of a verbally inspired Bible. This is hardly to be wondered at for a 'dynamic' view of translation goes hand in hand with a similarly 'dynamic' understanding of inspiration. This is to say, inspiration occurs not at the point of writing *but at the point of reading*. That which is important is the 'deed', that which is inherent in the act of reading itself.

If there is any inspiration in the text, it is to be found in the message at the very moment it comes across, the *truths*, according to Phillips (*Ring of Truth*, 1967), not the words. The reader knows that the Bible is God's Word for he recognises the 'ring of truth' in it *as he reads*. A similar view was expounded by the Swiss theologian, Emil Brunner, as long ago as 1935 in a book called *Unser Glaube* ('Our Faith'). The Word of God, he says, is *in* the bible even as the voice of a singer is *in* the gramophone record. Using the recording company 'His Master's Voice' as an analogy, he goes on to explain how through a rather scratchy wax recording the voice of the 'master' is heard. Brunner's bible is an imperfect and largely human book through which the scratchy voice of God is heard speaking. We are exhorted to ignore the scratches and listen to the voice of God. Inspiration is experienced *in the reading* as God speaks, and it has little to do with recording and preserving the written words. As a recording is nothing until played, so the bible is said to be nothing until it is read.

The link between a neo-orthodox perspective of inspiration and the translation methodology used for versions like the *New International Version* and the *Good News Bible* is readily acknowledged by those using and developing those methods. Inspiration is understood by them as being primarily the work of God's Spirit upon the reader rather than the writer. It means for them that emphasis can now be conveniently shifted from the 'details of the wording in the original'. Those with neo-orthodox views aim to 'inspire' present day readers in the same way that the original readers were 'inspired' by Scripture. Inspiration is understood not as a means of ensuring the accuracy of the divine originals, but is redefined as something that happens to the reader. It is the reader who is inspired by what he reads and not the writer who is enabled to record perfectly word by word what God has revealed to him. God speaks by giving the reader a 'dynamic' reading experience. This meshes very comfortably with the heterodox view of Scripture held by pentecostals and charismatics. An accurately transmitted and preserved text is of no consequence to any of these people. Those using the *New International Version* are announcing for all to see and hear their rejection of the biblical doctrine of verbal inspiration. They proclaim it as clearly as if they had the figures 666 tattooed on their foreheads.

## The advent of modern translations

Modern versions can be rejected on many grounds. First, they rely on questionable texts derived largely from the work of Westcott and Hort and others. Second, the translation methodology used violates the integrity of the biblical text and abandons all belief in verbal inspiration. They therefore obscure and pervert the Word God has given. Today, there are scores of new translations and each one claims for itself something the others do not possess. Clearly, if all these versions are different from each other, as they are, we must ask ourselves what has happened to the Word that God gave to the prophets and apostles, inspired as it is down to the last jot and tittle. All these different versions cannot be authentic.

Until the middle of the nineteenth century, few thought it necessary to try to improve on the 1611 *Authorised Version* and no other translation made any substantial impact. The rise in godless rationalistic theology at the same time as the appearance of new bible versions was not coincidental. The various revisions and translations fall into in three main groups: revisions, paraphrases and idiomatic translations, and the more recent translations resting on the modern 'scientific' linguistic analysis approach to language and translation.

New versions were initially undertaken more as a revision than a completely new translation based on the false assumption that the *Authorised Version* was riddled with errors in need of correction. First among these was the *Revised Version* of the New Testament, published in May 1881 by Thomas Nelson. Its appearance drew severe but scholarly critical reviews from godly theologians such as the Presbyterian, Robert L. Dabney, in the USA, who condemned it outright. The Old Testament was published in 1885, but caused hardly a ripple of interest. The *American Standard*

*Version,* an American variant of the English *Revised Version* was published in 1901. 1946 saw the appearance of the *Revised Standard Version* following this same tradition, a revision of the *American Standard Version.* These revisions pandered to a liberal view of Scripture, making changes to wording in the interests 'new scholarly accuracy'. They did not attempt any significant restructuring of the text or new experiments in idiomatic translation. In sheer disgust and anger, the *RSV* was publicly burned in more than one pulpit in the 1950s. The recently published *New King James Version* can similarly also be classed largely as a revision rather than a retranslation.

An idiomatic approach to bible translation was pioneered by James Moffatt. An appalling perversion, his *New Translation of the Bible* appeared in its final form in 1934. Others in this same category and equally as deviant include the paraphrases of William Barclay and J. B. Phillips. After the death of C. S. Lewis, J. B. Phillips in his book *'Ring of Truth'* (1967) describes an experience in which Lewis appeared to him and spoke a few words, sitting just a few away from him – "large as life and twice as natural!" Now either Phillips had completely 'lost it' and was a candidate for institutionalisation or this was an occult apparition. In either case, he disqualifies himself as a suitable instrument in God's hand. We can also include in this category 'common language' versions such as the *Good News Bible.* Although this particular bible in its final version also falls into the third group as it was produced according to 'linguistic analysis' methodology.

The translation of Moffatt and others such as Phillips and Barclay tend less to be a translation than a paraphrase interpretation of the text reflecting their own theological standpoint. In Matthew 1:23, Moffatt chooses the word 'maiden' rather than 'virgin', *"The maiden will conceive and bear a son".* In Isaiah 7:14, he chooses 'young woman'. Some will

**367**

argue that it can be a legitimate rendering in other contexts, but certainly not here. This event is supposed to be a sign from God, but what is unusual about a young woman conceiving and bearing a son? This happens every day of the week, how can *that* be a sign? A *virgin* conceives and bears a son (*AV*), now that really is a sign! These passages are reduced to meaninglessness to deny the virgin birth of our Lord.

The linguistic analysis methodology in bible translation was pioneered by the American scholar, Eugene Nida, who was translation secretary for the American Bible Society and the United Bible Societies. He also had connections with the Wyclif Bible Translators who adopted his methods in their work around the world. He was a leading influence in the production of the *Good News Bible*. His methods are based on Saussure's understanding of language and more specifically on the work of linguist Noam Chomsky's system of 'transformational grammar'. Chomsky was concerned to examine the 'deep structure' of the 'semantic components' below the surface structure of sentences. The *New International Version* was produced also by this method of translation.

## The art of translating

The task of translating can be defined technically as: the rendering of a passage from a 'source language' into a 'target language' so that the meaning carried by both is *approximately* the same. Yet, in translating the Word of God such a definition is inadequate. What the Bible translator must ensure under God is that the thoughts awakened in a reader's consciousness when reading the Scripture text in the original languages are identical to those experienced when reading the same text in the language of the translation. Under normal circumstances, such a goal would be difficult to achieve, although theoretically possible. In Bible translation, it can be achieved only by an extraordinary work of God.

A modern translator working on any text uses it as a pretext for his own new 'creative' work. He will frown upon any suggestion that his translation is to be servant to the text he is translating or that his work requires him in anyway to repress his own creative impulses. His status as a translator is not one of a servant, but he regards himself as a creative artist in his own right. There can be no master-servant 'hierarchy' between the text to be translated and the translator. Once more, the issue of authority raises its head. Do we submit to the given text of the Word of God or are we free to be creative? The translation must always serve the originals it cannot create anything new within the text. This concept runs counter to all that is at the heart of modern ideas of translation. The elevation of the translator to the position of a creative artist is nothing new. The poet Shelley expresses precisely this idea with the respect to the translation of poetry in *The Defence of Poesy*.

> "It were as wise to cast a violet into a crucible that you might discover the formal principle of its colour and odour, as to seek to transfuse from one language into another the creations of a poet. The plant must spring again from its seed, or it will bear no flower – and this is the burthen of the curse of Babel."

Perhaps in poetry no harm is done, but the translation of Scripture cannot be viewed as something creative in this sense. On the other hand, neither must it be simply grammatically mechanical. This would produce a rigid and lifeless text that would at times be unintelligible.

With respect to the Scriptures, the translator is not swapping one set of words for another, but neither is he being 'creative' in the manner just described. He is instead expressing in the words of the target language the thoughts generated in the mind from reading the text in the source language. The original is master, in this case the Word of God and not the translator, not the target language. The words of Scripture themselves ultimately determine the words that are to be used in translation, even when they may appear to allow some flexibility in the choice. Luther set the limits to such 'freedom'. He avoided senseless literalism, but at the same time, he wanted to produce recognisable German.

> "… we must inquire about this of the mother of the home, the children on the street, the common man in the market place. We must be guided by their language, the way they speak, and do our translating accordingly. That way they will understand it and recognise that we are speaking German to them." (*On Translating: An Open Letter*, Works Vol. 35; p.189)

In their Preface to the Authorised Version, the translators write,

> "For is the kingdome of God of God become words or syllables? why should we be in bondage to them if we may be free, use one precisely when we may use another no lesse fit, as commodiously?"

Those who would appropriate to themselves an irresponsible freedom in Bible translation often use such comments as these to justify their methods. They would do well to read a little more of Luther.

> "On the other hand I have not just gone ahead anyway and disregarded altogether the exact wording of the original. Rather with my helpers I have been very careful to see that where everything turns on a single passage, I have kept to the original quite literally and have not lightly departed from it. … But I preferred to do violence to the German language rather than to depart from the word." (*On Translating: An Open Letter*, Works Vol. 35; p.194)

Believing readers will say of a faithful translation, this is God speaking to me in my own language. The Bible translator is servant of the Scripture text not its master, nor can the target language ever be determinative of the translation. It must, if necessary, itself be changed to accommodate Scripture, *never the other way round.*

Meaning is bound to the words that carry it, in both languages.

> *What the Bible translator must ask himself is whether the thought arising in his consciousness when reading his translation is identical to that arising when reading the Scriptures in the Hebrew or in the Greek.*

Only then can we speak of a *faithful* translation. It will involve him in a mechanical process, and demand an intimate knowledge of the vocabulary and grammar of both languages and the way they are used. This is not translation by meaning or thought, but by a comparison of grammatical structure and of vocabulary. For example, identical tenses are not necessary used in the same way in two different languages – and a faithful translation will take account of that. Using the same tense in both languages may not give an identical meaning. Sometimes tenses in one language will be completely missing in another. The same, of course, is true of vocabulary. These are very complex matters to do with the structure of language and meaning rather than notions of 'freedom'.

Translation involves the transfer of the meaning carried in the words of one language, one set of language 'signs', into those of another language. The question now arises as to what extent similarity between the languages allows this. The leading Soviet linguistic semiotician of the 1970s, Jurí Lotman, maintained that language is steeped in the context of every culture; conversely, every culture has at its heart the structure of language. This is important for if this is the case, then it means that modern English carries at its heart the present degenerate nature of our culture. This renders it an unsuitable vehicle for the Holy Scriptures. The very idea of a modern version is then a non-starter. All this would have been equally true of English in 1611. It is often suggested that at the time of Shakespeare, the English language had reached some kind of literary pinnacle rendering it an eminently suitable vehicle for Scripture. This is debatable conjecture. Shakespeare certainly knew how to use English, but he also how to be vulgar, suggestive, and anything but pure-minded in his writing. Rather than being so much influenced itself by the language around it, the Authorised Version has given to the English language many words, phrases, and proverbs. As the Bible of Luther had done in German one hundred years previously, the Authorised Version had an impact on English prose that remains to this day.

The 1611 Bible was never the 'modern version' of its day. The Authorised Version possesses its own unique English. It gave to English far more than it ever took from it. Thinking to be up-to-date, an eighteenth century translator is said to have rendered Luke 15:11 "A certain man had two sons" (AV) as "A gentleman of splendid family opulent fortune had two sons." What about James 3:6 speaking of the tongue, "and it is set on fire of hell" (AV)? Another translator in the same century renders it as "tipped with infernal sulphur it sets the whole train of life in a blaze". Had the AV been a 'modern' translation couched in the language of its day, it would now sound ridiculous. We do not need a Bible written in modern language but one that is as clear as it can be, easily understood, timeless, and in a language that is appropriate to its purpose and content. It must also faithfully reproduce in English that which God inspired.

Roman Jakobson, who migrated to Prague from Moscow in 1920, to become a leading theoretician of Czech structuralism already begins with the assumption that *no complete equivalence is possible in translation.*

*To the modern linguist it makes no sense to say that the thought of one person can be replicated in the mind of another through the medium of language.*

In accord with structuralist thinking, as the link between a word or series of words in both languages is said to be an arbitrary one, the associations and connotations being irreconcilably different, they will be non-transferable between the two languages and possess no full equivalence. Translation can only be creative transposition, as that with which it must start and that which it produces are significations functioning each within their own given culture. Jakobson says that there can only be an adequate *interpretation* of another language and no precise equivalence. It is difficult to see how in these circumstances there can be any coincidence between two languages sufficient to speak of translation in any conventional sense.

Were all this true, an inspired Bible would have little meaning and a precise translation of it would be impossible. Translation cannot then have anything to do with an exchange of like for like, this is impossible. Linguists speak only of 'equivalence'. Having accepted structuralist presuppositions with respect to language and translation, Nida is faced with the enigma of equivalence in translation. Nida first formulated the classification 'formal' and 'dynamic' equivalence in translation. The term 'equivalence' of any kind with respect to Bible translation is entirely inappropriate. Following structuralist views of language, it suggests that the translation is something similar but not quite the same. A merely equivalent meaning, formal or dynamic, is not an identical one. It accommodates the notion that the reproduction of the thoughts of one person in the mind of another in another language through translation is not a credible purpose. It reiterates the remarks of the poet and writer, Hilaire Belloc, in his book on translation, *"there are, properly speaking, no such things as identical equivalents"*. This would mean that not only is access to the pure Word of God denied to all but those reading Hebrew and Greek, but ultimately even between those communicating in the same language. This means that no two readers will read even the originals in the same way, nor will they be able to communicate to each other the precise meaning of what they have read. Something that is an equivalent is not the same as its counterpart, therefore even the term 'formal equivalence' should not, strictly speaking, be applied to the *Authorised Version*. In accepting this distinction, we legitimise Nida's methodology.

Formal equivalence is said to be based on the principle of equivalent *form*, poetry to poetry, sentence to sentence, concept to concept and to preserve as much as possible the grammatical form of the original. Even then, it cannot be thought of as being in any sense precise. Dynamic equivalence aims at an equivalent *effect*. The effect that the original source language text had upon its readers should be the equivalent in the target language. The words, and therefore the meaning, may be quite different in the two languages. What is sought is the same *effect* rather than the same *meaning*. Nida himself gives the example in J. B. Phillips rendering of Romans 16:16 where Paul's 'holy kiss' is translated as 'a hearty handshake all round.' This whole distinction between formal and dynamic equivalence suggests a tension between form and content that does not in fact exist. Dynamic equivalence amounts to the creation of a new and different text.

Bible readers, it is claimed, can only respond to what they read when in a version written in their own language and within their own cultural context. In order to be a response in truth, such a response can only be expressed behaviourally as a deed, that is, in the act of reading itself. The concern of bible translators cannot be a formal matching of the message from one culture to another, but with the *dynamic relationship* of the various readers to the messages within their own respective languages and cultures. The reader in one language should be able to respond within his own culture to the message in the same manner as the reader does in an entirely different language or culture. The question for the translator must be not is it intelligible, but is it *meaningful*. This opens the door to almost limitless freedom in translation. Nida suggests that the expression in Scripture "white as snow" could equally be translated "white as egret feathers". In fact, where snow is unknown it could be substituted by anything very white!

By contrast, the production of a faithful translation will take account of and reproduce as closely as possible the grammatical units, phrases, sentences, figures of speech, and paragraphs. There will be a consistency in the translation of words, particularly 'key' words. Unlike in the processes of Chomsky's transformational grammar, the parts of speech will remain the same, noun for noun, verb for verb wherever possible. Idioms will be retained not exchanged. Many idiomatic expressions from the *Authorised Version* have past into everyday English. A dynamic translation changes all these things in the interest of obtaining an 'equivalent response'. It will 'naturalise' terms such as 'heart' for the appropriate equivalent in the culture into which the translation is going. This may mean translating 'heart' as 'liver' or 'kidneys' perhaps!

Translation theorists will say that a dozen different translators will produce a dozen different translations given the same text. They will also say at the same time that there exists an 'invariant core' in every text. The presence of this core can be shown by what is called 'semantic condensation'. There is a text of the Bible and a 'metatext', or core meaning within it. The variants, transformations, of this core do not affect the meaning but only influence the way in which it is expressed. The invariant core is that which all translations of a given text have in common. Only this is fixed, all else is variable, so there will be innumerable reading and translations none of which can said to be perfect, ideal, but nor can they said to be wrong. Each is valid to each individual and each context. There can be no single correct translation or interpretation. Many different translations of the text may emerge from this core, all of equal validity, none of which is 'wrong'. Whilst a translation seeks to communicate, it is also truly autonomous.

Translation and interpretation ought to be seen as two separate disciplines. However, for a structuralist, every reading is an interpretation. The reader, and therefore also the translator as a reader and re-interpreter of the text, has been re-evaluated by modern linguists. Roland Barthes sees the reader as a *producer* rather than a consumer of the text. The reader will 'translate' or 'decode' the text according to a different set of systems than that of the original writer and so again any idea of one 'correct' reading is gone. According to this view, the reader is also a translator of sorts. A translation is only a further translation of that already made by the reader. There can be no 'correct' reading, so there can be no 'correct' translation.

Modern structuralism and post-structuralism have much in common with the ideas of eighteenth century European romanticism. The rejection of cold rationalism and the formal harmony of neo-classicism saw their replacement by the vitalist imagination and the contingency of nature, often linked with political revolutionary idealism. The *Zeitgeist* moved on, as in *Faust,* from the sterility of cold reason to the vibrancy of the creative imagination whereby the universe was to be created afresh. The English writer and poet, Coleridge (1772-1834), held imagination to be the supreme creative power. Translation was even then perceived as a creative enterprise. We see that 'dynamic' translations are not quite as modern as many would have us believe. There were two approaches to translation at the time: that which saw the translator as a creative genius in his own right, recreating for his own time the creative genius of the original; and second, there were those who still saw translation as a function 'making known' the text.

Whilst his comments refer specifically to the translation of poetry, Henry Wadsworth Wadsworth Longfellow (1807–81) gives us a perspective that can to some extent be applied to Bible translation.

> "The only merit my book has is that it is exactly what Dante says, and not what the translator imagines he might have said if he had been an Englishman. In other words, while making it rhythmic, I have endeavoured to make it also as literal as a prose translation. ... In translating Dante, something must be relinquished. Shall it be the beautiful rhyme that blossoms all along the line like a honeysuckle on the hedge? It must be, in order to retain something more precious than rhyme, namely, fidelity, truth, the life of the hedge itself. ... The business of a translator is to report what the author says, not to explain what he means; that is the work of the commentator. What an author says and how he says it, that is the problem of the translator."

The modern structuralist translator begins with the assumption that on a purely linguistic level a phrase in one language cannot be translated into any other. He says that that this is due to lack of equivalent cultural conventions existing between languages. All possible phrases available in the target language must be considered in relation to the context of their meaning in the source language. The significance of the phrase must be considered in its particular context. He must then replace in the target language the invariant element drawn from the source language. The determinative factor in this kind of translating is *not* the text being translated, in the case of Scripture the original texts, *but the reader and his cultural environment*. God would presumably not be translated as 'Father' in a culture where deity is female! This would be regarded as imposing a 'value system' of the Scriptures upon that of the prospective reader.

## Linguistic analysis translation methodology and culture

The methodology of translators following linguistic analysis theory is based on modern developments in the fields of linguistics, anthropology, and psychology. It is the application of ungodly ideas to the world of bible translation. The ground for communication rather than being found in a common consciousness is instead said to be based in the 'common core of human experience'. Once more, we see a Faustian move from the 'word' to the 'deed'. A biblical view of the human psyche says that man is created in the image of God and shares a common unseen *internal* spiritual and mental constitution. Thus, men and God can communicate with each other through the medium of language and share each other's thoughts. This is denied by modern psychology. A shared 'experience' relates to that which is *external* to man. It has reference to that which men meet environmentally, and which modern psychology says largely makes men what they are. This can have no reference to an internal invisible mental world of the human soul, which they say does not exist. Only that which is done and experienced is real. For these people language is 'dynamic'; it is an 'event'. The text functions as symbols to reproduce not thought but response. Language, and therefore reading too, in this context exists *only as a present experience.*

Communication is not the transference of thought from one person to another, but the *behavioural event.* The meaning of human behaviour was at one time explained largely in terms of stimulus and response. Now psychologists set up 'behavioural predispositions' in order to examine what relationship exists between symbols (e.g. words) and human behaviour, and the response to meaning. Rather than the reproduction in the mind of the reader the *thoughts* of the writer, it now becomes the translator's goal to replicate the same *effect* on the reader as those of the original reader. Some have even suggested that structures of behaviour closely correspond to those of language. The emphasis is again that the truth is what is *done* rather than what is *thought.* This all reflects the views of Noam Chomsky that language is not just a series of sentences, but is a 'dynamic' mechanism capable of generating an infinite series of different utterances. From this *event,* all meaning is derived. We have an infinite anarchy of meaning.

According to this way of thinking, one word can never represent a single idea or object, but only a whole class of 'referents'. No word can have precisely the same meaning twice because no two reading or speech events can be identical. Each event is unique, the participants are never the same nor is that which is spoken of ever the same. What this thinking means, if it were true, is that there can be no true communication of the thoughts of one person to the mind of another, because due to the ever-changing nature of people and events nothing received can ever be the same as that which left the source. A Bible revelation of absolute truth becomes impossible as its meaning will always be defined by the subjective experience of the individual reader and not an objective meaning of the text. There are then as many meanings to the Bible as there are people who read it. It will mean different things to different people and all will be equally as authoritative. What is God's word to me may not be God's word to you.

With language being such an inherently unstable medium, the preaching of the absolute truth equally authoritative to all men is simply not possible. Even for any one person, the same word may also take on a different meaning each time he reads it. The Word of God cannot then be depended upon to say the same thing each time I read it. It will depend on circumstances for definition and meaning. This must then be multiplied by all those who read the Bible and by all the languages in which it is read. Clearly, no two people can ever have the same thoughts as an other, still less can they be communicated to another. Nor can any one person think exactly the same thoughts twice. Nothing is ever the same again. It is therefore quite impossible for God to replicate His thoughts in our minds. Words are never of a fixed meaning. According to this view, no word can by tied to any single object or meaning 'by virtue of some inherent formal identification'. This is a complete denial of what the Bible says. We must choose, do we accept modern linguistics or the teaching of Scripture? There is a choice to be made.

> "And out of the ground the LORD God formed every beast of the field, and every fowl of the air; and brought them unto Adam to see what he would call them: and whatsoever Adam called every living creature, that was the name thereof. And Adam gave names to all cattle, and to the fowl of the air, and to every beast of the field..." (Genesis 2:19-20)

Linguists drive a wedge between the form of language and the meaning this form carries, between 'letter and spirit', whereas in fact the one is inextricably linked with the other. The traditional and biblical view of language is that words and their grammatical arrangement carry certain meanings; meaning is an inherent property of the form. To alter the form is to change the meaning. Divorce form from meaning and nothing can be tied down. Meaning becomes something entirely arbitrary.

The pretext for a 'modern' version is that the Scriptures are unintelligible outside the 'social context' of which they are a part. To speak to us today the Bible must do so within that cultural context of which we are a part. Therefore, they will say, there is little point in reproducing an ancient text and expecting it to speak to us today as it did at the time it was written. That was a word unique to that day. Every writer and every reader in every age is different and even although the formal aspects of language on the printed page are identical, the way that they are handled will always be different as will be the ways in which words and sentences are understood. What is claimed is that despite some very general similarities no two persons can ever understand the same thing when reading the same text. If this is true when using the same language, it becomes infinitely more complex when dealing with a translation. Because no two individuals come from the same background, they will not extract the same meaning from the same passage. What this means is that meaning is derived subjectively from the experience of an individual; there can be no intrinsic and objective meaning to a text to be understood in the same way whoever reads it. In such a situation, it is impossible for there to be revealed to us a Word unchanged and unchanging, *"the faith which was once delivered unto the saints"* (Jude 3), one authoritative Word to all men in all ages. Meaning is never fixed. The environment, the 'social context' of an infinite and eternal God is not that of His creature man so that it is impossible for us to think the thoughts of God. Even as absolute communication is impossible between men, the same is true between men and God. Understanding Scripture is a 'dynamic' experience, a creative situation each time it is read. The early chapters of Genesis are thus bound to carry a different meaning and find a changing interpretation as times themselves change.

> We totally reject the convoluted word-games of these pseudo-scientific robber barons sent by the enemy of our souls to snatch from us the pure Word of God.

When translating, modern linguistic theory has wide repercussions for both the meaning of individual words and the arrangement of those words grammatically into sentences. First, individual words are not regarded as single points of meaning but as whole fields of meaning, 'semantic domains'. This means that a word may be translated in many different ways, or not satisfactorily at all in some cases. Etymology, or the origin of the word, no longer predominates. Second, sentences are broken down into 'kernel' or core constructions. This dismantling and reconstruction of the sacred text already sets to one side all thought of verbal inspiration and its essential role in the communication of meaning of Scripture. Third, the emphasis has moved from trying to establish the author's original intended meaning to asking after the likely *response* of the reader to the translation. Inspiration lies essentially not at the point of writing, but at that of *reading*.

The meaning of a word, it is said, can only be established in relation to the words preceding and succeeding it in the sentence. The meaning lies within the relationship between words and within sets of words. Such a series of meanings can be seen in numbers and colours. One is one by virtue of not being two, by looking at two one can be seen as one, or three as three. The same is true for colours. These are said to be 'chains' of meaning. This relativistic understanding of meaning is very different from a biblical understanding of language. Other series of words are sometimes described as 'hierarchies'. In such a series, the same object or idea will be described using different words. Some words are on the same level such as *peace* and *tranquillity*. Others operate at different levels such as *automobile, old banger* – all referring to the same thing. Sometimes the same word will occur on different levels. Whilst higher up the hierarchy, there will be a greater difference between languages, as for example in the area of abstract ideas, at the level of ordinary everyday terms such differences are not so striking. To find the meaning of an individual word the process followed is first to identify what class of word it is by contrasting it with other classes, for example, is it a greeting? Words in this class are then listed then the distinguishing features setting it apart from other similar words are identified. The translator must then isolate an equivalent word in the target language.

Attempts are made early on in the translation process to identify and analyse deeper and broader meanings in order to provide a picture of the whole meaning present in a single word. Words such as *logos, musterion, dikaiosune,* and *sarx* often present translators in this school with problems. They are consistently translated in the *Authorised Version* as 'word', 'mystery', 'righteousness', and 'flesh' respectively. A word such as *logos* will frequently be deemed untranslatable. *Musterion* will be variously translated, 'open secret', 'secret purpose'. *Dikaiosune* is rendered as 'goodness', 'integrity', 'moral truth' or 'justice'. *Sarx* comes out little better with 'sinful nature', 'natural inclinations' and many other renderings besides. Linguistic analysis says that the one word will encompass all of these ideas and nuances and many more besides in a 'semantic domain', many of them will be culturally and subjectively determined, depending upon who is writing or who is reading the word. Meaning is said to be almost completely open-ended, so that no one meaning can be tied to any one word. It is the world of *Alice in Wonderland*.

> 'When *I* use a word," Humpty Dumpty said in a rather scornful tone, "it means just what I choose it to mean — neither more nor less."
>
> "The question is," said Alice, "whether you *can* make words mean different things."
>
> "The question is," said Humpty Dumpty, "which is to be master — that's all."

On the contrary, Bible words must be defined for us by the way they are used in the Bible itself. Scripture is its own lexicon.

---

**The meanings of the words of the Bible are to be found in the Bible itself.**

---

Words like 'word' and 'flesh' have meanings determined by their use in the Scriptures. Unless there is some pressing need for an alternative, in the *Authorised Version* such 'key words' are invariably always translated using the same word. It is for preachers of the Word to explain and expound these words according to their very specific biblical usage, which will often be different from their secular use. For example, *dikaiosune* is translated 'righteousness' in our *Authorised Version*, but in English translations of the Greek philosopher, Plato, the same word is translated 'justice'. *Dikaiosune* when used in Scripture means to be right before God, to be as we ought before God, to stand in a right relationship to Him. Used in Plato, it means to be right with our fellowmen, to be as we ought with other men. In Scripture, the word is directed towards God, in Plato towards men. The word 'mystery' has a very different meaning in the Bible to that generally given to it in secular usage. Mystery identifies that which is known unto God but hidden from men, 'hidden wisdom' (1 Corinthians 2:7), God may or may not reveal 'them unto us by his Spirit' (v.10). We need to retain the word itself, if we are to retain its particular biblical meaning. Nida, following Chomski and others, has a very different understanding of meaning.

Before translation proper begins, the original text will already be broken up into a simple sentence or list of simple sentences called 'kernel' expressions.

> *In analysing and identifying Chomsky's 'below surface structures' of meaning in sentences, even before attempting a translation, the form of the original text is altered.*

It is from these ideas that the so-called 'dynamic' equivalence translation methodology, used in the *New International Version* and the *Good News Bible,* has been developed. Instead of transferring the text from one language to another by searching for 'equivalents' of the text as it stands, Nida suggests what is to him a more 'efficient' method.

1. Reduce the source text to its structurally simplest kernel structure, working from the transformed to the kernel level.
2. Transfer the meaning from the source to the receptor language by using and equivalent kernel structure.
3. Using the kernel structure chosen 'generate' the stylistic and semantically equivalent expression in the receptor language, working now from the kernel to the transformed level.

Ephesians 1:3-10 consists of around 130 words in Greek and is divided into just two sentences. The *Authorised Version* follows this precisely. The *New International Version* makes five sentences from the passage and the *Good News Bible* nine. Both versions change verses 4 & 5. The *Authorised Version* reads: *"without blame before him in love"*, whereas the *New International Version* tacks 'in love' onto verse 5, *"In love he predestined us…"* Before reaching this stage, the whole passage will have been broken up into simple 'kernel' sentences. Verses 3 and 4 in Nida's hands would look something like this:

| We thank | God | | |
|---|---|---|---|
| | God | blessed | us |
| | God | chose | us |
| | | | we would be holy |
| | God | loved | us |

The rest of the text would then be reconstructed around this (cf. *Good News Bible*). The passage is made to hinge on 'Let us give thanks…' By their own confession this type of translation is one in which the content itself has been altered in order to conform to the culture in which it is to be read and for this reason is to be considered a faithful rendering. ***In truth, what they are doing is rewriting Scripture.***

According to Chomsky's 'generative' grammar, similar phrases, which may be identical according to traditional grammar, are shown to be diverse. This system of grammar is based on the number of minimal 'kernel' sentences from which language builds up a much more elaborate structure using a variety of techniques of permutation, replacement, addition and deletion. Identical phrases may also be different because they have grown from different kernels and passed through different transformations. What this means in simple terms is that a translator will first dismantle the text to its minimal kernel sentences and then reconstruct it according to a set of predetermined rules.

Some of the more obvious 'transformations' would be:

*The passive derived from the active:*

      *Passive*        The thief was arrested by the policeman.

          *from*

      *Active*         The policeman arrested the thief.

*Questions from statements:*

      Did he shout?      from      He shouted.

*Negatives from positives:*

      He did not shout.    also from    He shouted.

Traditional grammatical structures are therefore said to have many different transformational structures within them.

| | | |
|---|---|---|
| *terminal utterance* | their beloved Saviour | |
| *kernel* | they love him | he saves them |

Transformation can move from kernel (minimal sentence) to terminal utterance (derived sentence) or the other way round. A whole series of terminal utterances can be developed from a single kernel (see 'he shouted' above). Every language will possess a certain number of kernel structures from which all other structures are derived. In all languages, there will be a similarity between these kernel sentences, far more than between those sentences derived from them and translation will take place at this level before the text is expanded.

Not only is the structure of the text changed but words are added to make it more readable. The modern 'science' of cybernetics can be defined as the study of control and communication. The area of cybernetics under which translation is considered is called 'information theory'. Information here is not meaning, but *unpredictability*. Nida gives the example that if an air raid siren goes off each

Saturday at noon, it does not tell us very much. If, however, it goes off at another time, we all dive for a bunker. Predictability in language tells us very little. Over against information stands 'redundancy' in language, this raises the predictability in a text. Redundancy is said to play an important role when reading and will often make up about fifty percent of any given communication. In other words, both in terms of vocabulary and grammar as well as context and culture many things will be very familiar to us as we read and therefore predictable, our mind will hardly register them.

One of the arguments brought against a literal translation, or one that follows the original text closely such as the *Authorised Version*, is that it will suffer from 'communication overload'. This means that the average reader will find it difficult to read because the information is too densely packed and that which is familiar, or redundancy in the text, is too sparse. Following the grammatical structures of the original biblical writers, seeking formal parallels to the words they use, are all said to produce overload because of their unfamiliarity to the modern reader. They say that to make the *Authorised Version* easier to read, translators must build in necessary redundancy. The *AV* is said to be an 'inferior' translation because it is difficult for modern readers to understand. To insist that readers make any effort to come to grips with such a Bible is viewed by Nida and others as cultural bigotry or paternalism. What impudence!

One way in which an element of redundancy can be introduced into the biblical text is by adding words. Not only is the text taken apart and reconstructed but words are added in order to make the Word of God 'easier' to read! This is what God says about adding to His Word!

> "Ye shall not add unto the word which I command you, neither shall ye diminish ought from it." (Deuteronomy 4:2)

By adding 'clues' that which is unfamiliar can be made less of a shock. Reading the Bible in the *Authorised Version* with such a heavy communication load generates fatigue!

## *The mark of all these distorters of Scripture is barefaced arrogance.*

Modern version propagandists and pompous academics delight to portray the average believer as being naïve and tradition-bound in ignorance, unable to discern the niceties of biblical exegesis and textual change. People read the *Authorised Version* because they are too ignorant to know any better! It is all a matter of education and within a generation or two the new will be accepted and the old completely forgotten! Let these people know this, ignorant many may be of the workings of these deceivers, but it is to their own blessing not to have understood their deviant nonsense.

A believer instructed in Scripture, illuminated by the light of God's Spirit, will immediately be alerted to anyone seeking to deprive him of the pure Word of God. For *that* no worldly university education is required, simply a modicum of the foolishness of God that is wiser than men! *"The fear of the Lord is the beginning of wisdom: and the knowledge of the holy is understanding"* (Proverbs 9:10). With God, the 'knowledge' of these pretend-wise-men is folly beyond words. They are the foolish ones, if they imagine for a second that we are going to fall for their puerile spin. In their writings, these men admit to a long-term goal and their never-ending series of translations and revisions serve this hidden agenda. According to Nida several generations of readers 'will obviously not find immediately acceptable a radically different translation, reflecting contemporary insights into text, exegesis, and lexicon.' Those born again of the Spirit of God may be temporarily deceived, but at some point they must jump off this madcap journey on the runaway train to perdition. In their blind arrogance, these corrupters of the pure Word of God suppose we do not 'comprehend the true nature of translating'. Of course we do! We have got behind their vile tricks! Furthermore, anyone who in pride claims that there are gross errors in our *Authorised Version* due to the ignorance of the translators is declaring his own spiritual blindness and obstinacy, to them we say,

> "Thou hast neither part nor lot in this matter: for thy heart is not right in the sight of God. Repent therefore of this thy wickedness, and pray God, if perhaps the thought of thine heart may be forgiven thee." (Acts 8:21-22)

Our belief about the nature of Scripture makes the text a given datum, preserved and kept by God, and is not one that can be reworked into another. The pre-eminence of the preserved text assumes there is but *one right* way of translating the text. Idiom by idiom translation may well be acceptable in purely literary texts, where the author may well be doing little more than playing elaborate games with the mind of the reader. It will not do for Scripture, where what we are trying to accomplish is a reproduction of the thoughts of God. The written text is a functional component in the revelatory process whereby God speaks to us and saves us.

The task of the Bible translator is to carry the biblical text from the source language to the target language in complete faithfulness. To do this he must acknowledge the existence of semantic identity. There will be a continuing identity of content and thoughts will be transferred accurately from one system of signs to another. This is only conceivable because man was created in the image of God, created with an innate pattern of 'grammatical' thinking. In the *Authorised Version*, we possess a 'translation' the language of which transcends time and culture and yet remains accessible. It possesses its own style, which rather than having been determined by the era from which it sprang, has instead influenced the development of the language itself.

Based on the assumption that we have genuine manuscripts today, we proceed by asking ourselves whether what we have can be translated into other than the original languages without being diminished. Is God's Word preserved as such through the process of translation? If not, then all but those familiar with Greek and Hebrew can have no access to God's Word. Once more, we are then thrown into the lap of other men, good or bad, and are denied direct access to Scripture ourselves. We need to ask whether we can have a translation in our own language that can truly be said to be the Word of God to the same degree as the original autographs. Should we not be able to read Hebrew and Greek are we to conclude we have no access to the pure Word of God? This view places the ordinary believer in the hands of a priestly class. We then need to be sure that the translation we read is a faithful translation.

> "If none could understand the Scriptures but those that had the original Greek, …then but a very few of the poorer sort would be saved; yet the Scripture saith, that 'God hides these things from the wise and prudent,' that is, from the learned of the world, 'and reveals them to babes and sucklings.'" (John Bunyan)

All translations in any language will be the Word of God to that extent that they reproduce for us the text that God has preserved.

---

*What we object to most strongly in modern versions is not any inadequacy in the translation, such as may be said of English versions before the* Authorised Version, *but the deliberate attempt to change, pervert, and deceive.*

By faith we accept the Bible as Word of God, equally it is by faith in promises of God that we believe that the Bible we now have in our possession to be word for word the inspired and inerrant Word of God. In that the *Authorised Version* in the providence of God is a 'correct' and faithful translation, we deem it not to be less the inspired Word of God than the divine originals. God has preserved His Word for us because He said He would and not one word of His can fail. This is the promise with which we begin.

Those who use modern versions such as the *Good News Bible* and the *New International Version* have separated themselves from the truth of God; they are no longer in touch with it or the God who gave it. They preach another gospel that is not another; they lead astray those who look to them for the truth, as blind leaders of the blind. They are blind to the glorious unveiling of the eternal purposes of God in Scripture, their eyes are closed to the 'big picture'. They cannot know the mind of God, for these perversions do not reflect it.

> *Those who read a different 'word', preach a different gospel.*

Modern bibles provide the ground for 'modern' preaching. 'Modernising' preachers expound a gospel changed in order to be intelligible within the 'social context' it seeks to address. This will be accompanied by the use of modern 'socially contextual' music and methods, creating an atmosphere that is amenable to the goats but which alienates the sheep. Those who trust themselves only to tread warily will take up a modern *Reversed Version* such as the *New King James Version* or some similar lighter perversion. Preaching and teaching from a different book *must and does* produce a different message.

This controversy is no small matter where opinions can safely be divergent. We are not among those deceived by these wicked men and we shall continue to expose their deeds. Let not any promoting these perverted scriptures imagine for a moment that we shall maintain a polite silence while they do their worst. We shall not! That which is done in secret shall be shouted from the housetops. The cry has gone up, they are on notice of our intentions. We shall wage an unceasing war, effectively clad in the amour of God's providing, skilfully using the sword of God's Word, cutting down all who suppose they can with impunity pervert Scripture and deceive the people of God. This is no namby-pamby exchange of quiet academic opinions as to which version anyone chooses to use, but a vicious and bitter struggle between the truth and apostasy. Use of the *New International Version*, the *New King James* revision and similar distortions, signals spiritual declension and backsliding. It marks a departure from the truth. The time has come to speak out in clear and unmistakeable language. The gloves are off, the issues are too important to tread lightly. The Bible calls down an anathema upon all who tamper with the Word of God and we stand with that! We cannot take kid gloves to grievous wolves who spare not the flock. Let us be very clear, the judgement of God will surely fall upon all who mutilate the Word of God in this way. Those who would follow the truth have no choice but to withdraw themselves from such lest being found in their company, they share their end.